iPad for Seniors

iPadOS 15 Edition

Kevin Wilson

iPad for Seniors: iPadOS 15 Ed

Copyright © 2021 Elluminet Press

This work is subject to copyright. All rights are reserved by the Publisher, whether the whole or part of the material is concerned, specifically the rights of translation, reprinting, reuse of illustrations, recitation, broadcasting, reproduction on microfilms or in any other physical way, and transmission or information storage and retrieval, electronic adaptation, computer software, or by similar or dissimilar methodology now known or hereafter developed. Exempted from this legal reservation are brief excerpts in connection with reviews or scholarly analysis or material supplied specifically for the purpose of being entered and executed on a computer system, for exclusive use by the purchaser of the work. Duplication of this publication or parts thereof is permitted only under the provisions of the Copyright Law of the Publisher's location, in its current version, and permission for use must always be obtained from the Publisher. Permissions for use may be obtained through Rights Link at the Copyright Clearance Centre. Violations are liable to prosecution under the respective Copyright Law.

Trademarked names, logos, and images may appear in this book. Rather than use a trademark symbol with every occurrence of a trademarked name, logo, or image we use the names, logos, and images only in an editorial fashion and to the benefit of the trademark owner, with no intention of infringement of the trademark.

The use in this publication of trade names, trademarks, service marks, and similar terms, even if they are not identified as such, is not to be taken as an expression of opinion as to whether or not they are subject to proprietary rights.

While the advice and information in this book are believed to be true and accurate at the date of publication, neither the authors nor the editors nor the publisher can accept any legal responsibility for any errors or omissions that may be made. The publisher makes no warranty, express or implied, with respect to the material contained herein.

Publisher: Elluminet Press
Director: Kevin Wilson
Lead Editor: Steven Ashmore
Technical Reviewer: Mike Taylor, Robert Ashcroft
Copy Editors: Joanne Taylor, James Marsh
Proof Reader: Steven Ashmore
Indexer: James Marsh
Cover Designer: Kevin Wilson

eBook versions and licenses are also available for most titles. Any source code or other supplementary materials referenced by the author in this text is available to readers at

www.elluminetpress.com/resources

For detailed information about how to locate your book's resources, go to

www.elluminetpress.com/resources

Table of Contents

About the Author 11

Acknowledgements 13

iPads 14
    What's New in iPadOS 15? 15
    Available iPads 19
        iPad Pro 12.9-inch (5th generation) 19
        iPad Pro 11-inch (3rd generation) 19
        iPad Air (4th generation) 20
        iPad (9th generation) 20
        iPad Mini (6th generation) 20
    A Series Chip 21
    M Series Chip 21
    Liquid Retina Displays 21

Setting up Your iPad 22
    Power Up 23
    Charging your iPad's Battery 23
    Unlock & Wake iPad 24
    Initial Setup 26
        Auto Setup 26
        Manual Setup 29
    Upgrading your iPad to iPadOS 15 36
    Adjusting Settings 37
        Opening the Settings App 37
        Searching for Settings 37
    Language & Region 38
    Keyboard 39
        Change or Add Keyboard 39
        Text Shortcuts 39
        Keyboard Settings 40
    Date & Time 41
    Display 41
    Dark & Light Mode 43
    Wallpaper 45
        Adjusting your Wallpaper 45
        Changing your Wallpaper 45
    Home Screen & Dock 47
    Apple ID 48
        Creating an ID 48
    FaceID 49
        Setup 49
        FaceID Unlock Settings 50

  Alternate Appearance...*51*
 TouchID 52
 Passcode 53
 Privacy 54
 Siri & Search.. 55
 Notifications 57
 Connecting to the Internet.. 59
  WiFi *59*
  Cellular *61*
  VPNs *63*
  School/Work Accounts *63*
 iCloud... 64
  Settings...*65*
  iCloud Sync *67*
  Storage Management *68*
  Forgot Password *69*
 Adding Email Accounts 70
 Add Social Media Accounts 73
 Connecting Devices 74
  Bluetooth *74*
  USB...*76*
  Video...*76*
 Connecting to a Computer.. 77
 Setup Universal Control 78
 Apple Pay 81
  Setup *81*
  Using Apple Pay *83*
 Family Sharing... 84
  Setup *84*
  Add a Family Member *87*
  Child Accounts...*88*
  Manage Family Sharing *91*
 Screen Time 92
  Downtime *94*
  App Limits..*95*
  Always Allowed..*97*
  Content & Privacy Restrictions...................................*97*
  Allowing and Blocking Content *98*

Getting Around Your iPad 100

 Your iPad 101
 Home Screen 105
  Anatomy *105*
  Arranging Icons *106*
  Switching Between App Pages *107*
  Removing Icons..*108*
  Status Bar *109*

- *The Dock* 109
- *Widgets* 110
- *Add to Home Screen* 110
- *Add to Today View* 112
- *Edit Widget* 114
- *Remove Widgets* 115
- App Library 116
- Control Center 118
- Notification Center 119
- Touch Gestures 120
  - *Tap* 120
  - *Drag* 121
  - *Zoom* 121
  - *Swipe* 122
  - *Switch Between Open Apps* 122
  - *Reveal Home Screen* 123
  - *Reveal Dock* 123
  - *Reveal App Switcher* 124
  - *Cut, Copy & Paste* 125
  - *Text Selection* 127
- Multitasking 128
  - *Switch to Another Running App* 128
  - *Close a Running App* 129
  - *Using Split View* 130
  - *Using Slide Over* 131
  - *Drag & Drop* 132
  - *Close Slide Over or Split View* 133
- App Shelf 134
- Universal Control 135
  - *Moving Between Devices* 135
- On-screen Keyboard 136
- Spotlight Search 139
  - *Searching for Things* 139
- Siri 141
  - *Using Siri* 141
  - *Siri Translate* 142
  - *Voice Dictation* 143
  - *Voice Control* 144
- Screenshot 146
- Screen Recording 147

Using Apps **148**

- App Store 149
  - *Browsing the Store* 150
  - *The Arcade* 153
  - *Search the Store* 155
- Taking Notes 157

- *Typing Notes*..*158*
- *Inserting Photos*..*159*
- *Handwritten Notes*..*160*
- *Paste Handwriting as Text*..*161*
- *Shape Recognition*..*162*
- *Dictating Notes*..*163*
- *Quick Note*..*164*
- *Organising your Notes*...*165*
- *Inviting other Users*..*166*

Reminders.. 168
- *Create a Reminder*..*168*
- *Create a New List*..*169*
- *Schedule a Reminder*..*170*
- *Reminder When Messaging Someone*......................*171*
- *Reminder at a Location*..*172*

Maps... 173
- *Guides*..*175*
- *Share Location*..*177*
- *Driving Directions*...*177*
- *Drop a Pin*...*180*
- *3D Maps*..*181*

News App... 183
Apple Books App.. 186
- *Browse the Store*..*187*
- *Search the Store*...*188*

Files App.. 191
- *Create New Folders*...*192*
- *Drag Files into Folders*...*193*
- *Delete Files or Folders*..*193*
- *Share a File*...*194*
- *External Drive Support*..*194*
- *Rename Files or Folders*...*195*
- *File Servers*...*196*

Voice Memos... 197
- *Recording Memos*..*198*
- *Renaming Memos*..*199*
- *Trim a Memo*..*200*

Clock App.. 201
- *World Clock*..*201*
- *Alarm*...*203*
- *Bed Time*...*204*
- *Stop Watch*...*206*
- *Timer*...*206*

Shortcuts... 207
- *Creating Shortcuts*..*207*
- *Shortcut Gallery*..*209*

- *Running Shortcuts* *212*
- Pages Word Processing 213
  - *Formatting Text* *215*
  - *Adding a Picture* *217*
  - *Collaboration* *218*
- Keynote Presentations 219
  - *Editing a Slide* *220*
  - *Adding Media* *222*
  - *Animations* *223*
  - *Formatting Text Boxes* *225*
  - *Formatting Text Inside Textboxes* *226*
- Numbers Spreadsheets 228
  - *Entering Data* *229*
  - *Simple Text Formatting* *230*
  - *Resizing Rows and Columns* *231*
  - *Inserting Rows & Columns* *231*
  - *Formulas* *232*
  - *Functions* *232*
- Fonts 233
  - *Downloading* *234*
  - *Installing from File* *235*
- Printing Documents 236
  - *Air Print* *236*
  - *Older Printers* *237*

Internet, Email & Comms **238**

- Using Safari 239
  - *Start Page* *239*
  - *The Toolbar* *240*
  - *The Sidebar* *240*
  - *Share Menu* *241*
  - *Browsing Tabs* *241*
  - *Tab Bar* *241*
  - *New Tab* *242*
  - *Show All Tabs* *242*
  - *Tab Groups* *242*
  - *New Tab Group* *243*
  - *Reopen Tab Group* *244*
  - *Bookmarking a Site* *245*
  - *Revisiting a Bookmarked Site* *246*
  - *Browsing History* *248*
  - *Reader View* *249*
  - *Page Zoom* *250*
  - *Download Manager* *251*
  - *Generate Automatic Strong Passwords* *252*
  - *Autofill Passwords on Websites* *253*
  - *Automatically add Password to Keychain* *254*

- *Forms Autofill* *256*
- *Add Contact Info* *256*
- *Adding Credit Cards* *258*
- *Using Autofill to Fill in a Form in Safari* *259*
- *Using Autofill to Fill in Payment Details in Safari* *260*
- *Password Monitoring* *261*
- *Website Privacy Report* *262*

Using Email 264
- *Reply to or Forward a Message* *264*
- *Email Threads* *265*
- *Add a Signature* *266*
- *New Message* *267*
- *Formatting Messages* *268*
- *Attachments* *269*
- *Flagging Messages* *270*
- *Create a Mailbox Folder* *270*
- *Move Message* *271*
- *Block Sender* *271*

Contacts 272
- *View Contact Details* *273*
- *New Contact* *274*
- *New Contact from a Message* *275*
- *Delete a Contact* *276*

Calendar App 277
- *Adding an Appointment* *278*
- *Add a Recurring Appointment* *279*
- *Adding an Appointment from a Message* *280*

FaceTime 281
- *Making a New Call* *282*
- *Adding Effects* *286*
- *Group FaceTime* *289*
- *Share Screen* *291*
- *SharePlay* *292*

Messages 294
- *Sending Photos from Photos App* *296*
- *Sending Photos from Camera* *297*
- *Adding Effects* *298*

Digital Touch in Message 300
Sending Payments with Message 305
Emojis 306
- *Using Emojis* *306*

AirDrop 307
- *To Send a file to Someone using AirDrop* *308*
- *To Receive a File from Someone using AirDrop* *310*

Using Multimedia **312**

Photos 313

- *Import Photos* 313
- *Browsing Through your Photos* 315
- *Editing Photos* 316
- *Adjusting Images* 317
- *Crop an Image* 318
- *Rotate an Image* 319
- *Creating Albums* 320
- *Search for Photos* 321
- *Sharing Photos* 322
- iMovie 325
  - *Creating a New Project & Adding Media* 325
  - *Editing your Movie* 327
  - *Reorder & Trim* 328
  - *Add Text to a Clip* 328
  - *Transitions* 330
  - *Add Additional Media* 330
  - *Add Audio* 331
- Camera App 334
  - *Adjusting your Photo* 337
  - *Panoramic Photos* 338
  - *Recording Video* 339
  - *Enhancing Video* 340
- Music App 341
  - *Apple Music* 342
  - *The Main Screen* 344
  - *Searching for Music* 345
  - *Add to Library* 347
  - *Creating Playlists* 348
  - *Importing CDs* 349
  - *Adding Tracks to your iPhone, or iPad Manually* 350
- Podcasts App 352
- iTunes Store 354
  - *Music* 355
  - *Films & TV* 356
- Apple TV App 358
  - *Watch Now* 358
  - *Library* 359
- Airplay 360
  - *Airplay to Apple TV* 361
  - *Airplay to your Mac* 362
- Apple Pencil 364
  - *Charge your Pencil (1st Gen)* 365
  - *Pairing your Pencil with your iPad (1st Gen)* 366
  - *Pair & Charge your Pencil (2nd Gen)* 367
  - *Using Apple Pencil* 368
- Scribble 371
  - *Handwrite in Text Fields* 371

  Delete Text..*371*
  Select Text...*372*
  Insert Text...*372*
 Document Scanner 373
 QR Code Scanner.. 377

iPad Accessories **378**

 Magic Keyboard.. 379
 Smart Keyboard 379
 Apple Smart Keyboard Folio 380
 Bluetooth Keyboards 381
 Mouse Support... 382
 Cases 384
 AirPods 385
  Setup *385*
  Charge *386*
  AirPod Controls..*386*
 Bluetooth Headphones 387
 Wired Headphones 387

Maintaining your iPad... **388**

 iPad Backups.. 389
 System Updates 390
 App Updates 392
 Deleting Apps... 393
 iPad Storage Maintenance 394
 iPad Recovery.. 396
 Connecting to a Computer... 400
  Sync your iPad/iPhone with your Mac.................................*401*
  Restore iPad *403*
 Erase iPad... 404

Video Resources **406**

 Using the Videos 407
 Scanning the Codes 408
  iPhone..*408*
  Android..*409*

Index.. **410**

About the Author

With over 20 years' experience in the computer industry, Kevin Wilson has made a career out of technology and showing others how to use it. After earning a master's degree in computer science, software engineering, and multimedia systems, Kevin has held various positions in the IT industry including graphic & web design, programming, building & managing corporate networks, and IT support.

He serves as senior writer and director at Elluminet Press Ltd, he periodically teaches computer science at college, and works as an IT trainer in England while researching for his PhD. His books have become a valuable resource among the students in England, South Africa, Canada, and in the United States.

Kevin's motto is clear: "If you can't explain something simply, then you haven't understood it well enough." To that end, he has created the Exploring Tech Computing series, in which he breaks down complex technological subjects into smaller, easy-to-follow steps that students and ordinary computer users can put into practice.

Acknowledgements

Thanks to all the staff at Luminescent Media & Elluminet Press for their passion, dedication and hard work in the preparation and production of this book.

To all my friends and family for their continued support and encouragement in all my writing projects.

To all my colleagues, students and testers who took the time to test procedures and offer feedback on the book

Finally thanks to you the reader for choosing this book. I hope it helps you to use your iPad with greater understanding.

Have fun!

1

iPads

The iPad is a tablet computer developed by Apple, and was originally released in 2010.

Up until 2019, the iPad used the same operating system as the iPhone (iOS), but as iPads continued to develop and evolve, they received more and more features not available on the iPhone. Because of this, iPads now have their own operating system called iPadOS.

The user interface is a touch screen, meaning you can manipulate sliders, switches, buttons and icons on screen using your finger.

The main screen is called the home screen and contains icons that represent apps. You can download countless apps from the App Store - you'll find an app for almost anything you can think of.

In this chapter, we'll take a look at

- What's New in iPadOS 15
- Available iPad Models
- A Series Chip
- M Series Chip
- A few Technical Terms
- Liquid Retina Displays

Let's begin by taking a look at the new features of iPadOS 15.

Chapter 1: iPads

What's New in iPadOS 15?

You can now place widgets among the apps on your Home Screen. A new mail & contacts widget allows you to keep in touch with people.

App library is now on iPad and automatically organizes your apps categories according to their function, such as productivity, social, etc.

Chapter 1: iPads

A new multitasking menu appears at the top of an app that lets you switch to split view, slide over, or full screen.

A new multi window shelf appears at the bottom of the screen and gives you quick access to all the open windows for an app.

Focus mode automatically filters notifications based on what you're doing. Turn on Do Not Disturb to switch everything off, or choose from ready made filters for work, personal time, sleep, fitness, or driving.

Tabs in Safari now have a rounder and more defined appearance and automatically adjust to match the colours of each site, extending the web page to the top of the window.

You can use Live Text to copy text out of an image and paste it into another app. Here, I've copied the title off the sign in the photo and pasted it into my notes aoo

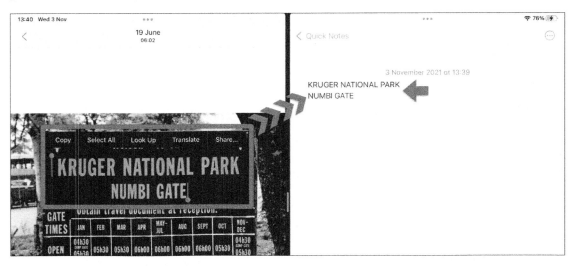

You can also look up information

Chapter 1: iPads

Currently only available in the US, Visual Lookup identifies objects and landmarks in photos. Here in the photo below, visual lookup has identified my dog as a dachshund, and offers extra photos and info on the object in a popup window.

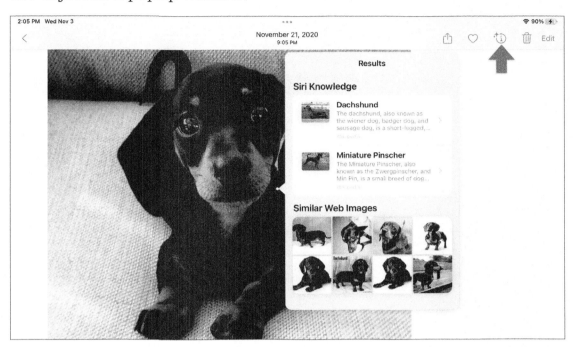

Universal Control allows you to use your keyboard and mouse across all your Apple devices such as an iPad and a Mac.

17

Chapter 1: iPads

SharePlay allows you to watch and listen to music in your FaceTime calls with your friends.

Available iPads

There are various different models available. Lets take a look at some of the main features of the latest iPads.

iPad Pro 12.9-inch (5th generation)

- Contains the M1 chip with up to 2TB storage
- Liquid Retina XDR display with 2388x1668 pixel resolution at 264 pixels per inch (ppi)
- Works with Magic Keyboard and Smart Keyboard Folio
- Works with Apple Pencil 2nd generation
- 12MP Wide and 10MP Ultra Wide cameras with video recording up to 4K
- USB-C connector with support for Thunderbolt / USB 4
- Nano and eSIM available on cellular models

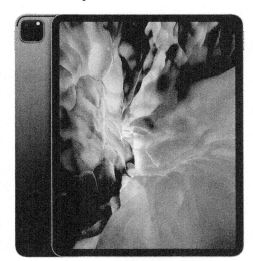

iPad Pro 11-inch (3rd generation)

- Contains the M1 chip with up to 2TB storage
- Liquid Retina display with 2732x2048 pixel resolution at 264 pixels per inch (ppi)
- Works with Magic Keyboard and Smart Keyboard Folio
- Works with Apple Pencil 2nd generation
- 12MP Wide and 10MP Ultra Wide cameras with video recording up to 4K
- USB-C connector with support for Thunderbolt / USB 4
- Nano and eSIM available on cellular models

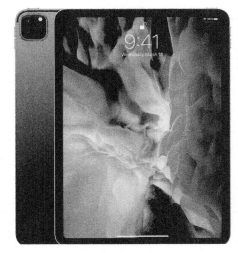

Chapter 1: iPads

iPad Air (4th generation)

- Contains the A14 chip with up to 256GB Storage
- 10.9-inch liquid retina display with 2360x1640 pixel resolution at 264 pixels per inch (ppi)
- 12MP wide camera
- USB-C connector
- Works with Magic Keyboard and Smart Keyboard Folio
- Works with Apple Pencil 2nd generation

iPad (9th generation)

- Contains the A13 Chip with up to 256GB storage
- 10.2 inch retina display with 2160x1620 pixel resolution at 264 pixels per inch (ppi)
- 12MP Ultra Wide front camera
- Lightning connector
- Note, this model is only compatible with the Apple Pencil 1st generation.
- Works with Smart Keyboard

iPad Mini (6th generation)

- Contains the A15 with up to 254GB storage
- 8.3 inch liquid retina display with 2266x1488 pixel resolution at 326 pixels per inch (ppi)
- 12MP Ultra Wide front camera
- USB-C connector
- Works with Bluetooth keyboards
- Works with Apple Pencil 2nd generation

Older models are also available from third parties.

Detailed specifications are available on Apple's website: www.apple.com/ipad/compare/

A Series Chip

The Apple A series is a series of microprocessors known as a system on a chip (SoC) used to power iPhones and iPads. The A series chips combine the CPU, Graphics Processor (or GPU), memory (or RAM), flash storage, and a neural engine which is a component designed to use machine learning and artificial intelligence for tasks such identifying objects in photos, or applying an automatic filter to a picture, analysing videos, voice recognition, and so on.

M Series Chip

This chip powers the high end iPad Pros and is the same chip found on the new Macs. The M1 chip combines the CPU, Graphics Processor (or GPU), memory (or RAM), SSD drive controller, and a neural engine which is a component designed to use machine learning and artificial intelligence for tasks such identifying objects in photos, or applying an automatic filter to a picture, analysing videos, voice recognition, and so on.

Liquid Retina Displays

A Retina Display is a screen with a high pixel density - meaning there are a lot more pixels per inch than a standard computer screen. This generates a high resolution, crystal clear image. A Liquid Retina Display uses Liquid Crystal Display (LCD) technology to display the image.

Liquid Retina XDR display is lit by multiple mini-LEDs, and supports resolutions of 2732x2048 pixels for a total of 5.6 million pixels with 264 pixels per inch, and delivers P3 wide colour giving richer and more vibrant colours.

ProMotion technology automatically adjusts the display refresh rate up to 120 Hz (twice the rate of typical LCD displays) to the optimal rate for the content.

High Dynamic Range (HDR) delivers detail in extremely bright parts of the image along with the subtle details in the darkest parts of the image.

True Tone uses multiple sensors to adjust the colour temperature of the display on your iPad depending on the ambient light, to make the display look more natural.

A nit is measurement of the brightness of light. Computer monitors usually range from 200 - 600 nits. Higher nits allow you to brighten the display so you can see the screen clearly on a sunny day.

2

Setting up Your iPad

If you've just bought your new iPad and taken it out the box, the process to set it up to use for the first time is very simple. You don't even have to connect it to your computer.

In this chapter, we'll take a look at

- Powering Up & charging your iPad's Battery
- Unlock & Wake iPad
- Initial Setup
- Upgrading to iPadOS 15
- Adjusting Settings
- Changing Wallpaper
- Home Screen & Dock
- Apple ID
- FaceID, TouchID & Passcode
- Privacy
- Siri & Search
- Notifications
- Connecting to the Internet
- iCloud
- Adding Email Accounts
- Add Social Media Accounts
- Connecting Devices
- Connecting to a Computer
- Setting up Universal Control
- Apple Pay
- Family Sharing & Screen Time

Take a look at the video resources, open your web browser and navigate to the following website.

elluminetpress.com/using-ipad

Chapter 2: Setting up Your iPad

Power Up

To power on your iPad, press and hold the power button on the top right of the device for a couple of seconds until you see the Apple logo on the screen.

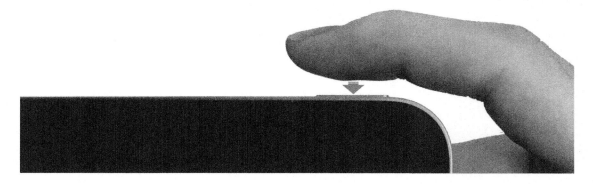

Once your iPad powers up, you'll land on the lock screen, see page 24.

If you have a new iPad, you'll need to run through the initial setup. See page 26.

Charging your iPad's Battery

Plug your iPad directly into the charger to charge the battery. Plug one end of the lightning or USB-C cable into the charger.

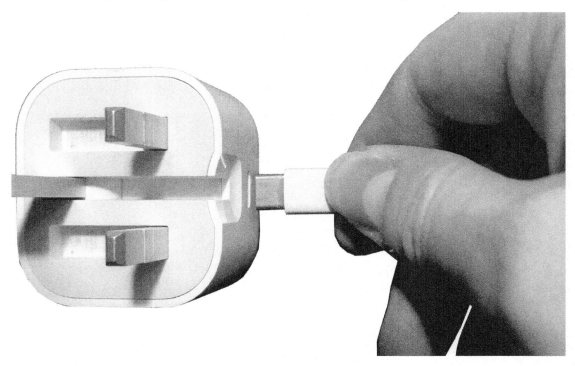

Chapter 2: Setting up Your iPad

Plug the other end of the lightning or USB-C cable into the port on the bottom of your iPad.

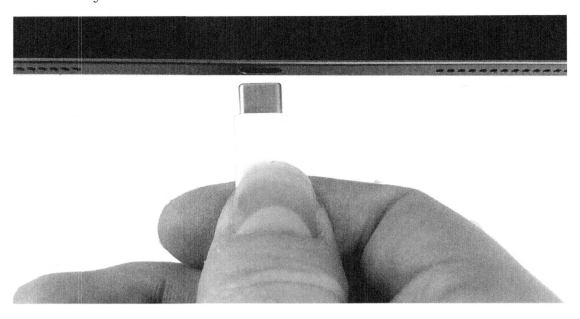

Your battery will take a few hours to charge. Best practice is not to let your battery deplete completely, charge it up when you still have about 20% charge left.

Unlock & Wake iPad

The home button also contains a finger print scanner and is usually configured during the initial setup.

On the iPads with a home button, place your finger on the home button so your thumb fits snugly into the button's indent, then press the button once to unlock your iPad - **don't** hold the button down.

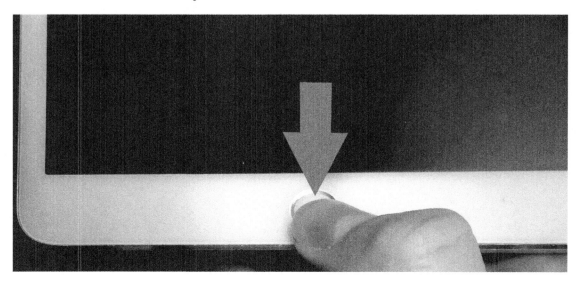

Chapter 2: Setting up Your iPad

On the other models, press the power button on the top - allow the finger print scanner to identify your fingerprint.

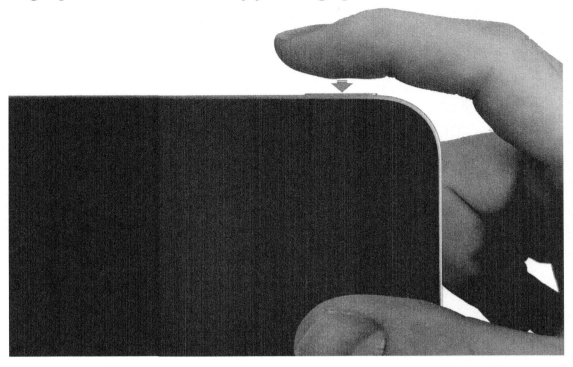

On the iPads Pros, press the power button on the top right of the device, then swipe up from the bottom edge of the screen when prompted.

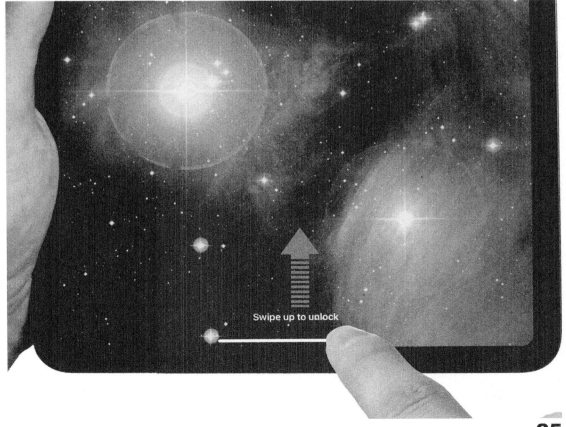

Chapter 2: Setting up Your iPad

Initial Setup

To use iPad, you need an internet connection and your Apple ID. There is an automated setup feature that allows you to transfer settings from another device, such as an iPhone or an iPad. The other device must be running iOS 11 or later, or iPadOS 13 or later. If not, you can still set up your iPad manually (see page 29). First lets take a look at the auto setup feature.

Auto Setup

Turn on your iPad. On the welcome screen, slide your finger across the screen, or press the home button to start.

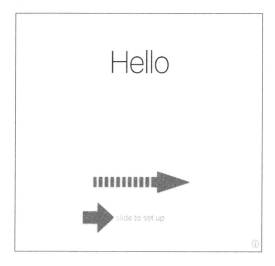

Select your language and country/region.

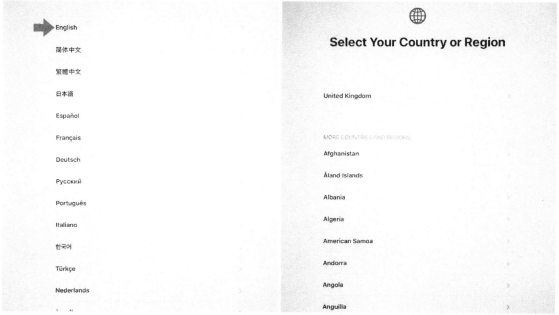

Chapter 2: Setting up Your iPad

When you land on this screen, place your old iPad or iPhone next to your new iPad.

Unlock your old iPad or iPhone. You'll get a prompt on your old device, tap 'continue'.

Chapter 2: Setting up Your iPad

Now, you'll see a strange looking pattern appear on your new iPad's screen. Holding your old iPhone/iPad, position the pattern in the circle on your old device as shown below.

Keep your old iPad/iPhone next to your new one until the setup is complete.

Enter the passcode from your old iPad/iPhone, into your new iPad.

Set up Touch ID, sign in with your Apple ID when prompted.

Tap 'continue' on the 'go home' screen, 'quick access to the dock' screen, 'switch between apps' screen, and the 'quickly access controls' screen.

Chapter 2: Setting up Your iPad

Manual Setup

Turn on your iPad, then from the welcome screen, swipe your finger across the bottom of the screen, or press the home button.

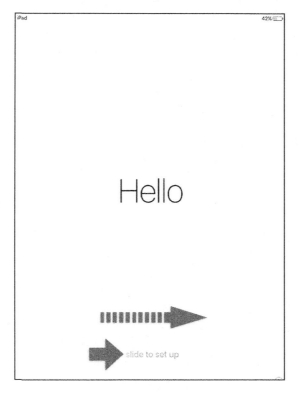

Select your language and country/region.

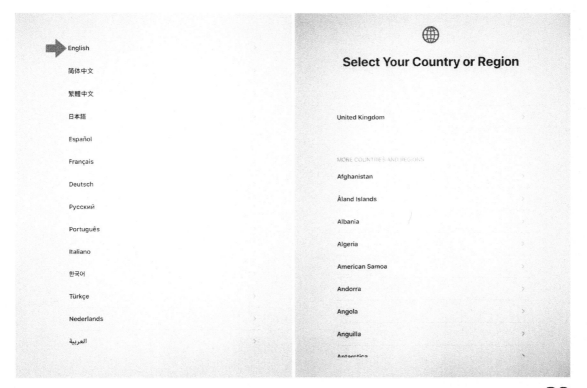

29

Chapter 2: Setting up Your iPad

Select 'set up manually' on the bottom of the screen.

Select your WiFi network and enter your WiFi password when prompted.

Tap 'continue' on the data privacy screen.

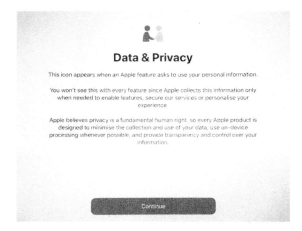

Chapter 2: Setting up Your iPad

Tap 'continue' to set up Touch ID.

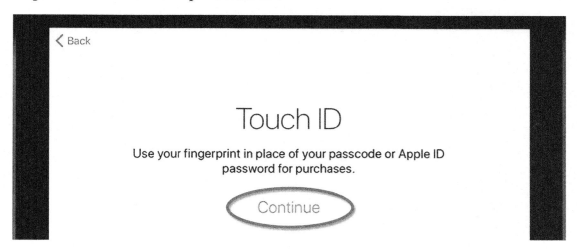

Now you need to scan your finger print. Scan the finger you are most likely to use to press the home button with. In most cases this is your thumb, so it makes sense to scan this finger. *If you're using a new iPad air, the finger print scanner is on the top button - so use your right index finger.* Follow the instructions on the screen.

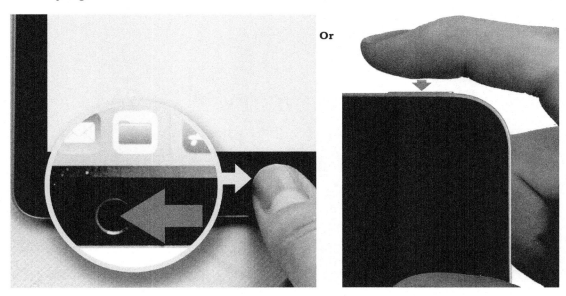

You'll need to scan your finger a few times, so the system can account for different variations as you wont always put your thumb on the home button in exactly the same position every time. Do what it says on the screen. When you're done, tap 'next' on the top right.

Check out the Touch ID demo in the 'using iPad' section of the video resources on how to scan your fingerprint. Scan the code with your iPad or go to the following website.

elluminetpress.com/using-ipad

Chapter 2: Setting up Your iPad

Enter a 6 digit passcode. This code is used to unlock your iPad if Touch ID isn't available.

Tap 'restore from iCloud backup'. This will ensure all your settings, messages, contacts, apps, photos, music, and email are restored.

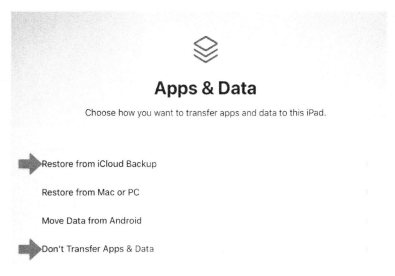

If you are setting up from scratch or are a new user, tap 'don't transfer apps & data'.

Chapter 2: Setting up Your iPad

Sign in with your Apple ID email address and password. Tap 'next' on the top right..

Choose a backup if prompted. Choose the latest one on the list.

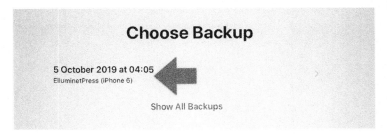

Tap 'enable location services'. This allows your iPad to work out your physical location so you can get local information, weather, and map directions.

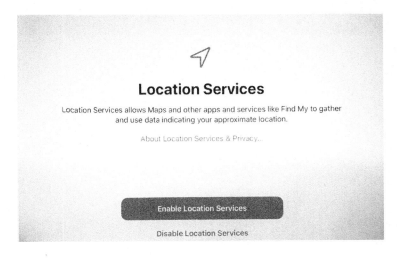

Chapter 2: Setting up Your iPad

Tap 'continue' to set up Apple Pay. Follow the prompts to add your credit/debit cards.

Tap 'continue' to set up Siri. Follow the prompts on screen.

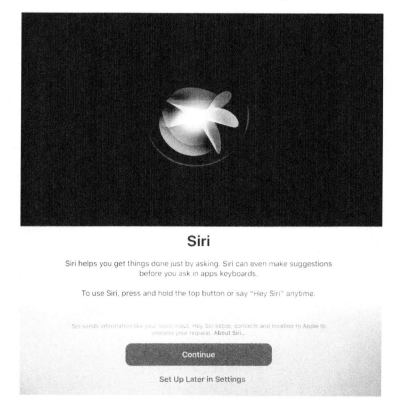

Tap 'don't share' on iPad Analytics.

Chapter 2: Setting up Your iPad

Tap 'continue' on the 'true tone display' screen.

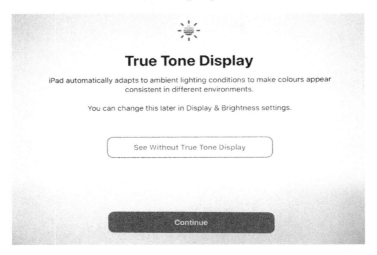

Select light or dark mode. Dark mode is much easier on the eyes and is good for low light and night time usage.

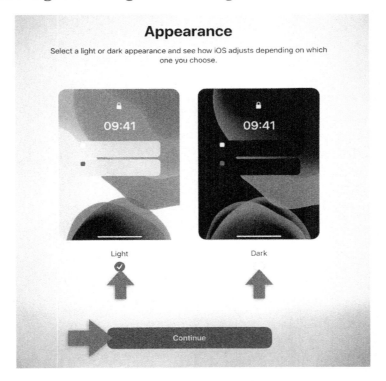

Tap 'continue' on the 'restore completed' screen if prompted.

Tap 'continue' on the 'keep your iPad up to date' screen

Tap 'continue' on the 'go home' screen, 'quick access to the dock' screen, 'switch between apps' screen, and the 'quickly access controls' screen.

Once you're completed the initial setup, you'll land on the home screen.

Chapter 2: Setting up Your iPad

Upgrading your iPad to iPadOS 15

New iPads will come shipped with iPadOS 15, but if you're upgrading an older iPad, iPadOS 15 will run on the following devices:

- iPad Pro 12.9-inch (5th generation)
- iPad Pro 11-inch (1st - 3rd generation)
- iPad Pro 12.9-inch (1st - 4th generation)
- iPad Pro 10.5-inch
- iPad Pro 9.7-inch
- iPad (5th - 9th generation)
- iPad Mini (5th & 6th generation)
- iPad Mini 4
- iPad Air (3rd & 4th generation)
- iPad Air 2

Make sure your iPad is plugged into a power outlet, and you are connected to your WiFi.

Once you have done that, go to the settings app, tap 'General', then select 'Software Update'.

Tap 'Download and Install' on the available update.

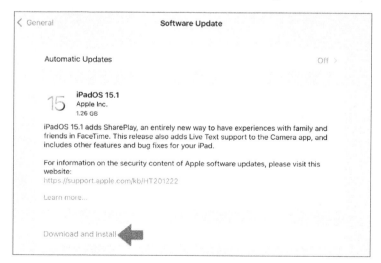

To update now, tap 'download and install'. Enter your passcode when prompted. Your iPad will restart and the update will install. This might take a while.

Chapter 2: Setting up Your iPad

Adjusting Settings

To adjust any settings on your iPad, you'll need to use the settings app.

Opening the Settings App

You'll find the icon on the dock or on the home screen.

Settings are grouped into sections based on the feature the settings control. You'll find a section for display, sound, or home screen settings among many others. These sections appear down the left hand side of the screen.

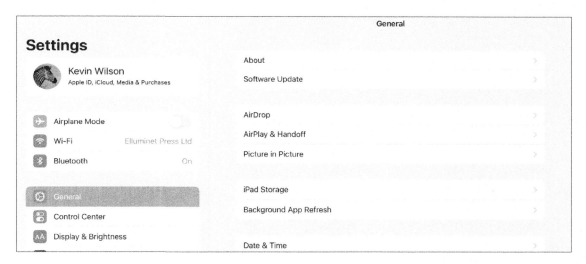

When you select a section, the settings in that section appear down the right hand side. In the screenshot above, I've selected 'general'. The settings in the 'general' section appear on the right.

Searching for Settings

On the top left of the settings app, you'll see a search field. Drag the list on the left downwards if the field doesn't show.

37

Chapter 2: Setting up Your iPad

Type in the name of the setting or device you want to change.

In the drop down list, you'll see suggested settings. Select the closest match from the drop down list.

Language & Region

You can change the language of your iPad, and the region if it's incorrect or if you've accidentally changed it. To do this, open the settings app, then select 'general' from the list on the left. Tap on 'language & region'.

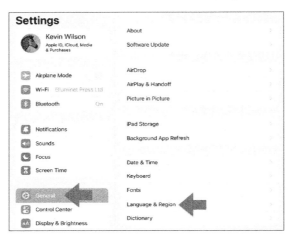

To change the display language, tap 'ipad language', then select a language from the list.

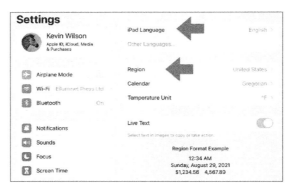

To change the region, tap 'region', then select a region from the list. If you use a different calendar, tap 'calendar', select a calendar from the list. To change the temperature units, click 'temperature unit', then select F for Fahrenheit, or C for Celsius.

Chapter 2: Setting up Your iPad

Keyboard

You can add keyboards for other languages, you can also turn on or off turn typing features, such as spell checking, on or off and change the layout of your on-screen or wireless keyboard. To do this open the settings app, select 'general' from the list on the left, then select 'keyboard.

Change or Add Keyboard

In the keyboard settings, tap on 'keyboards'.

Tap 'add new keyboard'.

Select a keyboard from the list.

Text Shortcuts

You can create shortcuts for sentences or phrases you use most often. So for example, you can create a shortcut for "I'm on my way, see you in a bit". So instead of typing that out every time, you can shorten it to perhaps OMY, then all you need to do is type, OMY each time you want to use the phrase.

To do this in the keyboard settings, tap 'text replacement'.

39

Chapter 2: Setting up Your iPad

Tap the '+' icon on the top right to create a new shortcut.

Type your sentence into the field marked 'phrase'. Then type in the shortcut. Tap 'save' when you're done.

Now, when you're typing, all you need to type when you want to use the phrase is the shortcut.

Keyboard Settings

You can change certain settings that are designed to make typing easier. This includes spelling auto correct, predictive text, punctuation and so on. You can change these in the 'all keyboards' section of the keyboard settings page. Tap 'general', then 'keyboards'.

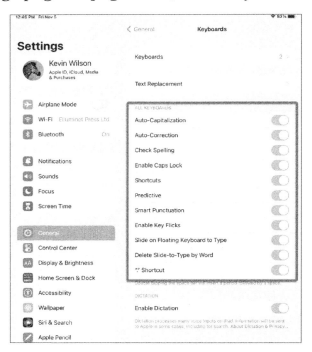

Chapter 2: Setting up Your iPad

Date & Time

The date and time is usually set automatically for you depending on your location. However, sometimes you want to change these if you're travelling or in another country.

To do this, open the settings app then select 'general' from the list on the left hand side. Tap on 'date and time'.

Here, you can change to 24 hour clock, add or remove the AM/PM markers or remove/show the date on the status bar on the top left of your iPad screen or on the top of the lock screen.

To set your time zone manually, turn off 'set automatically', then tap on the time zone location. Type in the country you're in or want to use.

Tap on the country in the search results.

Display

Using the display settings you can change various options. To do this, open the settings app, then select 'display & brightness' from the list on the left.

Here, you can switch between dark and light mode... see page 43.

41

Chapter 2: Setting up Your iPad

Further down you can change the screen brightness and enable/disable true tone. Now true tone is a feature that adapts the screen colour, brightness and contrast according to the ambient light in the room you're physically in

Under 'night shift', you can remove the bright blue light from your screen. This gives your screen a orange tint that is supposed to make it easier on your eyes.

To do this tap on 'night shift'. Under 'scheduled', turn this on, then select the time you want night shift to start and when you want it to end.

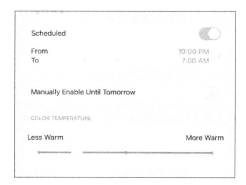

To change the amount of blue or orange, use the slider under 'colour temperature'. When you slide this to the right, you'll see the screen go orange. If you slide to the left, you'll see the screen go more blue.

Chapter 2: Setting up Your iPad

At the bottom of the screen, you'll see 'auto lock', this allows you to change the time it takes for your screen to lock after you stop using your iPad. Tap on the time to change.

At the bottom, you can change the text size. To do this just tap on 'text size' then drag the slider to resize the text

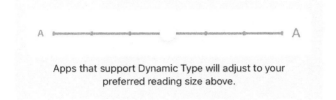

Dark & Light Mode

Dark mode reduces the amount of white on the screen and is perfect for low-light environments making it easier on your eyes. Here below, you can see light mode on the left, and dark mode on the right.

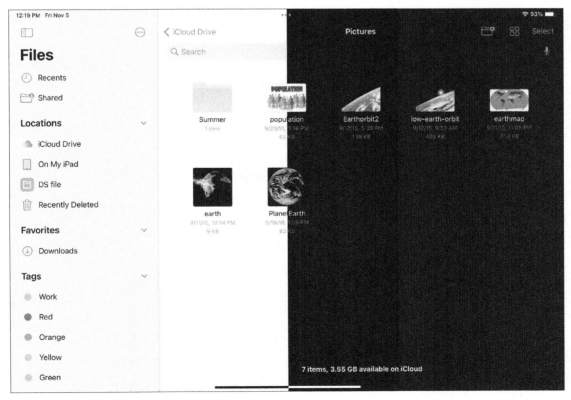

Chapter 2: Setting up Your iPad

To enable dark mode, open your settings app, and select 'display and brightness'.

On the right hand side, select 'dark' to switch to dark mode.

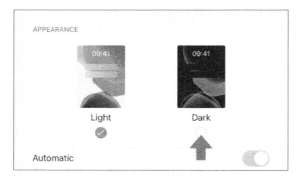

You can also set your iPad to switch to dark mode automatically. This means your iPad will switch to light mode during the day, and dark mode at night. To do this, tap the switch next to 'automatic'.

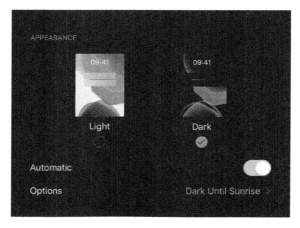

Tap 'options' to change when your iPad changes between dark and light mode. To set your own schedule tap 'custom schedule' and enter the times.

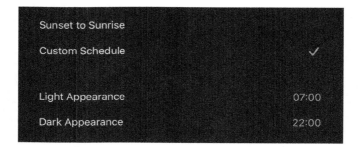

Chapter 2: Setting up Your iPad

Wallpaper

You can set a photograph as a background on your lock screen and home screen.

Adjusting your Wallpaper

First, open the settings app, then select 'wallpaper' from the list on the left hand side.

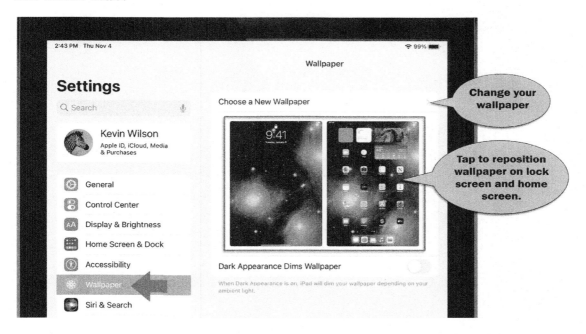

Here, you'll see two previews, the one on the left is your lock screen, the one on the right is your home screen. You can reposition the wallpapers using these previews. Just tap on the one you want to reposition, then drag the image.

Underneath you'll see a setting called 'dark appearance dims wallpaper. This, as the name suggests, reduces the brightness of the wallpaper to match dark mode.

Changing your Wallpaper

To change the wallpaper image, on the wallpaper section of the settings app, click 'choose a new wallpaper'.

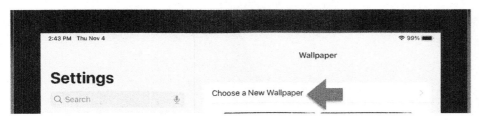

45

Chapter 2: Setting up Your iPad

Choose one of the presets at the top, or tap 'all photos' if you want to select one of your own photographs

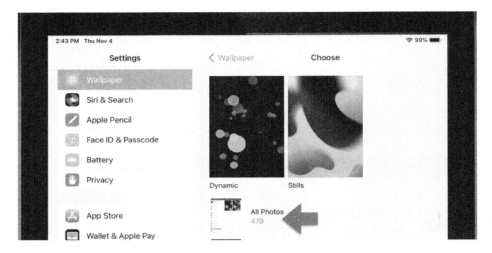

Select the photo you want to use.

Drag the photograph with your finger until it's in the desired position. You can also make the photograph bigger or smaller by pinching the screen with your thumb and forefinger. Tap 'set' on the bottom right when you're done.

Chapter 2: Setting up Your iPad

To set as both home and lock screen tap 'set both'. If you just want the photo on your home screen, tap 'set home screen'. Likewise for lock screen.

Home Screen & Dock

You can change the size of the apps on your dock, you can also select where you want new apps to appear (on home screen or in library). You can choose to show app library link on the dock or recent apps you've either used or downloaded, as well as show the notification badges on the icons in the library. To change these settings, open the settings app, then select 'home screen & dock' from the list on the left.

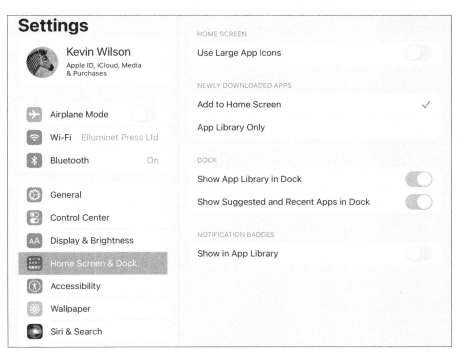

Chapter 2: Setting up Your iPad

Apple ID

Your Apple ID contains all your personal information, messages, calendar, contacts, email, and various settings.

Creating an ID

To create an Apple ID open safari and go to the following website:

`appleid.apple.com`

From the website click 'Create your Apple ID' on the top right.

Fill in the form with your details, scroll down to the bottom and click 'continue'.

Keep a note of the email address and password you entered. You will need this Apple ID if you want to purchase Apps from the App Store, use iCloud, Apple Email, or purchase songs from iTunes Store.

Chapter 2: Setting up Your iPad

FaceID

Face ID is only available on the iPad Pro series with the TrueDepth HD camera, and uses a digital scan of your face to unlock your iPad.

Setup

To setup FaceID, open your settings app, select 'Face ID & Passcode' from the list on the left. Enter your passcode when prompted.

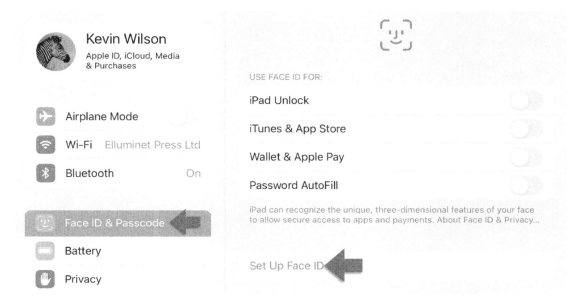

Tap 'Set Up Face ID'. Now, look straight at your device, then rotate your head around in a circular manner - keep looking at your device, rotate your head left, then down, then right, then up, until the green marker makes it all the way around the circle. Tap 'done' to accept.

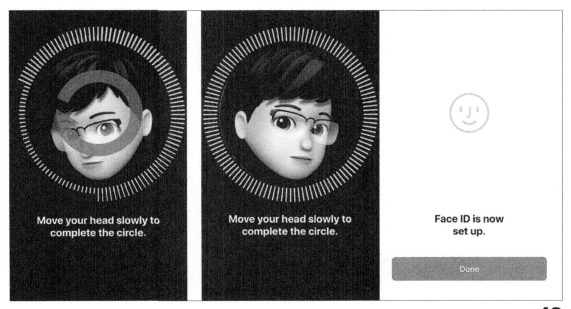

49

Chapter 2: Setting up Your iPad

FaceID Unlock Settings

You can use FaceID to unlock your iPad, authenticate a purchase in the iTunes or App store, or Apple Pay. You can also use FaceID to authenticate password autofill in Safari or another app. To enable these turn on the green switches next to the settings.

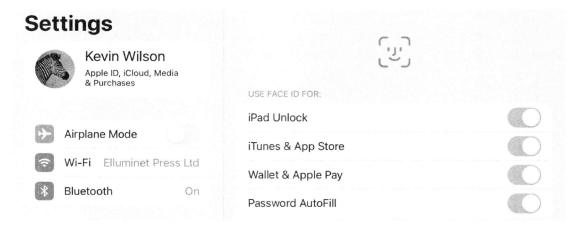

At the bottom, you can change your attention settings. Read the explanations underneath the settings for details on what they do.

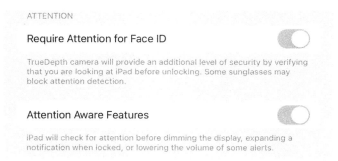

At the bottom, you can allow or disallow access to features when your iPad is locked. This means features someone can access from the lock screen. For example, if we enabled control center, or search using the green switches below

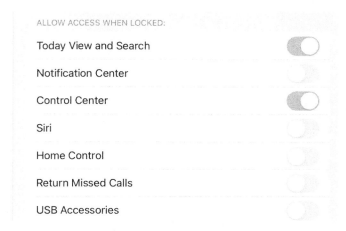

50

Chapter 2: Setting up Your iPad

You would be able to access the control center from the lockscreen without unlocking your device, as I've done so below. You can turn these off if you want to lock down your iPad.

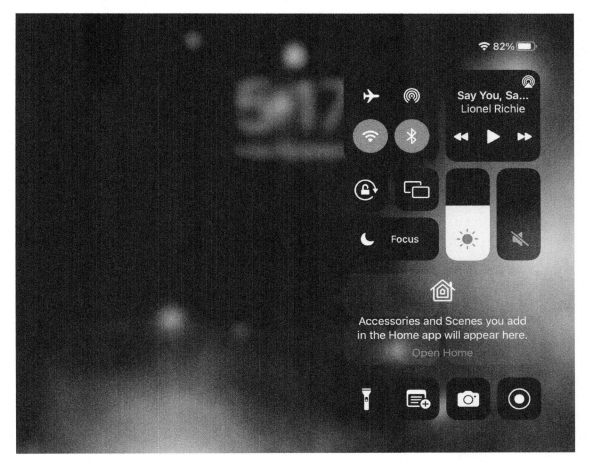

Alternate Appearance

You can set up an additional face, called an alternate appearance. This is useful if your significant other needs to use your phone, or you use your phone in situations where you need to wear a mask, heavy makeup, or sunglasses.

To set this up, first make sure you're wearing your mask, sunglasses, makeup etc, then in the 'faceid & passcode' settings, tap 'set up an alternate appearance'.

Run through the setup on page 49.

Chapter 2: Setting up Your iPad

TouchID

Open your settings app, tap Touch ID & Passcode. Enter your passcode when prompted.

Tap 'add fingerprint'.

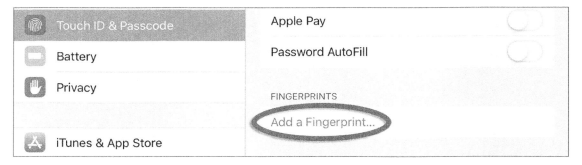

Scan the finger you are most likely to use to press the home button with. In most cases this is your thumb, so it makes sense to scan this finger. *If you're using the new iPad Air, the finger print scanner is on the top button - so use your right index finger.* Follow the instructions on the screen.

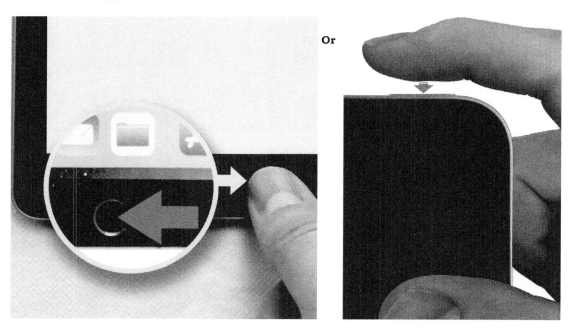

You'll need to scan your finger a few times, so the system can account for different variations, as you wont always put your thumb on the pad in exactly the same position every time. Do what it says on the screen. When you're done, tap 'next'.

Check out the Touch ID demo in the 'using iPad' section of the video resources on how to scan your fingerprint. Scan the code with your iPad or go to the following website

Chapter 2: Setting up Your iPad

Passcode

You can change your passcode using the settings app. To do this, select 'FaceID & Passcode' or 'TouchID & Passcode'. Enter your current passcode when prompted to unlock the settings.

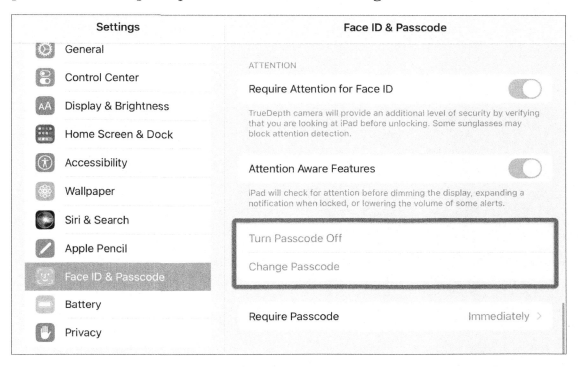

Here, you can turn off passcode. This is not always a good idea, because once unlocked, anyone can access your bank, send emails or texts in your name, or steal sensitive information. However, if you need to turn the passcode off, tap 'turn passcode off'.

To change your passcode, tap 'change passcode'. Enter your current passcode when prompted, then enter your new passcode.

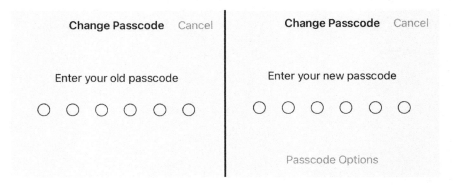

At the bottom, select 'require password'. This allows you to set a timer for how long your iPad waits before locking your screen when you leave your device. If TouchID or FaceID is enabled, the only option immediately. If not, you can select a duration.

53

Chapter 2: Setting up Your iPad

Privacy

The privacy settings give you control over which apps can access certain resources such as Location Services ie your physical location, contacts, calendar, or reminders, your photos, camera, as well as other hardware devices such as microphone, bluetooth, files and folders. Apps are required to request permission to access these resources. You can grant or deny this permission. For example, here in the image below, I'm using Facebook to take and post a photograph. The first time I do this with the app, it will ask me for permission

To view privacy settings, open the settings app, then select 'privacy' from the list on the left hand side. Here, you can see which apps are allowed to access different resources such as location services, tracking, contacts and so on.

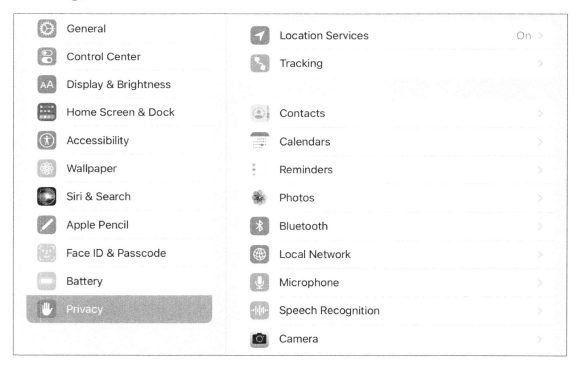

Tap on a resource to view which apps (if any) have requested access to the information.

Chapter 2: Setting up Your iPad

For example, if I tap on camera, I'll see all the apps that have requested permission to use the camera. Tap on the green switches to grant or revoke access.

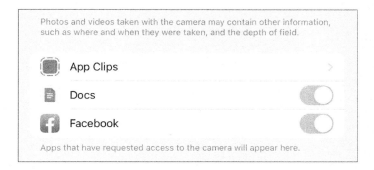

You can see I have granted Facebook access to the camera. To revoke access, tap on the switch to turn it off.

Siri & Search

To change Siri settings, open the settings app, then select 'siri & search' from the list on the left hand side.

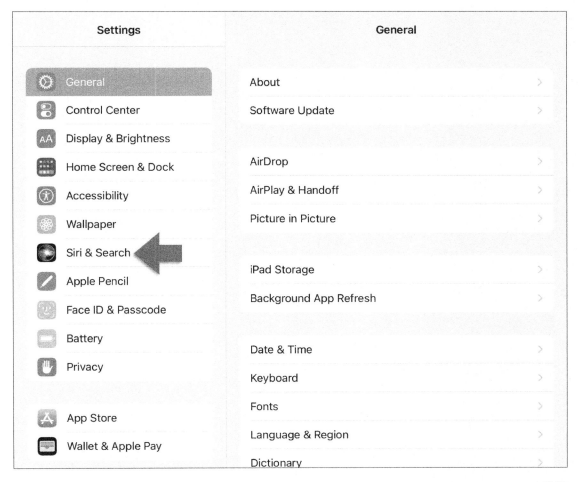

Chapter 2: Setting up Your iPad

Here, you can customise Siri. Lets take a look at the settings:

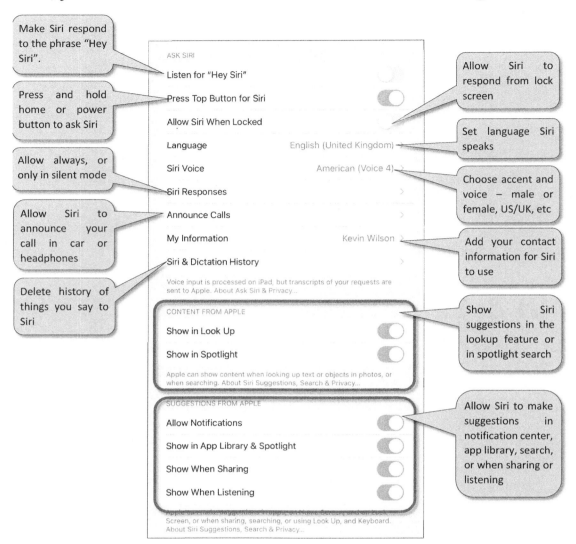

At the bottom, you can select an app. Here, you can allow Siri to learn from how you use the app, as well as allow a particular app to appear in search or Siri's suggestions.

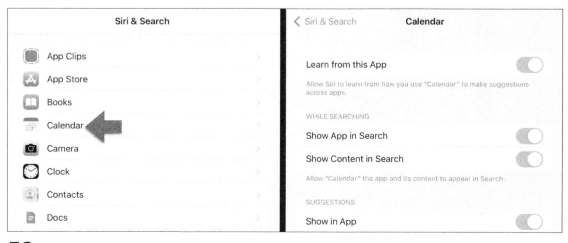

Chapter 2: Setting up Your iPad

Notifications

You can customize the Notification Center and select which apps that are allowed to display notifications in Notification Center. You can also customize notifications for individual apps. To do this, open the settings app, select 'notifications' from the list on the left hand side.

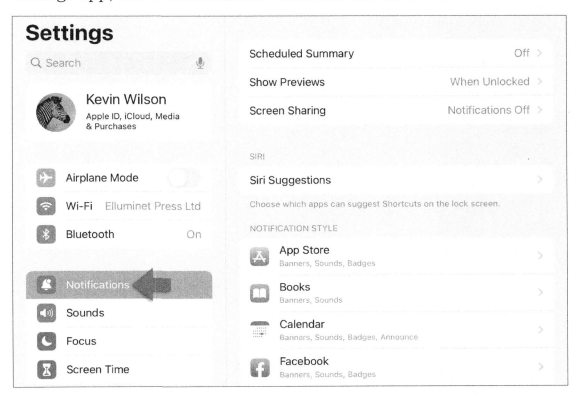

At the top, you'll see three settings. A scheduled summary is a list of notifications for each day. Show previews allows you to show a preview of a notification when the iPad is locked or unlocked. For sensitive apps, you might want to set this to 'when unlocked', so no private message appear on your iPad when the screen is locked. Screen sharing allows you to configure whether you want notifications to appear when you're sharing your screen or using SharePlay. Good idea to set this to 'notifications off' to prevent notifications appearing while you're presenting, sharing your screen, or watching together on SharePlay.

You can change the notification style of a particular app. To do this tap on the app in the 'notification style' section.

Here, you can specify whether you want the notification to appear on lock screen & notification center, as well as what sound the notification makes when it pops up.

Siri Suggestions allows you to choose which apps Siri is allowed to suggest on the lock screen.

Chapter 2: Setting up Your iPad

At the bottom of the page, you'll see a list of apps. Here, you can select an app and customise the notification banners on the lock screen, and notification center. For example, I selected 'calendar'.

If you want the notifications to stay on your lock screen all the time, change 'banner style' to persistent. If you want the notification to popup, alert you, then disappear, change 'banner style' to temporary

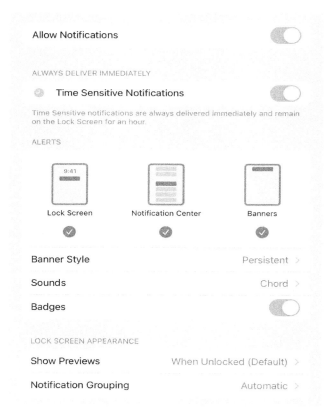

If you want to change the sound, tap sound, then select a sound from the options.

Badges are the little indicators on app icons.

Chapter 2: Setting up Your iPad

Connecting to the Internet

You can connect your iPad to the internet using WiFi or Cellular (if you have the cellular model).

WiFi

WiFi is often faster than cellular data networks, but may not be available in some locations.

To locate nearby WiFi networks, open the settings app. Select 'WiFi' from the list on the left hand side, then tap the name of the network you want to join.

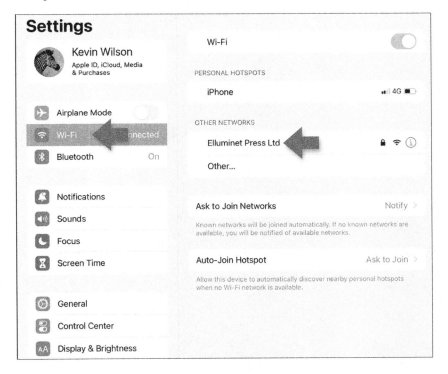

Enter the WiFi password or network key.

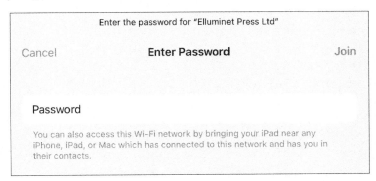

Once you have done that tap 'join'.

Chapter 2: Setting up Your iPad

For your home WiFi, the network key or password, is usually printed on the back of your router.

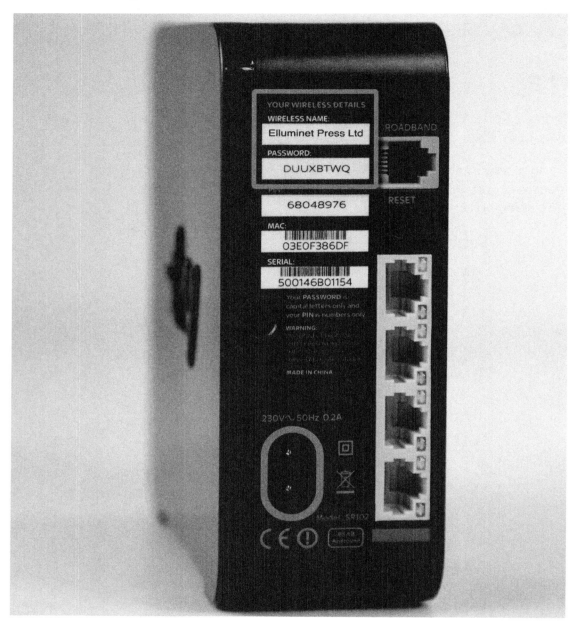

The network name is sometimes called an SSID.

Use the same procedure if you are on a public hotspot such as in a cafe, library, hotel, airport and so on. You'll need to find the network key if they have one. Some are open networks and you can just connect.

When using public hotspots, keep in mind that most of them don't encrypt the data you send over the internet and aren't secure. So don't start checking your online banking account or shop online while using an unsecured connection, as anyone who is on the public WiFi hotspot can potentially gain access to anything you do.

Chapter 2: Setting up Your iPad

Cellular

Make sure your device is off before doing this. If you're using an iPad with cellular features, you'll need to insert a SIM card from your network provider.

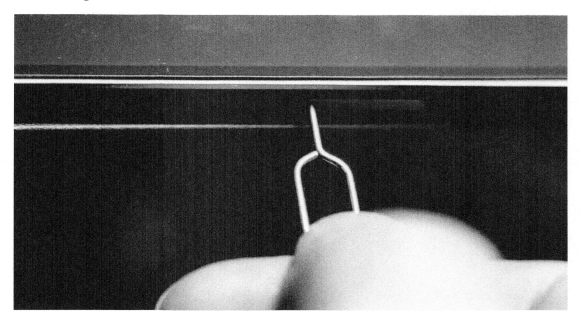

To do this, push the end of a paper clip into the release hole on the side of your device. Pull out the little tray and insert your SIM.

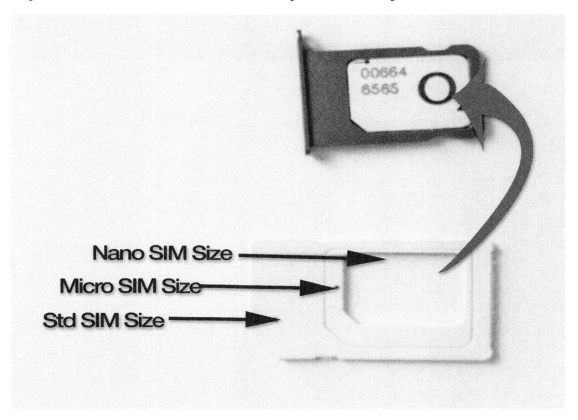

Chapter 2: Setting up Your iPad

Slide the little tray back into your device, until it fits firmly into place against the side.

You're now ready to power on your iPad. To do this, hold down the power button located on the top of your device, until you see the Apple logo on the screen.

Give your iPad a few seconds to start up.

Open the settings app, select 'cellular data' or 'mobile data' from the list on the left.

Turn on cellular data. Under cellular data options, you can select 3G, 4G, 5G, LTE, depending on your network provider. You can also enable/disable data roaming.

You can use your iPad as a hotspot to share your data connection with another device such as your Mac.

Chapter 2: Setting up Your iPad

Underneath, you'll see details of your data plan. Tap on your plan to view details, or tap 'add a new plan' to add a new data plan from your provider.

At the bottom of the page, you'll see which apps are allowed to use this data connection.

If you want to save your data, turn off the apps you don't use. Apps you turn off will be blocked from using your cellular data but will reconnect when you switch to WiFi.

VPNs

If you're really concerned about security or use your devices on public hotspots for work, then you should consider a VPN or Virtual Private Network. A VPN encrypts all the data you send and receive over a network. There are a few good ones to choose from, some have a free option with a limited amount of data and others you pay a subscription.

You can download an app from the app store to automatically configure the VPN. Take a look at www.tunnelbear.com, windscribe.com & speedify.com

To set one up manually, open the settings app then select 'general' from the list on the left. Tap 'VPN and device management'. Tap 'VPN', then enter the connection details. You can get these from your VPN provider, school, college or work.

School/Work Accounts

If your school/college or work provides you with an account, open the settings app, then select 'general' from the list on the left. Tap 'VPN and device management'. Tap 'sign in to work or school account', then enter your account email address and password.

Chapter 2: Setting up Your iPad

iCloud

If you've set up your iPad from new and been through the initial setup, then your iPad will normally be signed in to your iCloud account. However if you need to sign into another iPad then you can do so from the settings app.

To **sign in**, open your settings app, tap on 'sign in to your iPad' then enter your Apple ID email address and password. Tap 'sign in'.

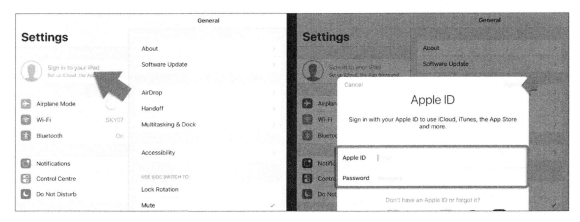

To **sign out**, open your settings app, tap on your Apple ID.

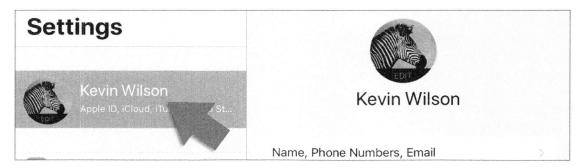

On the bottom right hand side, tap 'sign out'.

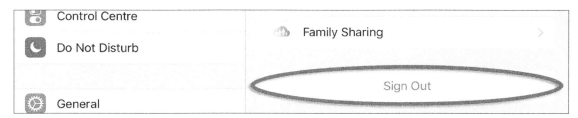

Chapter 2: Setting up Your iPad

Settings

Once you've signed into your iCloud account, you'll see some settings down the right hand side.

Here, you can change your name, add phone numbers or email addresses people use to contact you. Just tap 'edit' next to the section you want to change.

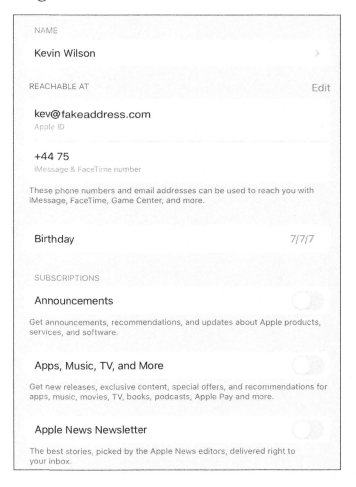

65

Chapter 2: Setting up Your iPad

Under 'password & security', you can change your iCloud password, as well as enable/disable 2 factor authentication. If you forgot your iCloud password, go to `iforgot.apple.com` then follow the instructions on screen.

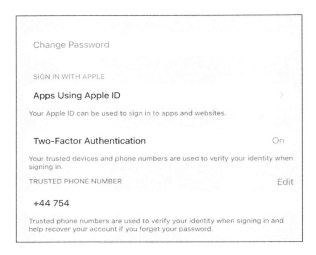

Under 'payment & shipping', you can add apple pay and credit cards to buy things online, in the app store, apple music, apple TV, etc. Tap 'add payment method' to add a new card, or tap 'apple pay' to edit apple pay settings.

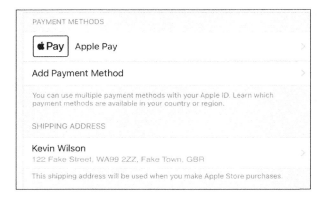

Under subscriptions, you can manage subscriptions to apple music, apple one, iCloud+ and so on.

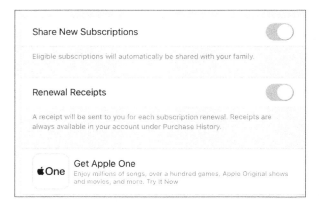

Chapter 2: Setting up Your iPad

iCloud Sync

From the settings app, select your Apple ID, then click 'icloud'.

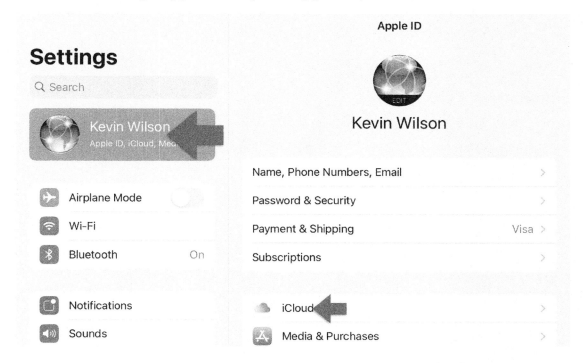

Under 'apps using icloud', you can select which apps you want to synchronise across all your devices.

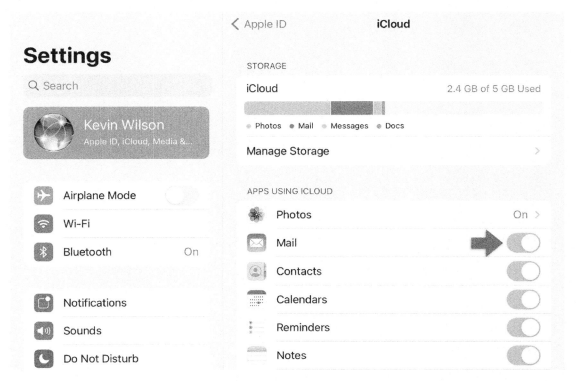

Click the switch on the right to turn on and off.

Chapter 2: Setting up Your iPad

Storage Management

From the settings app, select your Apple ID, then click 'icloud'. You'll see a chart at the top of the screen giving you a breakdown of what is taking up space on your iCloud storage. Tap 'manage storage'

Here, you'll see a more detailed breakdown of the apps using storage on iCloud and the amount of space they've taken up. Now the data stored on iCloud isn't the app itself, it's the data such as your messages, photos you've taken, device backups etc.

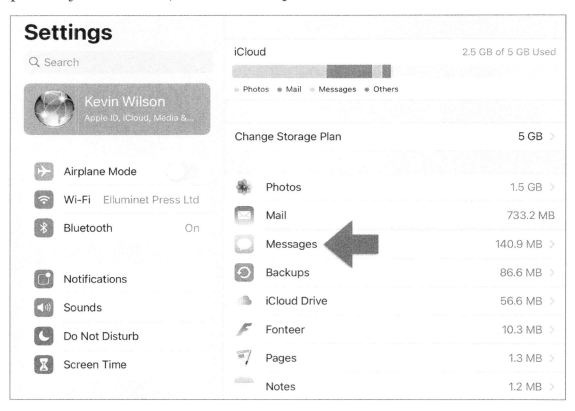

Tap on the app to view details and delete any data. This is useful if your iCloud storage is running low.

Tap 'change storage plan' if you need more than 5GB of iCloud storage. There is a charge for larger storage plans.

Chapter 2: Setting up Your iPad

Forgot Password

If you've forgotten your iCloud password, you can attempt to recover it.

On your iPad or another computer, open your web browser and navigate to

`iforgot.apple.com`

Enter your Apple ID email address, click 'continue'.

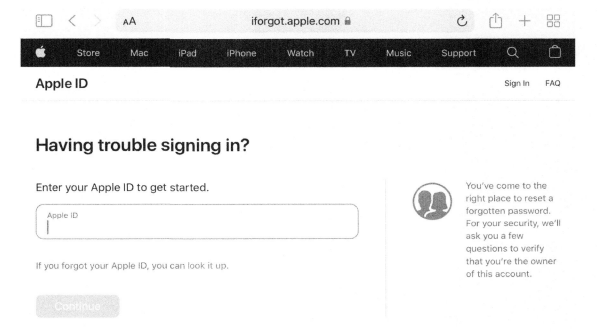

Enter your phone number if prompted, click 'continue'.

You'll receive a 'reset password' prompt on one of your Apple devices, such as your iPad, iPhone or Mac. In this example, this is on my iPad. Tap 'allow' on the prompt.

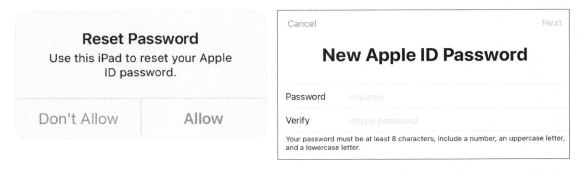

Run through the instructions. Then enter a new password when prompted.

Tap 'next'.

69

Chapter 2: Setting up Your iPad

Adding Email Accounts

If you have multiple email accounts, perhaps one for home, work, school etc, you can add them all to the email app. To do this, tap the settings app icon on your home screen

On the left hand side of the screen, scroll down to 'mail'.

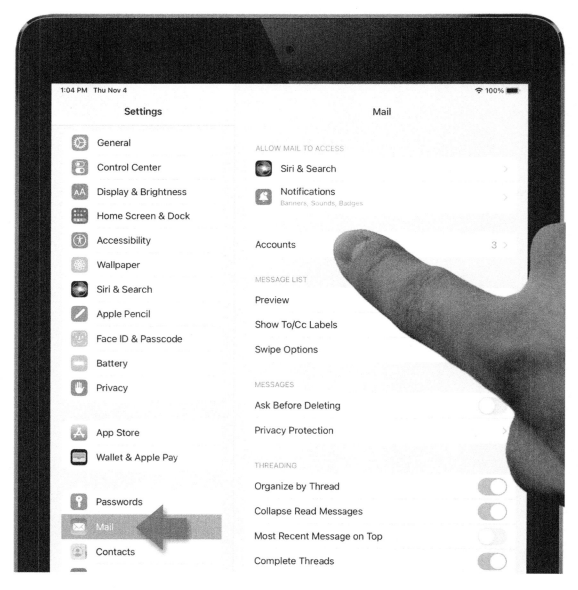

On the right hand side at the top, tap 'accounts'.

Chapter 2: Setting up Your iPad

Under the 'accounts' section, tap 'add account'.

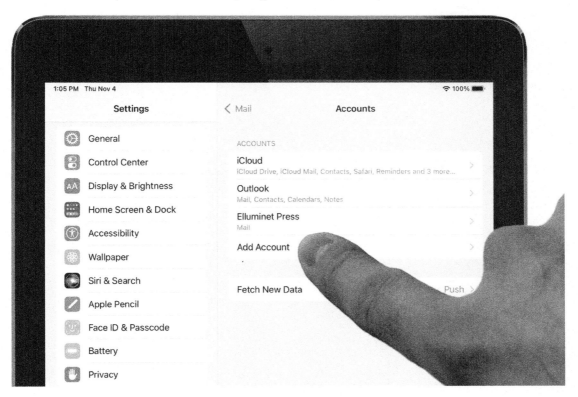

Tap the type of account you want to add.

If you have a Yahoo account, tap 'yahoo', if you have a Google/GMail account, tap 'google', or a Hotmail or Microsoft Account, tap 'outlook.com'. In this example I am going to add a Microsoft Account. So I'd tap on 'outlook.com'.

71

Chapter 2: Setting up Your iPad

In the box that appears, enter your account email address, tap 'next', then your password. Tap 'next'.

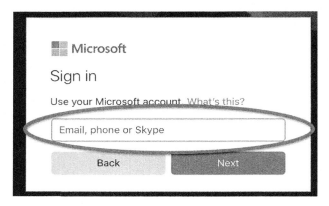

Select 'yes' to the permission confirmation, to allow your iPad to access your email account.

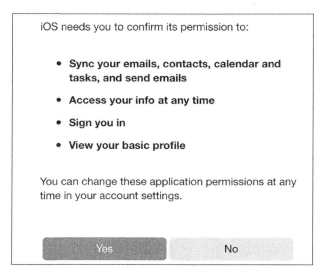

Select what you want your iPad to sync from the mail server. You can copy email, contacts, your calendar and any reminders onto your iPad by turning all the toggle switches to green, as shown below.

Tap 'Save'.

Chapter 2: Setting up Your iPad

Add Social Media Accounts

You can add your Facebook and Twitter accounts to your iPad. The easiest way to do this is to go to the App Store and download the app for Facebook, Instagram, Twitter, and whatever else you use.

Tap on the 'app store' icon on your home screen. Tap 'search' on the bottom left.

In the search field on the top right type 'facebook'.

Tap 'get', next to the Facebook icon to download it. This icon might also look like a cloud if you have downloaded it before on another device, such as an iPod or iPhone.

Once the app has downloaded, hit your home button, then tap the Facebook icon on your home screen.

You can now sign in with your Facebook username and password.

You can use the same procedure to setup any other social media apps you want to use.

Chapter 2: Setting up Your iPad

Connecting Devices

You can connect various devices to your iPad most of which use bluetooth to connect wirelessly.

Bluetooth

You can pair bluetooth keyboards, headphones, and bluetooth capable hardware in some cars.

To pair a device, first put the device into pairing mode. You'll need to refer to the device's instructions to find specific details on how to do this. On most devices, press and hold the pairing button until the status light starts flashing. This means the device is ready to be paired with your iPad.

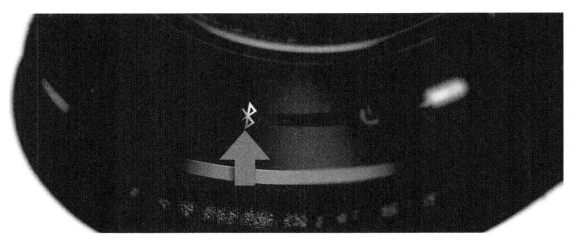

On your iPad, open the settings app. From the settings app, select 'bluetooth'.

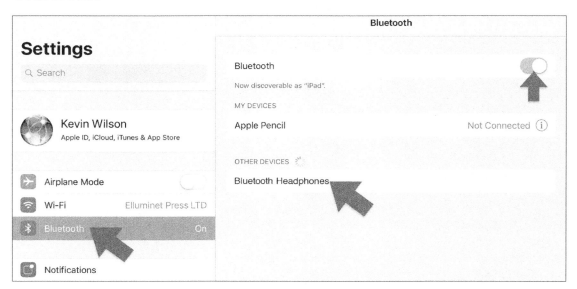

Chapter 2: Setting up Your iPad

Turn it on, if it isn't already.

Your iPad will scan for devices nearby. You'll need to give it a few seconds to work. Any devices found will be listed. Tap on the device in the list to pair it.

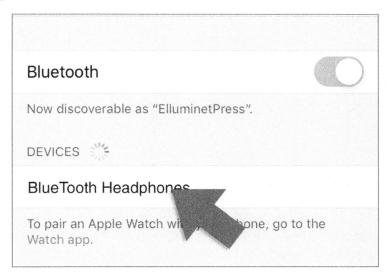

Some devices require a PIN code, enter it if prompted. Refer to the device's instructions to find out what the PIN code is. On most devices the default PIN is 0000, 1111 or 1234, but not always.

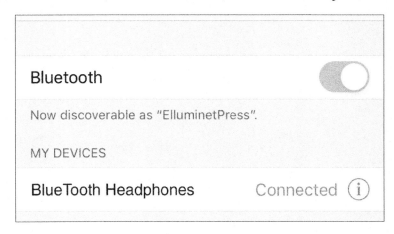

To remove a device, tap the 'i' info icon, then tap 'forget this device'.

Chapter 2: Setting up Your iPad

USB

These come in useful when you want to connect something to your iPad and most peripherals, if they are not wireless, connect via USB.

These can be keyboards, mice, external hard drives, USB memory sticks, cameras, some models of printers and memory card readers.

For standard iPads (iPad 9.7", iPad 10.5", and iPad Mini) you'll need one with the lightning plug, for other iPads such as iPad Mini, iPad Air and iPad pro, you'll need USB-C

Video

AV Adapters are useful if you want to connect your iPad to a TV, Monitor or Projector.

You can buy a small adapter that plugs into the port on the bottom of your iPad and will enable you to connect to an HDMI or DVI/VGA connector on your TV or Projector. Most modern TVs and Projectors are HDMI.

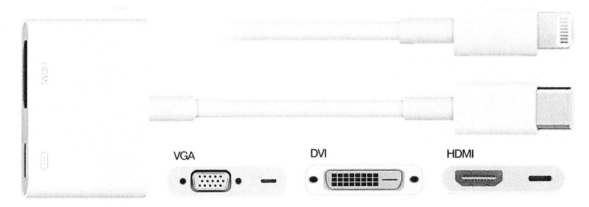

For standard iPads (iPad 9.7", iPad 10.5", and iPad Mini) you'll need one with the lightning plug, for other iPads such as iPad Mini, iPad Air and iPad pro, you'll need USB-C

Chapter 2: Setting up Your iPad

Connecting to a Computer

Your iPad lightning cable connects to the port on the bottom of your iPad.

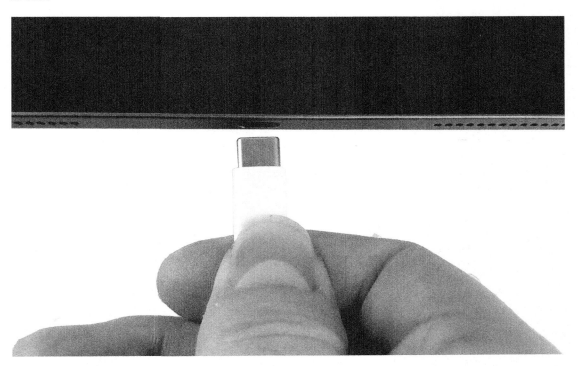

The other end of the cable can be plugged into a PC or Mac to allow you to load on music, photos, apps etc.

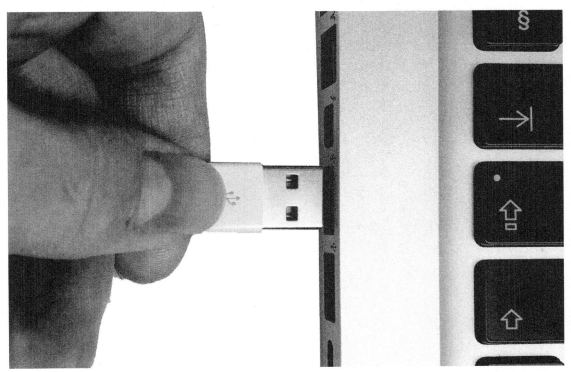

Chapter 2: Setting up Your iPad

Setup Universal Control

This feature usually works automatically when compatible devices are nearby. Here below is our little setup. We have an iMac on the right with an iPad Pro next to it.

To set up Universal Control, on one of your Macs - I'm going to start on the iMac - click on the Apple icon on the top left, then select 'system preferences'. Then click on 'displays'.

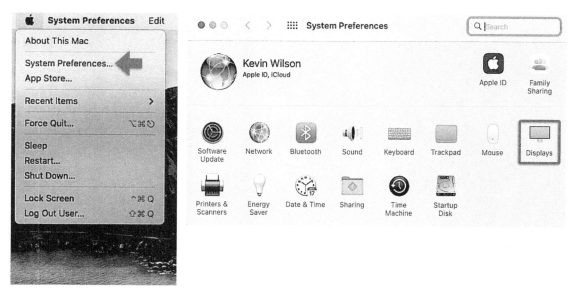

Chapter 2: Setting up Your iPad

Click on 'add display' on the bottom left. In the drop down menu, you'll see a section called 'link keyboard and mouse'. Select the machine you want to link to, in this demo iPad Pro.

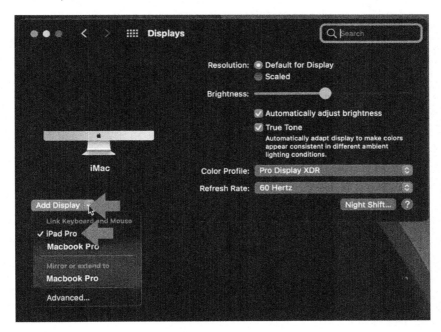

Now arrange the displays on the screen to match your physical setup. My iPad is on the right, so I moved the 'iPad' icon to the right of the iMac icon.

Chapter 2: Setting up Your iPad

On the 'add display' drop down menu, select, 'advanced'.

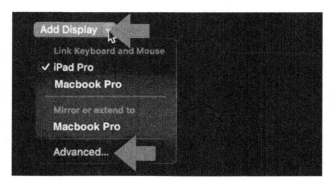

Here, you can allow your mouse pointer to switch between nearby Macs and iPads.

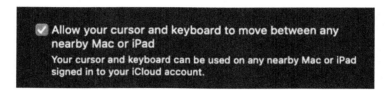

Here, if you turn this option off, you allow your mouse pointer to move freely between your Macs and iPads.

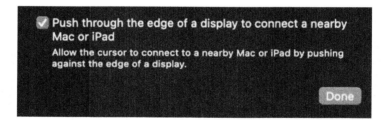

If you turn this feature on, you'll see a purple marker when you move your mouse pointer to the edge of the screen. You'll need to push through to get to the other Mac or iPad.

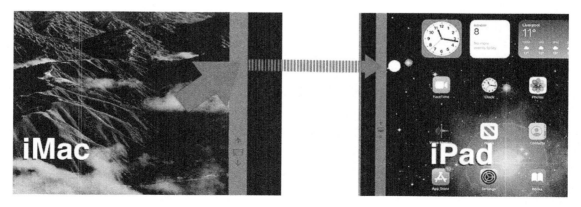

Click 'done', when you're finished.

See "Universal Control" on page 135.

Chapter 2: Setting up Your iPad

Apple Pay

Apple Pay allows you to keep digital copies of your bank cards, and lets you pay for things using your iPhone or iPad. You can use this feature on an iPad but it is more convenient with an iPhone.

Apple Pay will run on iPhone SE, iPhone 6, iPhone 6 Plus, and later as well as, iPad Pro, iPad Air 2, iPad mini 3, and later.

Setup

Make sure your bank supports Apple Pay. If so, go to your settings app then scroll down the left hand side and tap 'wallet & apple pay'. Then tap 'add credit or debit card' link. Tap 'continue' on the apple pay popup.

Now, in the 'add card' window, if you already have a credit/debit card registered with your Apple ID, then apple pay will ask you to add this one.

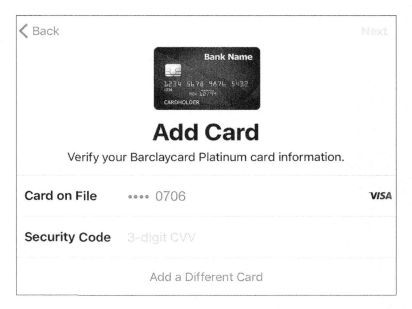

If this is the card you want to use, then enter the 3 digit security code and tap 'next' on the top right. Hit 'agree' on the terms and conditions; your card will be added.

Chapter 2: Setting up Your iPad

If you want to add a different card, tap 'add a different card', at the bottom of the 'add card' window. You can scan your card with the iPad's camera.

Position the card so it fills the white rectangle on your screen. Apple Pay will scan your card and automatically enter your details

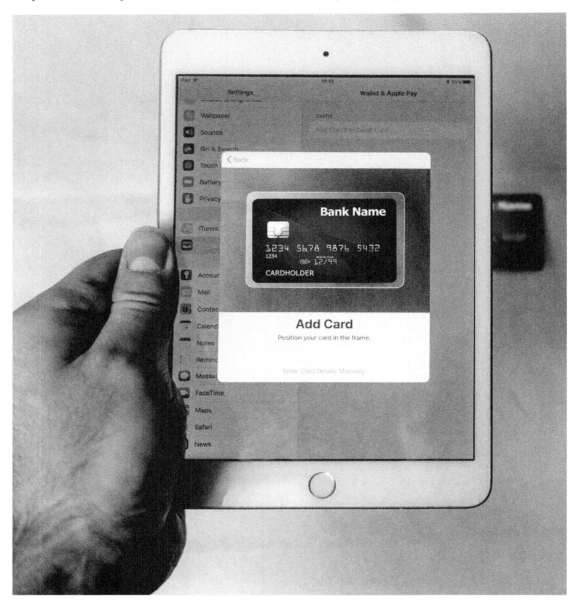

If you can't get the camera to scan the card, tap 'enter card details manually' then key in your card number, exp dates and so on.

Enter the security code from the back of your card. The bank will authorise your card. Accept the terms and conditions.

If you also have an iPhone, these cards will be synced with your iPhone so you can use Apple Pay on there too.

Chapter 2: Setting up Your iPad

Using Apple Pay

You can use Apple Pay at any store that supports this feature. You will usually see the logo displayed in store. You can also use Apple Pay on some online stores.

First, make sure your shipping and contact details are correct for Apple Pay. Open the settings app, select 'Wallet & Apple Pay'. Set a shipping address, email and phone number if you haven't already.

During checkout, tap the 'Apple Pay' button.

Review the payment information. Then authorise the payment either using your Touch ID or Face ID.

To authorise on the iPad Pro series with Face ID, double-press the top button, then authenticate with Face ID.

On an iPad with Touch ID, authenticate with Touch ID using the home button on standard iPads, or the top button on the new iPad Air.

83

Chapter 2: Setting up Your iPad

Family Sharing

You can add up to six other family members. You can share iTunes and Apps, Apple Music, iCloud Storage, your location and authorize your kid's spending on the app store.

You can set up an Apple ID for each of your kids, set permissions remotely with screen time and approve spending or downloads from a your device with the 'Ask to Buy' feature.

Setup

To setup family sharing open the settings app on your device, select your Apple ID. Tap 'Family Sharing'.

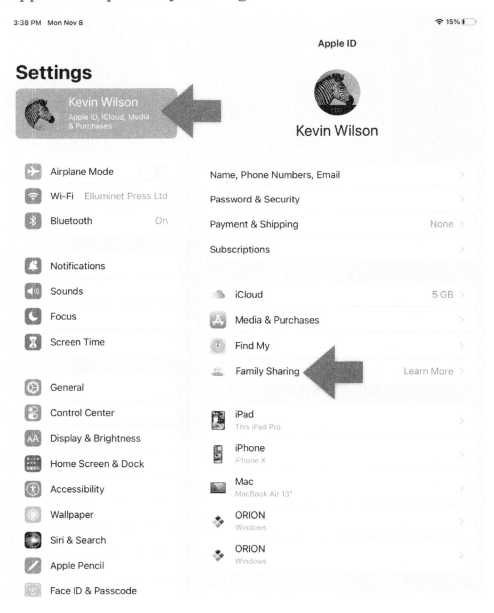

Chapter 2: Setting up Your iPad

Click 'set up your family'

Click 'invite people'

Click 'invite in person'

85

Chapter 2: Setting up Your iPad

Enter the person's Apple ID and password, tap 'next' on the top right of the screen.

On the other person's iPhone or iPad, they'll receive an email asking them to join the family.

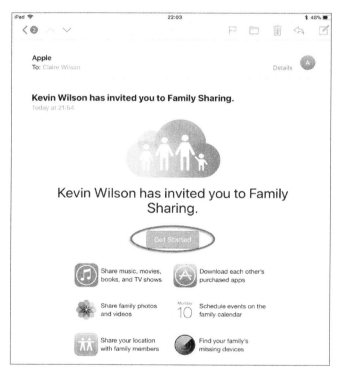

Tap 'get started', then tap 'accept' at the bottom of the invitation.

Chapter 2: Setting up Your iPad

Add a Family Member

Go to settings, select your Apple ID. Tap 'family sharing' then tap 'add member'. Tap 'invite people'

Now select how you want to invite them. You can invite them 'in person', or send an invitation via iMessage or email.

In this example I'm going to invite 'in person' as this person is in the same house hold. Select 'invite in person' from the popup. Enter the person's Apple ID email address and password.

Click 'next' on the top right of the screen.

Chapter 2: Setting up Your iPad

When the person checks their email, they'll see an invitation to join the family.

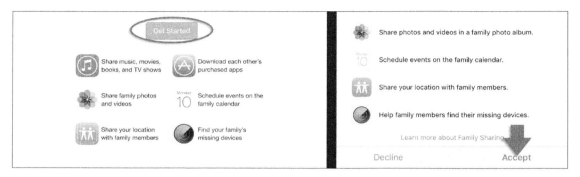

Click 'get started', then click 'accept' on the confirmation.

Child Accounts

If you have young children it makes sense to create separate accounts for them rather than allowing them to use yours. This helps to protect them and to help you monitor what your child is up to.

To create a child account, go to settings, select your Apple ID. Tap 'family sharing' then tap 'add member'. From the bottom of the popup select 'create an account for a child'.

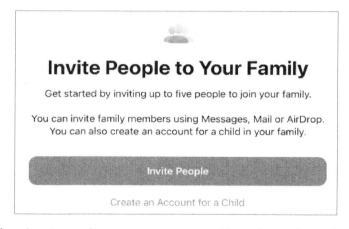

Now follow the instructions on screen. Tap 'continue' on the 'create child account' screen.

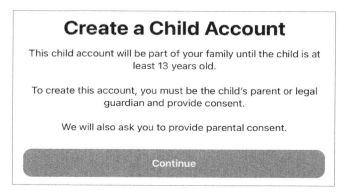

88

Chapter 2: Setting up Your iPad

Select a payment method for verification, then on the next screen enter your card details. This does not take any payment, the card details are used to verify your identity. Click 'done' on the top right.

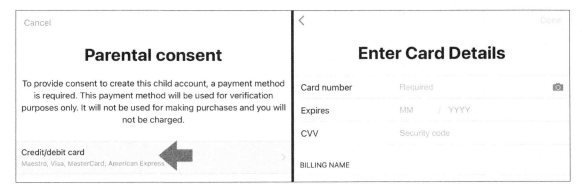

Scroll to the bottom, tap 'agree'.

Enter your child's first name, surname, and date of birth, then tap 'next'.

89

Chapter 2: Setting up Your iPad

Enter an Apple ID email for them. Tap 'next'. Enter a password for them and tap 'next'.

Click 'use...' at the bottom of the screen.

Click 'turn on' at the bottom of the screen. 'Ask to buy' means that if your child tries to buy an app from the app store, a music track, tv show or film, you will receive an authorisation request where you can approve the purchase or deny it. You'll also be able to track their physical location.

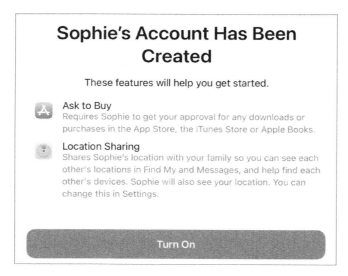

Now allow your child to sign into their iPad with the Apple ID email address and password you just created. In this example it would be sophie20077@icloud.com

Chapter 2: Setting up Your iPad

With 'ask to buy' enabled, kids can send purchase requests for apps, music, movies, and more to their parents provided this service is set up correctly.

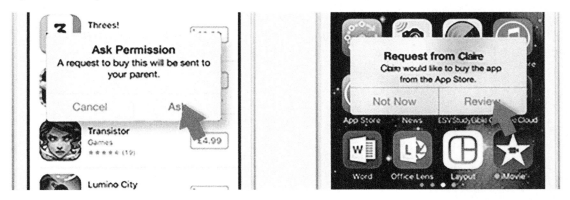

On your device, tap 'review' from the prompt to see details of the request.

Manage Family Sharing

To manage your family sharing settings, open the settings app on your device, select your Apple ID. Tap 'Family Sharing'. Let's take a look at the sections on the 'manage' screen...

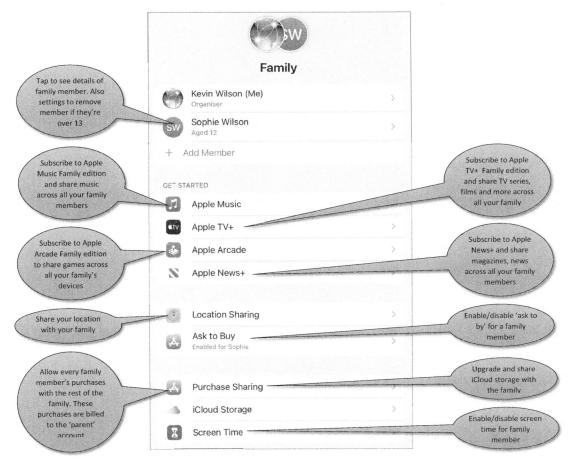

91

Chapter 2: Setting up Your iPad

Screen Time

Screen Time collects usage statistics on the various apps you use on your iPad. It records how much time you've spent using a particular app, can generate activity reports, allows you to set app time limits, and can be useful for monitoring your kid's activity.

You can find screen time on your settings app. On the left hand side of the settings app, select 'screen time'.

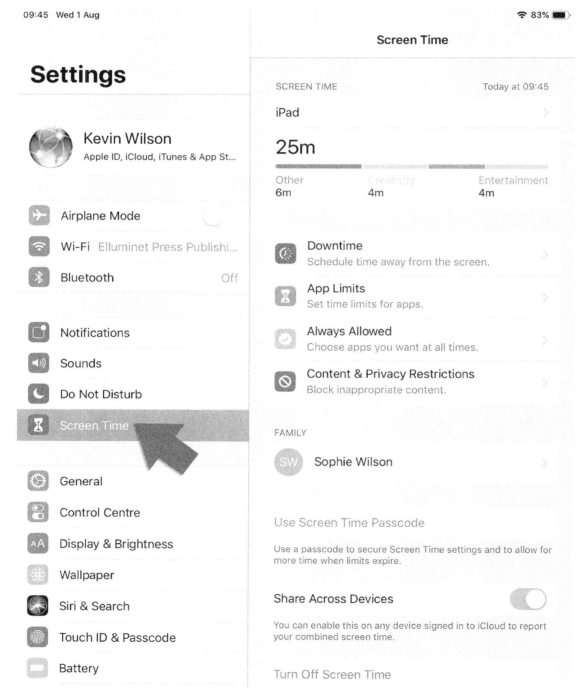

Chapter 2: Setting up Your iPad

Lets take a look at the main screen.

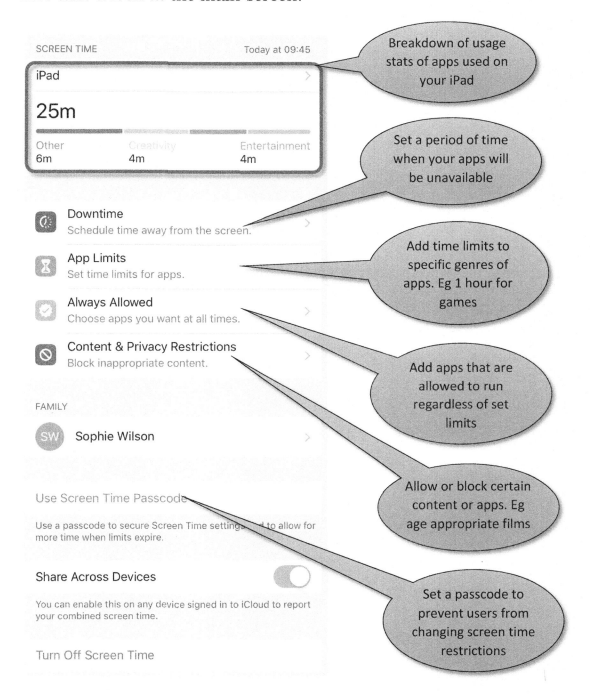

Starting from the top of the screen, you'll see a breakdown of the total time spend using your iPad

Below that, you'll be able to make some adjustments to the settings as shown in the image above.

From here, you can also block different apps and various web sites and content.

93

Chapter 2: Setting up Your iPad

Downtime

With downtime, you can set a period of time, say a couple of hours, that your iPad apps are unavailable.

Select 'downtime' from the main screen, and turn it on using the switch at the top.

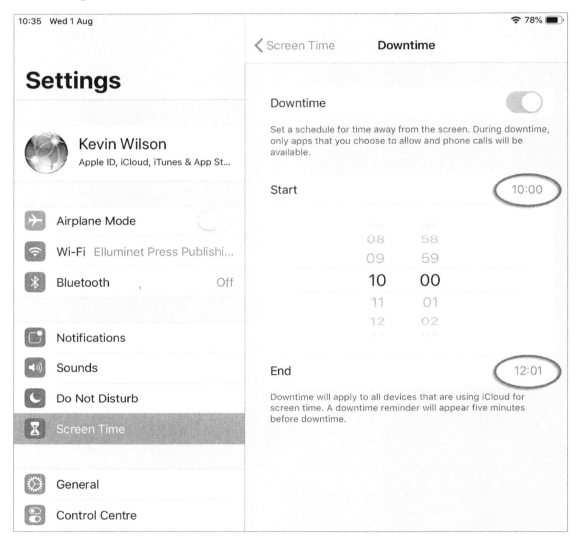

Below, you'll see two options appear. Use this to set the start and end times you want apps to be unavailable. Tap on the times to change them.

For example, you could set it from 9pm to 7am. This would mean, from 9pm, your iPad apps will turn off until 7am the next morning - preventing you from using your iPad late at night.

You could also set a limit so if your children use the iPad, they can't use it until a certain time - perhaps after they've done their homework.

Chapter 2: Setting up Your iPad

App Limits

You can set the length of time you want a particular app to be available. To do this, select 'app limits' from the main screen, then tap 'add limit'.

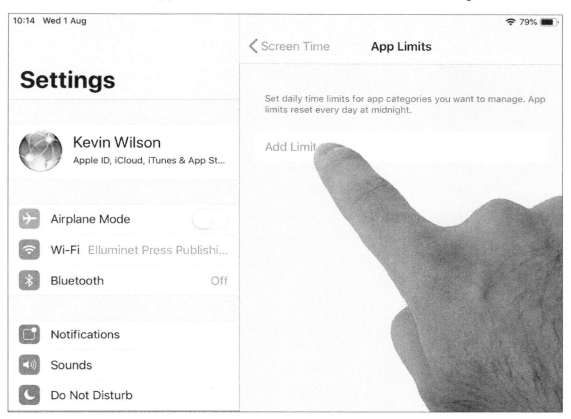

Choose the genre of apps you want to add the limit to. In this example I'm adding a limit to all social networking apps such as facebook, instagram and so on, then tap 'add'.

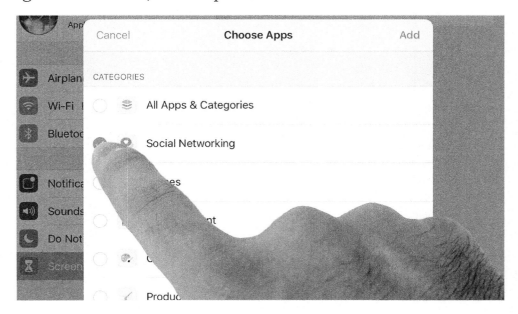

Chapter 2: Setting up Your iPad

Set the length of time using the sliders indicated with the red arrow.

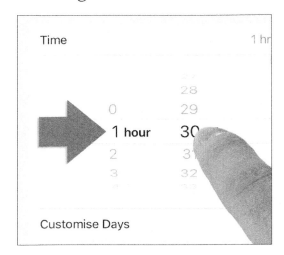

If you want different times on different days, select 'customise days'. This will allow you to input different time limits on different days. Eg, you might want to allow more time at the weekends. Tap on the time limits to change them.

Tap 'back' to return to the previous screen.

Tap the set time on the top right to confirm.

Chapter 2: Setting up Your iPad

Always Allowed

This allows you to choose the apps you want to be available regardless of any content restrictions or time restrictions that are set. Tap the green + to add an app from the list, or tap the red - to remove an app.

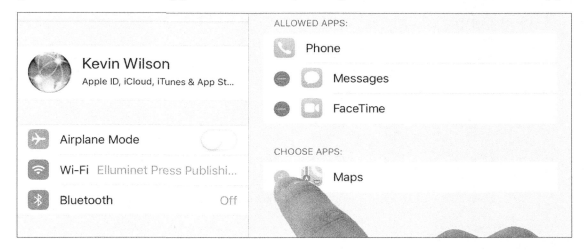

Content & Privacy Restrictions

Content & Privacy allows you to set restrictions on certain content such as age appropriate films and television programs, or songs, websites, and books with adult themes. This is useful if your kids are using the iPad.

To set content & privacy restrictions, from the settings app, on the screen time page, select 'content & privacy restrictions'.

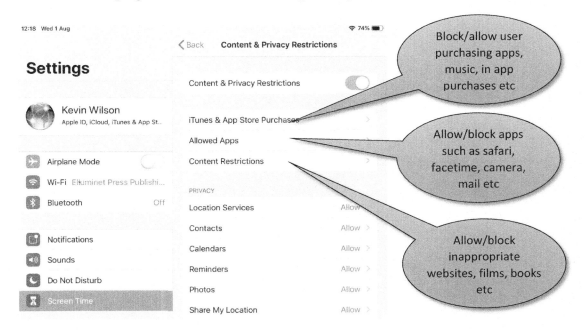

97

Chapter 2: Setting up Your iPad

Allowing and Blocking Content

Go to the 'content & privacy restrictions' section of screen time. From here you can add restrictions on content, apps and websites.

Tap the options to make your selections about what content to allow and what content to block.

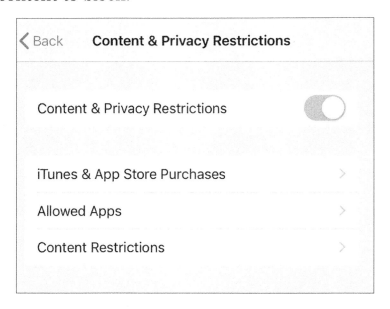

For example, to allow or block app store purchases, tap 'iTunes & App Store Purchases'

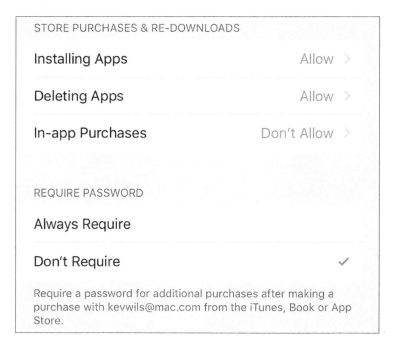

Change the setting to 'allow' to allow the feature, change it to 'don't allow' to deny the feature.

Chapter 2: Setting up Your iPad

You can do the same for content restrictions such as age appropriate apps, films and websites.

To change these settings, tap 'content restrictions'

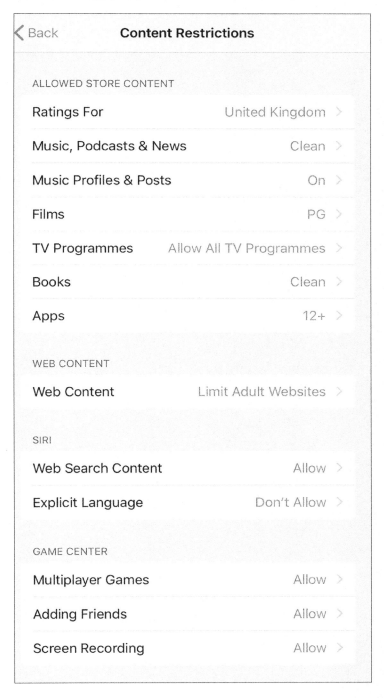

Tap on and change the settings appropriately. For example, to only allow PG rated films, tap 'films' and select 'PG'

Do the same for websites, web search content and language. Tap and set these to the appropriate settings, as shown in the example above.

3 Getting Around Your iPad

iPads have a touch screen user interface allowing you to interact with the apps on the screen using touch gestures.

In this chapter, we'll take a look at:

- Around the iPad's Hardware
- The Home Screen
- The App Library
- Control Center
- Notification Center
- Touch Gestures
- Multitasking
- The App Shelf
- Using Universal Control
- The On-screen Keyboard
- Spotlight Search
- Siri
- Translation
- Taking Screenshots
- Screen Recording

Take a look at the video resources, open your web browser and navigate to the following website.

elluminetpress.com/ipad-nav

Chapter 3: Getting around your iPad

Your iPad

Let's take a look around the iPad itself. If you're using the new iPad Air, Mini or iPad Pro, you'll have something like this.

Along the top bezel, you'll find the front facing facetime camera. This is also where you'll find the TrueDepth camera on the iPad pro for use with FaceID.

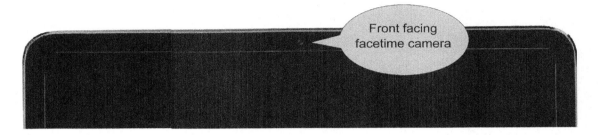

Along the top edge, you'll find the power button. On some models such as the new iPad Air and iPad mini, the power button also houses the TouchID fingerprint scanner.

Along the bottom edge, you'll find either a USB-C port, or a lightning port on older models, or the 10.2" iPad.

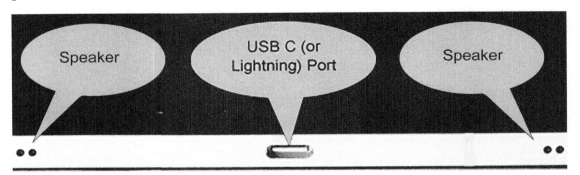

You'll also find two speakers either side.

101

Chapter 3: Getting around your iPad

On the back, you'll see your cameras, front mic, and camera flash/flashlight, as well as a LIDAR scanner on some models.

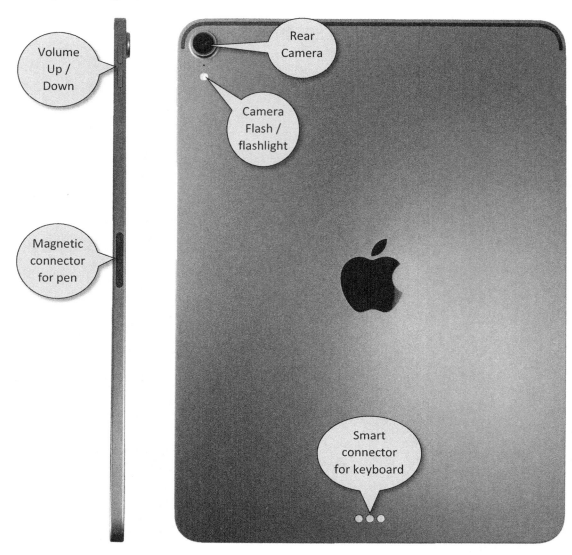

Along the side you'll find your volume controls and a magnetic connector you can use to hold and charge your Apple Pencil (2nd Gen).

Along the other side, you'll find your SIM card tray (only on cellular models). This allows you to connect to the internet using the cellular network much like a cell/mobile phone.

Here, you can insert a SIM card from your network provider.

See page 61 for more details on how to insert a SIM card.

Chapter 3: Getting around your iPad

If you have an older iPad or the 10.2" model, the physical layout of your iPad will be slightly different from other models.

At the bottom of the iPad itself, we have the home button. Whenever you want to get back to the home screen from any app, just press this button.

103

Chapter 3: Getting around your iPad

This diagram below shows the rear. You can see volume controls and SIM card tray on the left of the diagram. On the back you'll see your camera, the headphone jack along the top and the dock connector along the bottom.

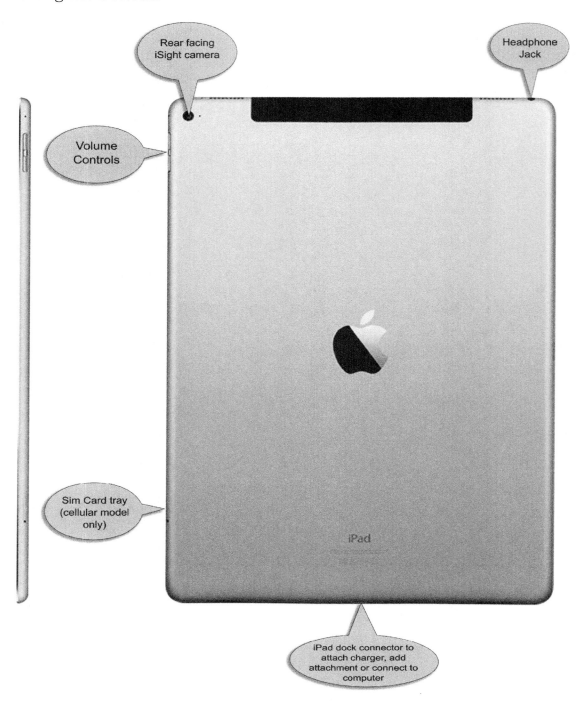

You can see volume controls and SIM card tray on the left of the diagram. On the back you'll see your camera, the headphone jack along the top and the dock connector along the bottom.

Chapter 3: Getting around your iPad

Home Screen

The home screen is a launch pad where you'll find icons for all your apps.

Anatomy

Along the top, you'll see the status bar. This shows date, time day on the left hand side, with WiFi/Cellular and battery status on the right hand side.

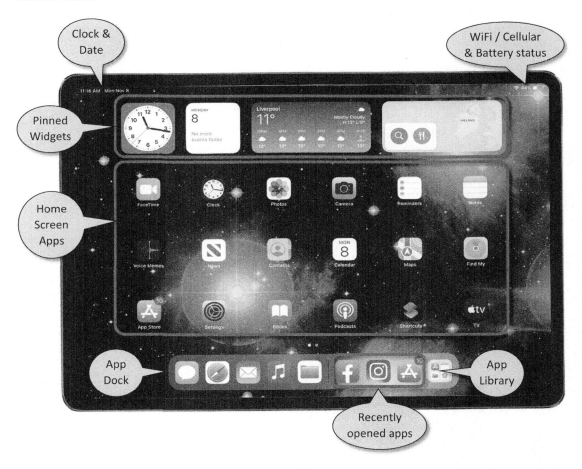

With iPadOS 15, you can add widgets to the home screen. These appear along the top, however you can put them anywhere on the home screen.

Underneath you'll see icons for all apps installed on your iPad. Swipe left or right to move between app pages. Along the bottom, you'll see the App dock. This allows you to access popular apps, as well as apps you use most often. On the far right of the app dock, you'll see an icon to open the app library.

Chapter 3: Getting around your iPad

Arranging Icons

To move an icon, tap and hold your finger on the icon, then drag your finger across the screen.

The other icons on the screen will automatically move and rearrange themselves around the icon you're moving. To move the icon onto another page, drag the icon to the right or left edge of the screen. Once the icon page turns, release your finger.

Tap 'done' on the top right when you're finished.

Chapter 3: Getting around your iPad

Switching Between App Pages

You can get to the other pages by swiping your finger left or right to turn the page.

The two little dots, circled in the illustration above, show you what page you are on and how many pages of icons you have. This will vary depending on what apps you have installed. In this example, there are two pages. You can identify what page you are on by looking at this icon, the one in bold is the page you are on. In this example, page 1.

Take a look at the 'arranging icons' video demo of the accompanying video resources. Scan the code or go to the following website.

elluminetpress.com/ipad-nav

Chapter 3: Getting around your iPad

Removing Icons

To remove an app, tap and hold your finger on the app's icon, until you see the drop down menu.

Select 'remove app' from the drop down menu.

This will uninstall the app. To put it back on your home screen, you'll need to download it again from the app store.

Chapter 3: Getting around your iPad

Status Bar

The status bar runs along the very top of the screen. On the left hand side you'll see your clock and date.

On the right hand side you'll see your system icons for wifi, cellular, and remaining battery capacity.

The Dock

The dock runs along the bottom of your screen, and is a place where you can access your most used apps.

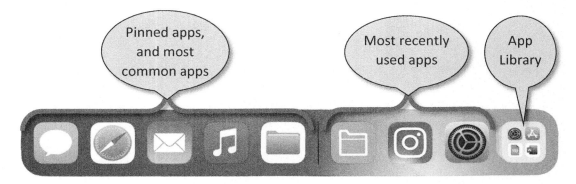

On the far right, you'll see an icon that opens the app library.

You can also add your favourite apps to the dock at the bottom of the screen. To do this, tap, and drag an icon from the home screen to the dock.

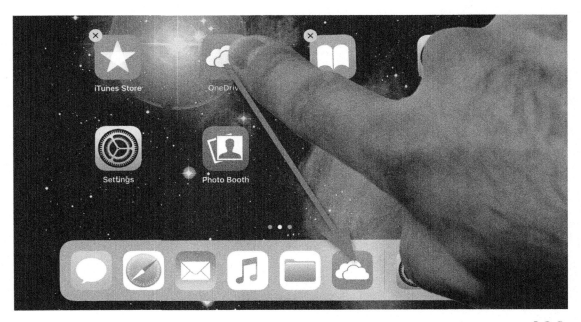

Chapter 3: Getting around your iPad

Widgets

Widgets are small applets that give you quick access to information and actions. You can add widgets to your 'today view', or you can add them to your home screen.

Add to Home Screen

To add widgets, tap and hold your finger on the home screen. You'll see a '+' icon appear on the top left of the screen.

Select the widget you want to add from the list on the left hand side.

Chapter 3: Getting around your iPad

Swipe left/right across the widget to select a size. Tap 'add widget' when you're done.

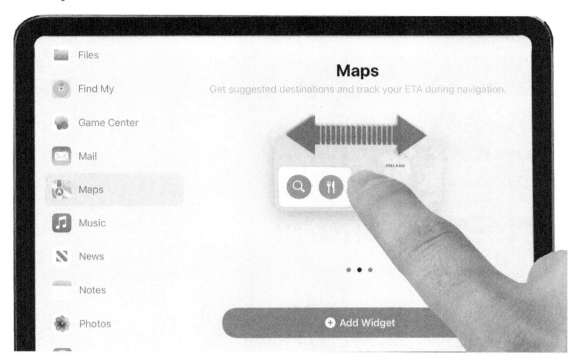

Tap and drag the widget into position, then tap 'done' on the top right when you're finished.

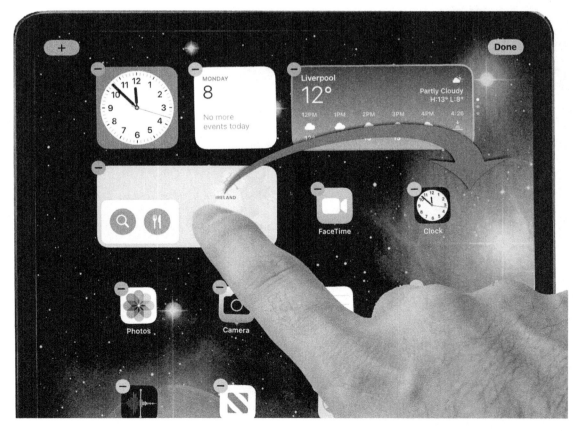

Chapter 3: Getting around your iPad

Add to Today View

To open the 'today view' panel swipe left to right across the home screen until you see the panel open. Tap and hold your finger on the screen.

Tap the plus sign icon on the top left.

From the popup window, tap the widget you want to add.

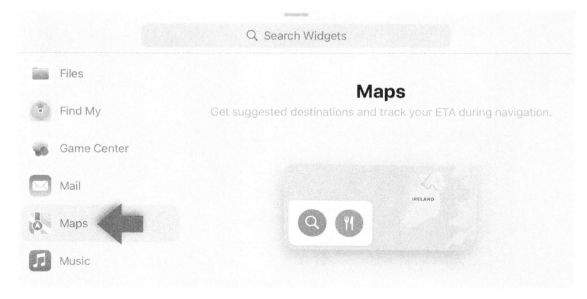

Chapter 3: Getting around your iPad

Swipe, left and right to select the size of the widget.. Tap 'add widget'.

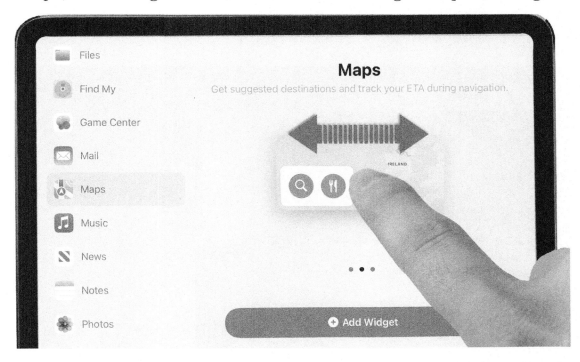

The widget will appear in the 'today view' on the left hand side. To move a widget, tap and drag the widget to a new position on the list.

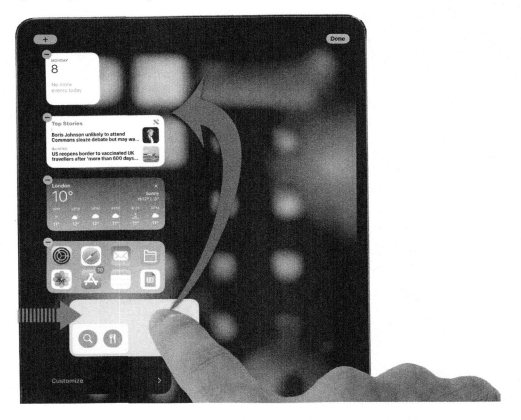

Tap 'done' on the top right of the screen when you're finished. Or press the home button.

Chapter 3: Getting around your iPad

Edit Widget

Some widgets you can edit, such as weather, or calendar. To do this, tap and hold your finger on a widget, select 'edit' from the popup menu.

In this particular widget, you can select a location. Tap on the location and select one from the list.

Chapter 3: Getting around your iPad

Remove Widgets

If you want to remove widgets from the home screen, tap and hold your finger on the screen, then tap the '-' icon on the top left of the widget.

Similarly on the 'today view' side bar. Tap and hold, then tap the '-'.

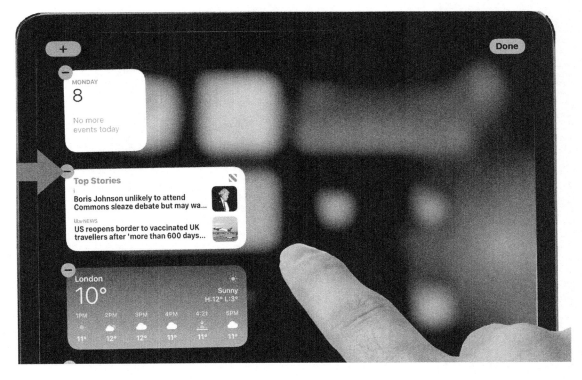

Tap 'done' on the top right when you're finished.

115

Chapter 3: Getting around your iPad

App Library

The app library a quick access location for all of apps installed on your iPad. To open the app library, tap on the icon on the far right of the dock. You can also swipe left until the app library appears.

Apps are grouped according to their function, so you'll see groups such as entertainment, productivity, recently added and so on. Frequently used apps appear as larger icons.

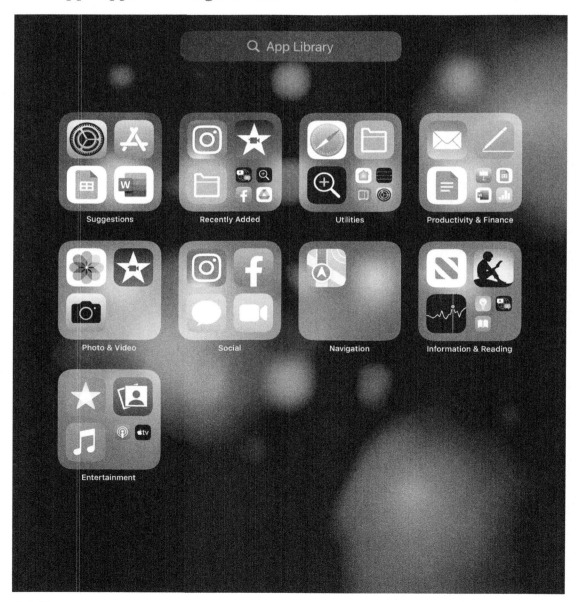

116

Chapter 3: Getting around your iPad

You can also search for apps, to do this tap the 'app library' search field at the top.

Underneath, you'll see an alphabetised list of all of your apps. Select and app from the A-Z list.

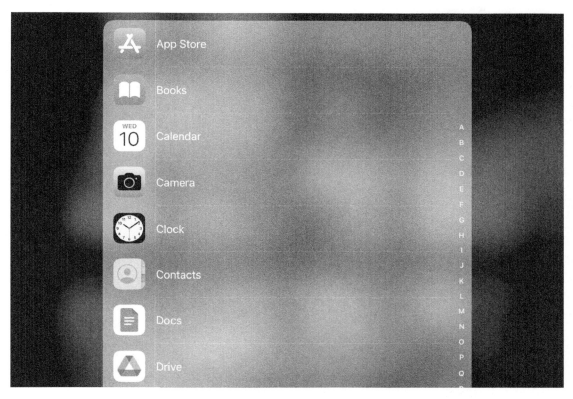

If you want to search for an app, type the name into the search field at the top of the screen. Tap on an app in the search results.

Chapter 3: Getting around your iPad

Control Center

The control center is your control hub where you can adjust screen brightness, volume, access WiFi/bluetooth controls, access your camera, and other controls.

To open control center, swipe downwards from the top right edge of your screen.

Here you can control the volume of playing music, turn on and off WiFi, blue-tooth, access your camera, set the orientation lock to stop the screen shifting - this can be useful if you are reading a book etc.

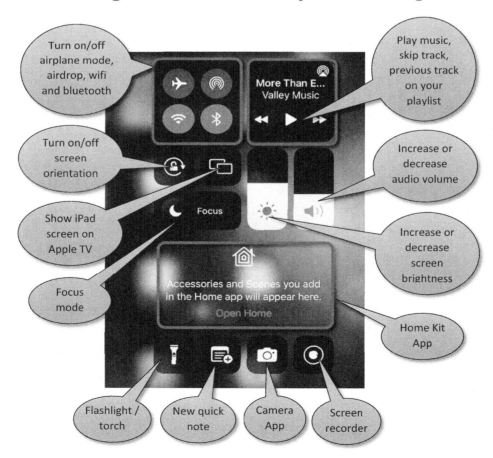

118

Chapter 3: Getting around your iPad

Notification Center

This is where you'll find notifications from various apps. Notifications will also appear on the lock screen. To open notification center, swipe your finger downwards from the top center edge of the screen.

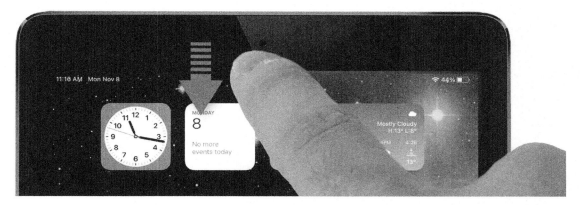

Notifications such as news headlines, new email, sms/text messages, reminders and various others will appear here.

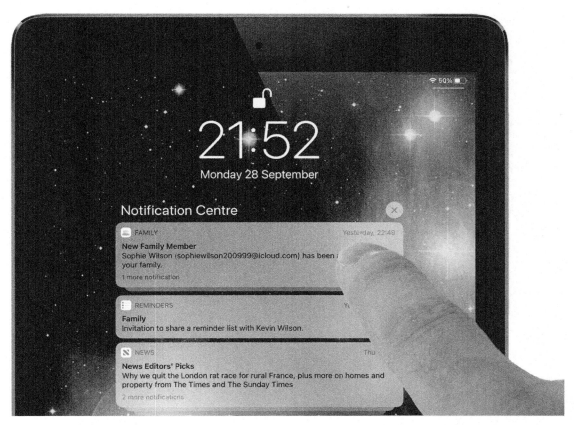

Multiple notifications from the same app are grouped. Tap on one of the groups to open it up.

Swipe right to left over the notification to see additional options such as manage, view and clear notification.

119

Chapter 3: Getting around your iPad

Touch Gestures

Gestures, sometimes called multi-touch gestures, are what you'll use to interact with the touch screen on iPad.

While you work through this part, take a look at the 'navigation' section of the accompanying video resources. Scan the code or go to the following website.

`elluminetpress.com/ipad-nav`

Tap

Tap your index finger on an icon or to select something on the screen. For example, you can tap on an app icon, a link in safari, or even a song you want to download.

You can also tap and hold your finger on the screen to access other options that might be available (this is like right-clicking the mouse on your computer).

Chapter 3: Getting around your iPad

Drag

Tap on the screen and without lifting your finger off the glass, slide your finger around the screen to drag up and down, left or right, and any other direction on the screen.

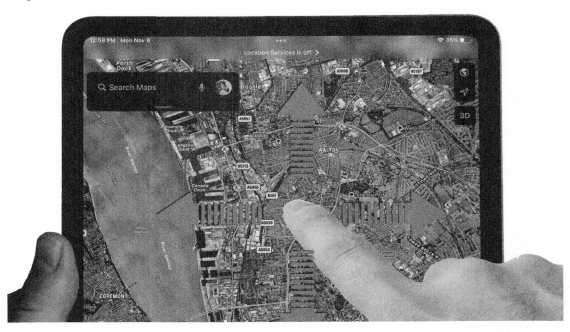

Zoom

Hold your index finger and thumb on the area you want to zoom in or out of, then pinch the screen to zoom out and spread to zoom in.

Pinch is shown in the illustration above, with the large red arrow, spread is shown with the small red arrow.

Chapter 3: Getting around your iPad

Swipe

This allows you to flip through photos, pages in an e-book, pages on the home screen. You swipe across the screen almost like striking a match. You can swipe up, down, left, and right.

Switch Between Open Apps

Hold your four fingers (not your thumb) on the screen and swipe across to switch between open apps. You can swipe left and right.

Chapter 3: Getting around your iPad

Reveal Home Screen

On the new iPad Air, Mini and iPad pro, you'll see a small horizontal bar along the bottom of the screen. To reveal the home screen, swipe this bar upwards.

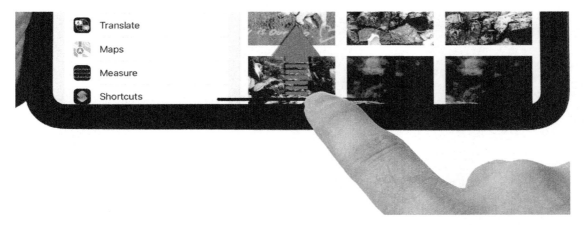

For older iPads or the 10.5" model, press the home button once to get back to your home screen.

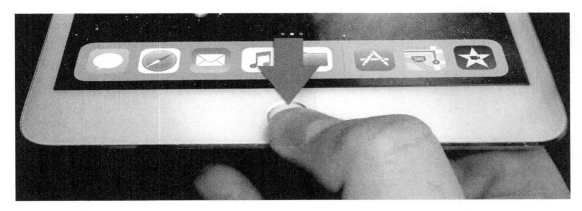

Reveal Dock

If you're using the iPad pro or the new iPad Air or Mini, you can reveal the dock by dragging the bar along the bottom of the screen up about 1 inch.

Chapter 3: Getting around your iPad

Reveal App Switcher

To reveal the task switcher, so you can see all your running apps, press the home button twice. You can also swipe upwards from bottom edge to the center of the screen, until the app thumbnails appear.

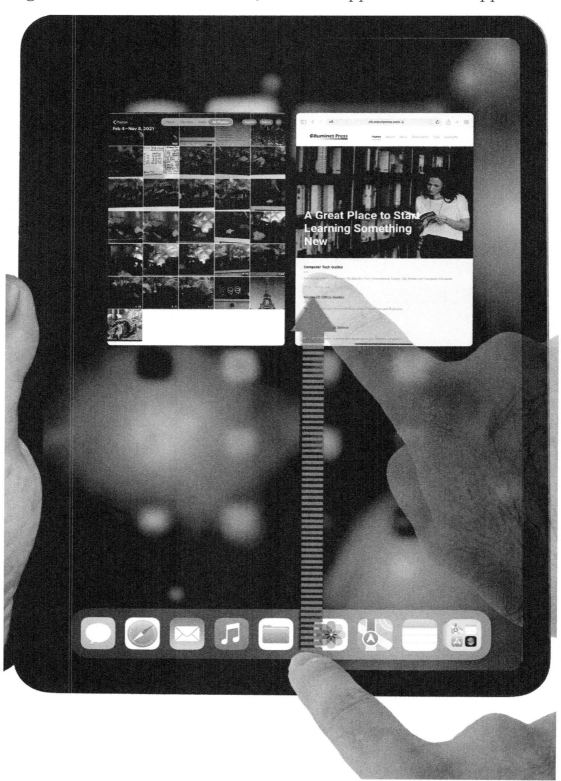

Chapter 3: Getting around your iPad

For older iPads or the 10.5" model, double press your home button - that is pressing twice in quick succession - to bring up your multitasking app switcher, where you can view all your running apps, switch to a running app, or close apps.

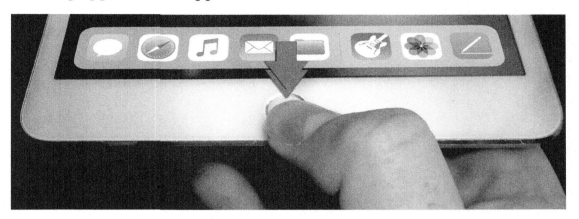

You can also swipe upward from the bottom edge to the center of the screen, until all the app thumbnail icons appear.

Cut, Copy & Paste

Select the text you want to copy or cut. To cut text, pinch with three fingers twice in a row. To copy text, pinch with three fingers once.

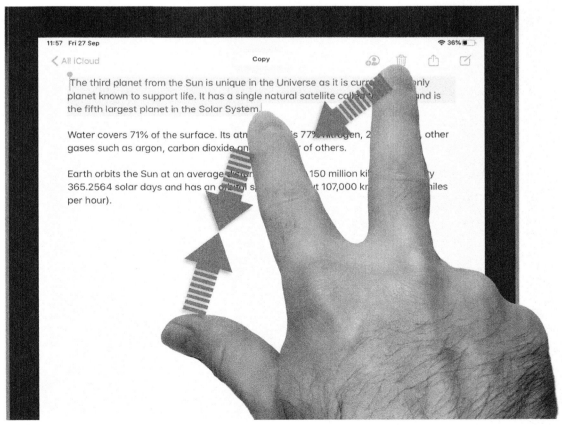

125

Chapter 3: Getting around your iPad

Pick up the cursor and drag it to where you want to paste the text.

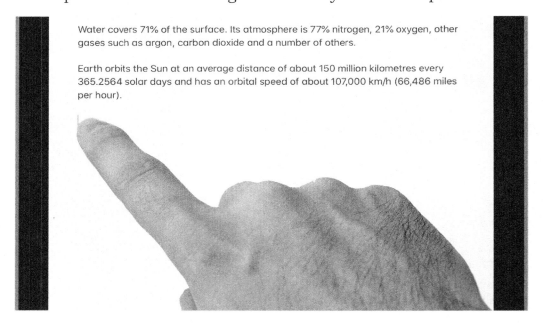

To paste text, spread with three fingers to paste.

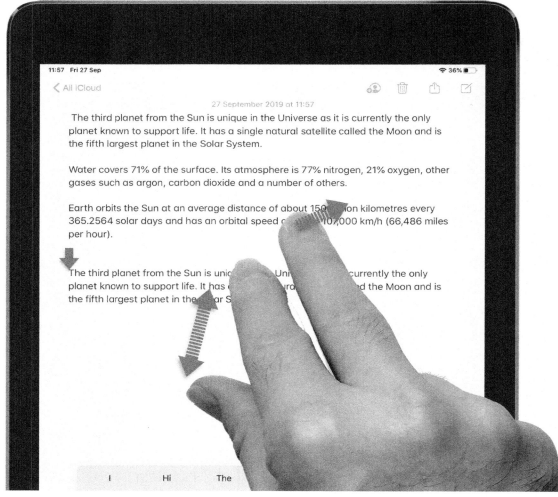

Chapter 3: Getting around your iPad

Text Selection

Quickly select a block of text by dragging your finger over it. You can also select a word with a double tap. A sentence with three taps. Or a whole paragraph with four taps.

To select a word, double-tap on it.

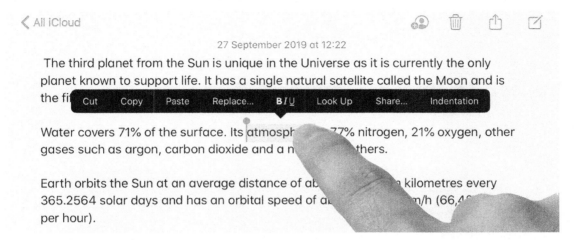

To select a sentence, tap on the text three times.

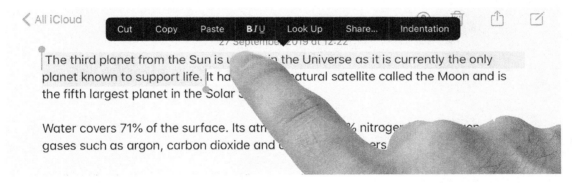

To select a paragraph, tap on the text four times.

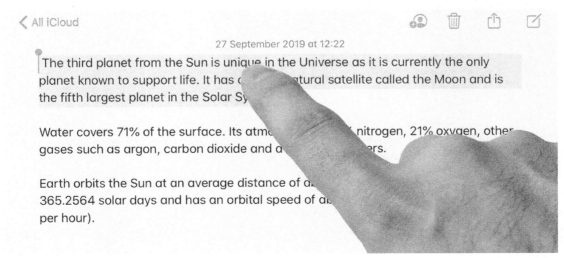

127

Chapter 3: Getting around your iPad

Multitasking

iPads run an operating system called iPadOS. iPadOS is a multitasking operating system. This means that you can run more than one app at the same time. Open apps that are not currently on your screen will be running in the background. To quickly see what apps are running, press your home button twice, or swipe upwards from the bottom edge to the center of the screen, until the app thumbnail icons appear. See "Reveal App Switcher" on page 124.

Switch to Another Running App

To switch to another app, open the task switcher. You'll see thumbnails of all running apps. Tap on an app to switch

Chapter 3: Getting around your iPad

Close a Running App

After using your iPad, you will find that there are a lot of apps running, this can severely affect the performance of your iPad and drain your battery more quickly.

To close apps, open the task switcher, then swipe your finger upwards on the app you want to close, as illustrated below.

This will close the app.

Do this on all the apps you want to close.

Chapter 3: Getting around your iPad

Using Split View

While running an app, you'll see a three dots icon at the top of the app. This allows you switch to split view, slide over, or full screen. To use split view, tap the middle icon.

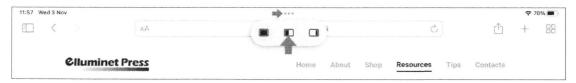

The app you're currently running will move aside, allowing you to select another app from your home screen.

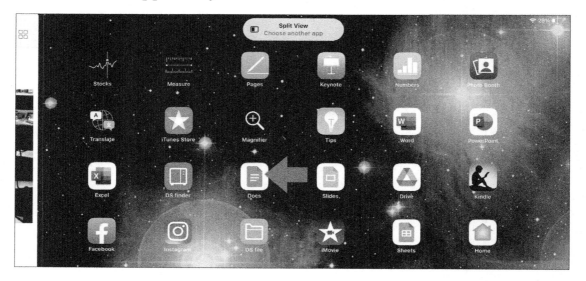

Your screen will split and you'll see one app on the left hand side and the app you just opened on the right.

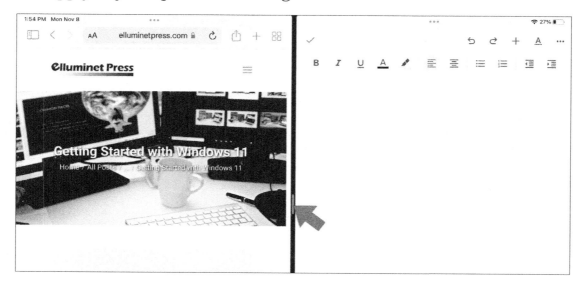

Drag the divider left or right to resize the apps.

Chapter 3: Getting around your iPad

Using Slide Over

While running an app, you'll see a three dots icon at the top of the app. This allows you switch to split view, slide over, or full screen. To use slide over, tap the right hand icon.

The app you're currently running will move aside, allowing you to select another app from your home screen.

You'll see all the apps you have open in the slide over panel.

Chapter 3: Getting around your iPad

Drag & Drop

The Drag and Drop feature allows you to drag text, photos or documents from one app to another. You can drag items within the same apps or across different apps. Open the two apps in split view as demonstrated in the previous section.

In the demonstration above, I have the safari app running in split view with the notes app.

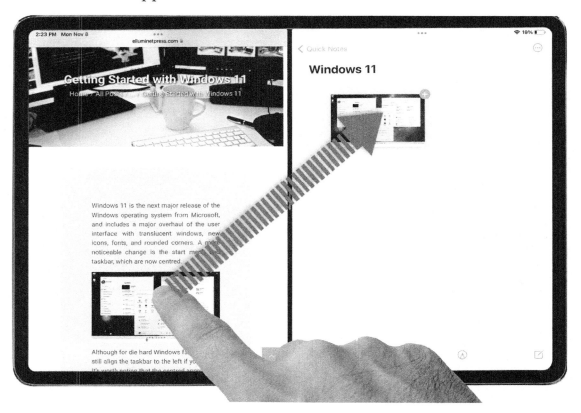

To drag the image from the website, tap and hold your finger on the image in the safari app, then drag it across to the notes app.

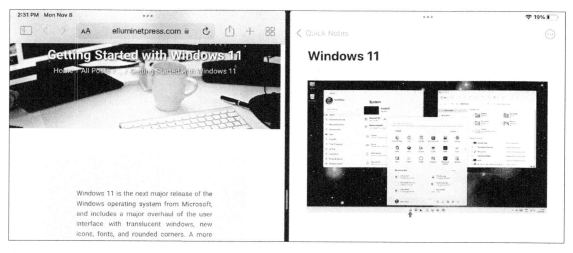

Chapter 3: Getting around your iPad

Close Slide Over or Split View

To close the slideover app, swipe the app off the edge of the screen.

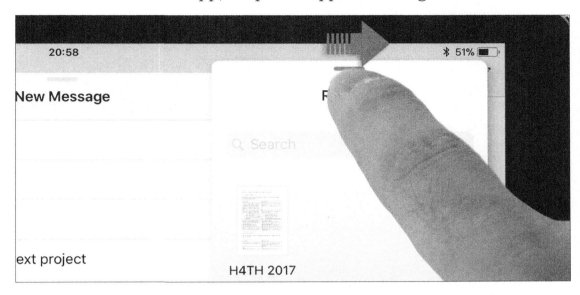

To close your splitscreen, swipe the handle on the divider off the screen.

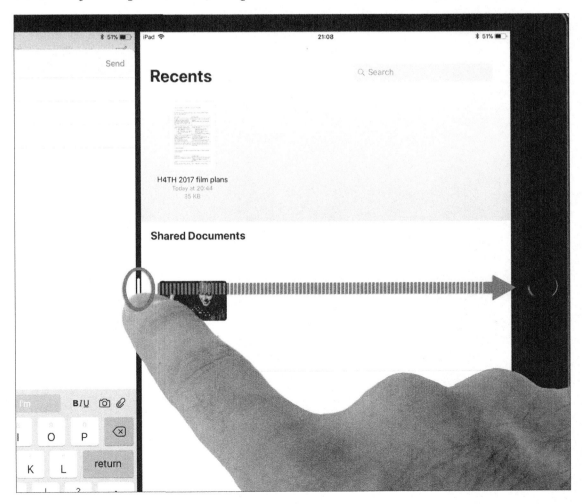

133

Chapter 3: Getting around your iPad

App Shelf

A new feature introduced in iPadOS 15 is the shelf. The shelf shows all open windows of the same app at the bottom of the page, and works for apps that support multiple windows.

To view the shelf, tap the three dots icon on the top middle of the screen.

Here in the mail app, I have a reply message window open and the main app window.

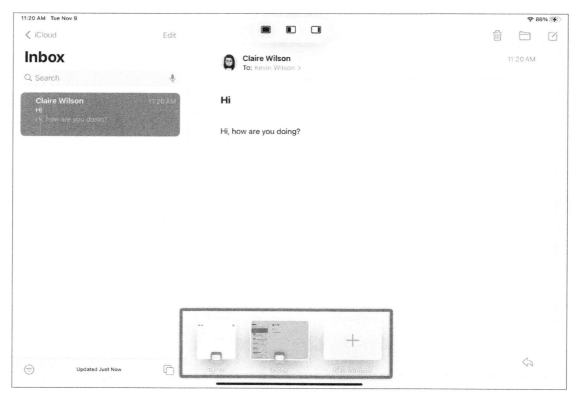

Tap on any of the thumbnails on the app shelf to switch to another window.

You can also open a new instance of the app. To do this tap 'new window'.

134

Chapter 3: Getting around your iPad

Universal Control

Universal Control allows you to use your keyboard and mouse across all your Apple devices such as an iPad and a Mac. You can also drag and drop files, documents or photos across your devices. This feature is only available on the newer iPads and Macs. See page 78 for details on setup.

Moving Between Devices

Here on my desk I have my iMac and iPad Pro. I'm going to use the mouse and keyboard connected to my iMac to move between both devices.

To do this, move the mouse pointer off the edge of the screen. If you have 'push through the edge of the display' setting enabled (see page 80), then you'll see a purple marker. Push your mouse through to the other Mac.

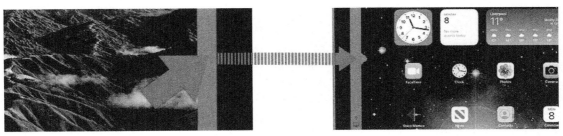

135

Chapter 3: Getting around your iPad

You can drag and drop files from and iPad to a Mac. Useful if you want to use Apple Pencil to create a design on your iPad, or take a photo, and then drop it into a project you are building on your Mac. Just use the mouse to move the pointer over to the iPad, then click and drag the file into the project on your Mac. Here in the demo below, I'm dragging a photo from the photos app to a Pages document on the iMac.

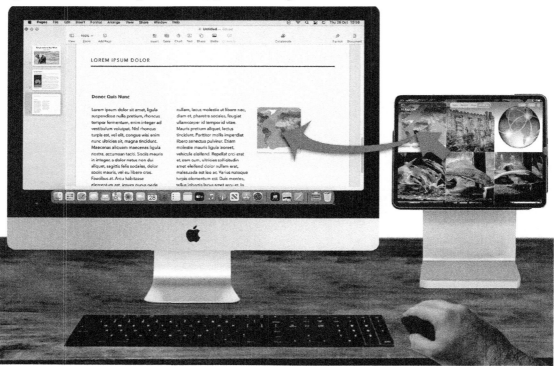

On-screen Keyboard

Typing on an iPad is easy using the on-screen Multi-Touch keyboard. Tap in any text field, email, document or message, and the on screen keyboard will pop up on the bottom of the screen.

You can tap on the keys to type your message.

People's typing styles are different, but most seem to use one finger for each half of the keyboard.

Chapter 3: Getting around your iPad

To access the numbers and symbols on the top half of the key, slide your finger down on the key. This is like holding down the shift key on a computer. For example, to type 4, slide your finger down on the letter R - the letter R will turn into a 4.

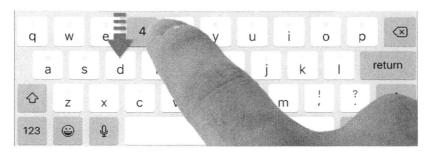

Lets take a closer look at the keyboard. You'll notice some icons and information along the top of the keyboard. Some of these will depend on which app you are typing in but most have a similar function.

Here is an example from the mail app. Along the top you will see some predictive text suggestions that appear according to what you're typing in. If the correct word appears, you can quickly tap on the appropriate suggestion instead of typing in the whole word.

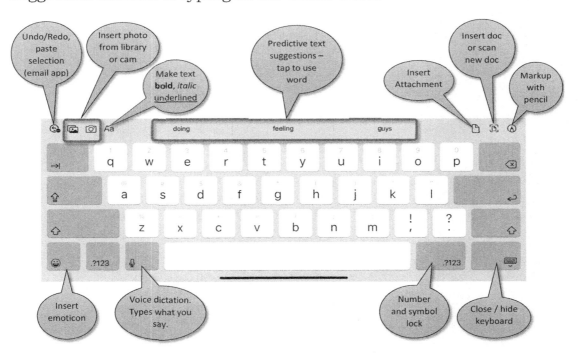

There are some icons along the bottom worth noting. The '123' key, locks in numbers and symbols so you can quickly enter a series of numbers just by tapping the keys. The 'smiley face' icon allows you to insert emojis or emoticons - small smiley faces, thumbs up, expressions, and small images that are intended to show how you're feeling in your messages. Finally the 'microphone icon' is a dictation tool that transcribes or types out voice dictations.

137

Chapter 3: Getting around your iPad

On the top left of the keyboard, you'll find icons to paste, or undo.

The next two icons allow you to select a photo from your photos app, or take a photo with your camera.

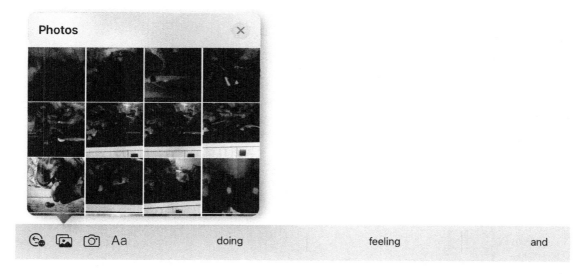

You'll find an icon for formatting your text. Here, you can change the font, size, colour, indent, text alignment, and add lists.

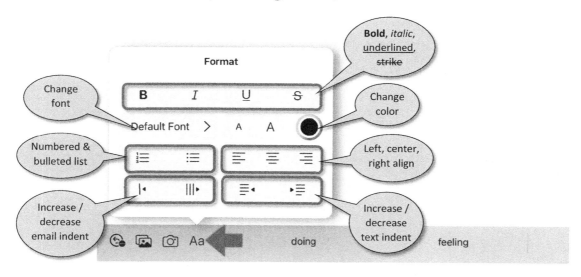

On either side of the predictive text section, you'll see some app specific icons. You can use these to insert a file, scan a document, or use your pen to insert a drawing.

Chapter 3: Getting around your iPad

Spotlight Search

Spotlight is integrated with a number of web services so that users can search using Wikipedia, Bing, or Google. Other services include: news, nearby places, suggested websites, movie show times, and content that is not already on the device from the iTunes Store

Searching for Things

You can activate spotlight search by swiping your finger downwards from the centre of your home screen.

Once you have spotlight's search screen, you can type your search into the search field at the top of the screen.

Search also gives you some Siri suggestions. These are taken from your most commonly used apps. Underneath you'll see some shortcuts from some of your most used apps.

139

Chapter 3: Getting around your iPad

In the example below, I am searching for my computer notes. Spotlight will search through the web, your apps, documents, books, recently visited sites in safari.

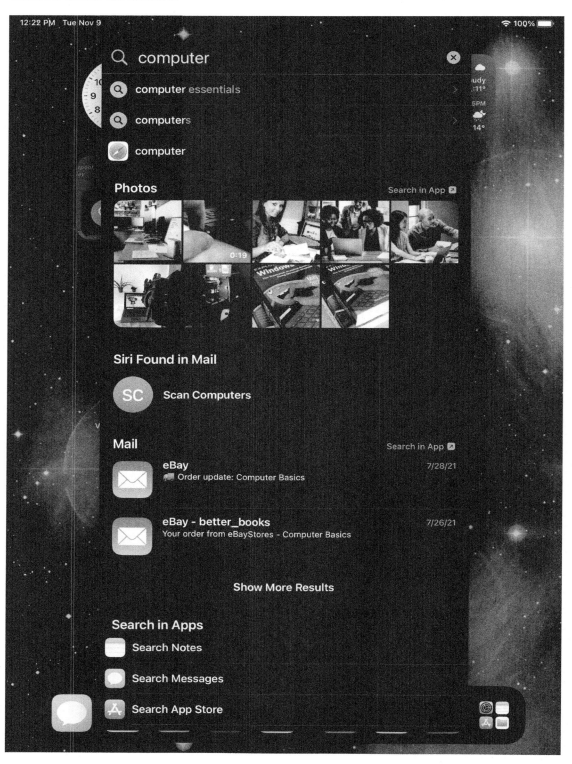

Scroll down the list, select the best match. Tap 'show more results' to view more results.

Chapter 3: Getting around your iPad

Siri

Siri is an extremely useful feature. She allows you to talk to your iPad, sometimes referred to as a virtual assistant. She can help you with all kinds of things. You can ask Siri to send messages, schedule meetings, and search for nearby restaurants, all without having to type a single letter.

Using Siri

To use Siri, press and hold the home button until you see Siri appear on the bottom right of your screen.

If you're using an iPad Pro or a new iPad Air / Mini, then press and hold the power button until you see Siri appear on the bottom right of your screen.

You can also say "Hey Siri!".

Try some of the following phrases...

Try saying: "Hey Siri"
Try saying: "Send email to..." (pick a name from your contacts list)
Try saying: "What is the weather like tomorrow"
Try saying: "Find me a website on baking a cake"
Try saying: "Remind me to pick up milk on the way home"
Try saying: "Call..." (pick a name from your contacts list).

141

Chapter 3: Getting around your iPad

Siri Translate

Here's a good one for those who love to travel but don't speak the local language. At the time of writing, Siri can only translate from US English to French, German, Italian, Mandarin and Spanish.

To use the translator, hold down the home button, or the power button until Siri appears on the bottom right.

Say "How do I say where is the train station in Spanish?"

Just replace the underlined bits of the phrase for the phrase and language you want to translate into.

Siri will translate the phrase and speak it out aloud.

Chapter 3: Getting around your iPad

Voice Dictation

Another useful feature of Siri is voice dictation, which allows you to enter text without having to use the keyboard. You can search the web, take notes, post an update to Facebook, and more just by speaking.

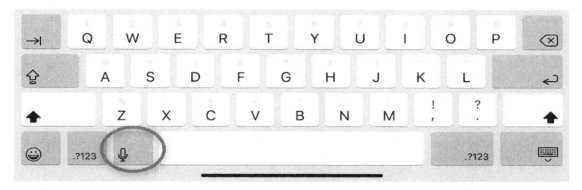

To use voice dictation, tap the microphone icon on your on screen keyboard.

If the icon isn't there go to your settings app, tap 'general', then 'keyboard'. Go down to 'enable dictation' and switch the slider to on.

Then start dictating the text you want Siri to type. She listens to what you say, and types it. The more you use it, the better Siri gets at understanding you.

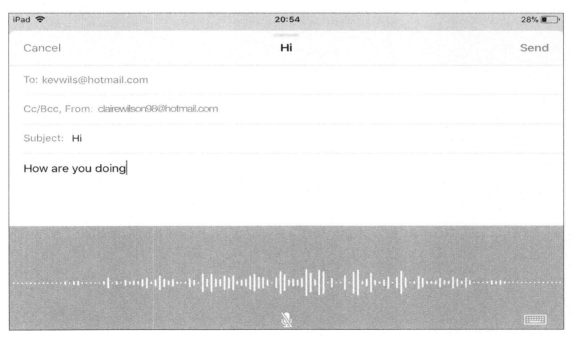

You can even add punctuation by saying words like "period" or 2 "question mark" when you reach the end of a sentence. Tap the keyboard icon on the bottom right to close dictation mode.

143

Chapter 3: Getting around your iPad

Voice Control

You can use voice commands to navigate around your device, launch apps and get things done without using your fingers.

To enable voice control, open your settings app then select 'accessibility'.

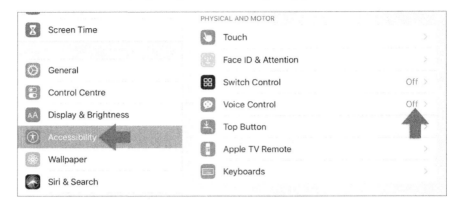

Select 'voice control', then tap 'set up voice control' at the top.

Tap 'continue'.

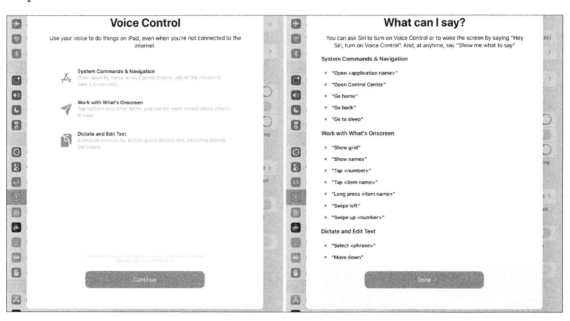

Have a look through all the voice commands you can give. Tap 'done' when you're finished.

Now, try a few voice commands. For example, say "open safari".

144

Chapter 3: Getting around your iPad

You can customise voice control. Here, you can turn on/off voice control, select your language, customise commands, add words to vocabulary if voice control doesn't recognise a particular word or phrase. You can also allow voice control to show confirmation, play a sound when activated or show hints.

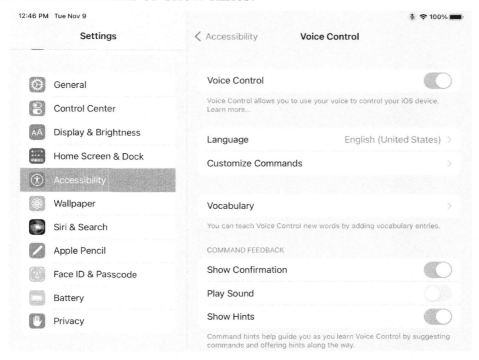

You can customise commands. Open settings app, select 'accessibility', then select 'voice control'. Tap on 'customise commands'. To create a new command tap 'create new command'.

In the 'phrase' field, type in a phrase. This is the phrase you'll say to execute the command. Eg "Insert Claire's address". In the 'action' field, select the action this command is going to carry out. Tap 'insert text', then type in the text to be inserted. Eg an address. In the 'application' field, set this to any app, or tap and select the app you want the command to work in.

You can also record commands. Say "Start recording command". Perform the command on your iPad, then say "stop recording command", when you're done.

Chapter 3: Getting around your iPad

Screenshot

Press the top button and the home button at the same time. You'll hear a camera sound.

If you're using an iPad Pro, or new iPad Mini / Air, then press the top button and the volume up button at the same time.

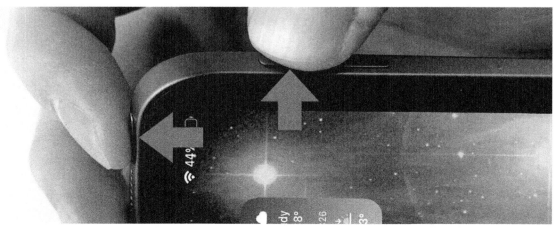

Chapter 3: Getting around your iPad

Screen Recording

To enable the screen recording function, to the settings app, select control center, then tap the + next to 'screen recording'.

To record your screen, open control center, tap the 'screen recording' icon.

Wait for the three-second countdown. Your recordings will appear in the photos app. To stop recording, tap the recording icon again in control center.

147

4

Using Apps

You can pretty much get an app for virtually anything, and these are all available from the app store.

Some are free and others you have to buy. There are games, productivity apps and apps just for fun.

Your iPad comes with some apps built in. You can also download millions more from the App Store.

In this chapter, we'll take a look at

- App Store
- Taking Notes
- Reminders
- Maps App
- News App
- Apple Books App
- Files App
- Basic File Management
- Voice Memos
- Clock App
- Shortcuts
- Pages, Numbers & Keynote
- Printing & Fonts

Take a look at the video resources, open your web browser and navigate to the following website.

elluminetpress.com/ipad-apps

Chapter 4: Using Apps

App Store

The app store has over 1 million apps available for download direct to your iPad without even going on a computer. To start app store, click App Store app on your main screen.

Once on the app store's main screen, tap the icon on the top right to sign in with your Apple ID if you haven't already done so. If you are already signed in, your Apple ID will be displayed here, you won't need to sign in again.

On the app store, you will find everything from games and entertainment to productivity tools such as word processing, drawing and photo apps. These are split into games and app sections and you'll find these on the bar along the bottom of the screen.

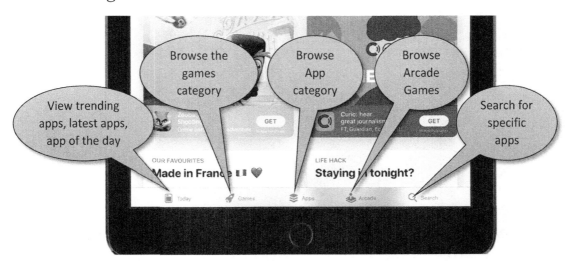

Also along the bottom you'll find updates to your installed apps, it's worth checking this from time to time, as apps are updated all the time. The last icon on the bar along the bottom allows you to search the app store for a specific app name or type/genre of app. You can search for recipes, travel details, maps. There is an app for almost anything you can think of.

Chapter 4: Using Apps

Browsing the Store

If you are more the browsing type, app store has grouped all the apps into categories according to their use. Select 'apps' from the bar on the bottom of the screen. Here you'll see some of the most popular apps, new apps and top selling apps. You can tap on any of these apps to view or download.

Tap on the app's image to view more details, Tap 'see all' at the top of each section to see all the apps in that section. Tap on 'get' or the price to download the app. Scroll down the page to see all the apps in the sections.

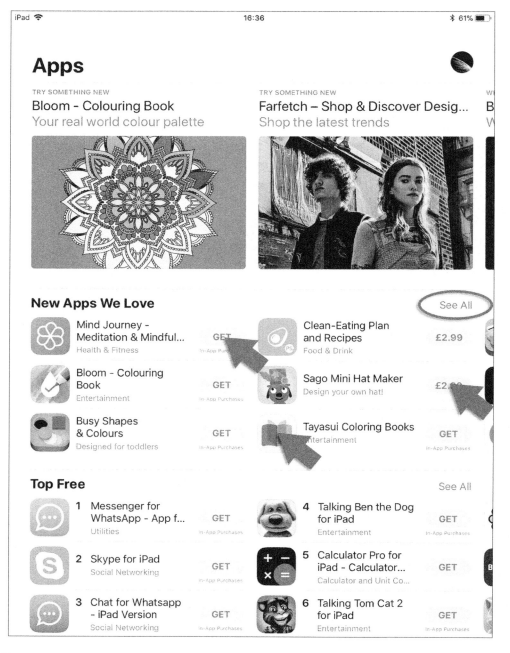

Chapter 4: Using Apps

If you scroll down a bit, you'll see a section called 'top categories'.

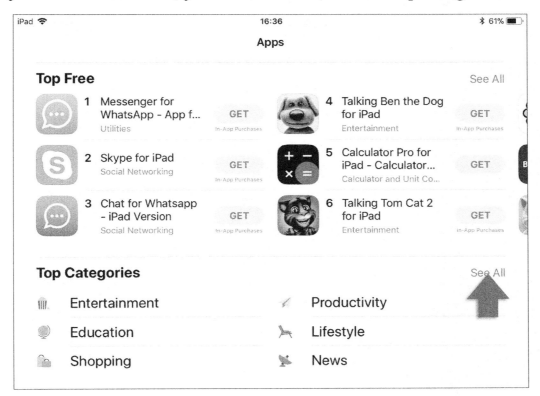

Tap on a category to browse the available apps. In this example, I'm going to explore the 'reference' category.

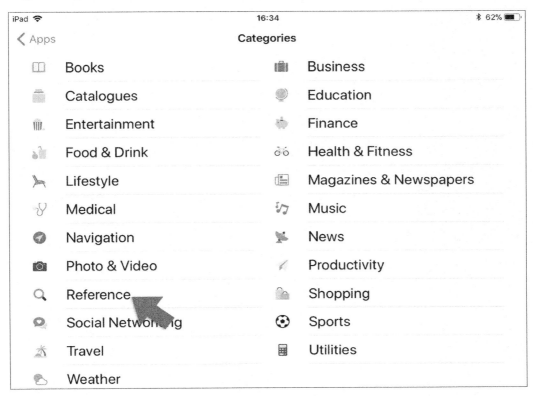

Chapter 4: Using Apps

Here, you'll see a list of all the apps available for that category. Again, tap 'see all' on the top right to see the full lists in the different sections.

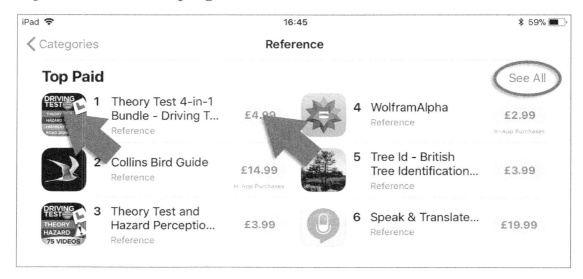

Claire is 18 and learning to drive, so two apps might be of use to her: Theory Test and Hazard Perception. Tap on the apps icon to view more details about the app

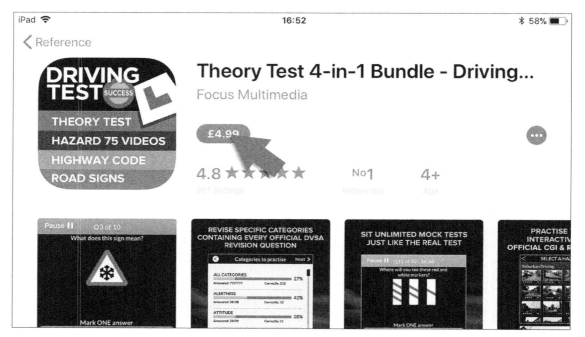

Tap the price tag to download and install the app on your iPad

This gives you information about what the app does, what it costs, some screen shots of the app in action and the device requirements in order to run the app.

To purchase an app, just tap on the price tag.

Chapter 4: Using Apps

The Arcade

Apple Arcade is a subscription service that allows you to play the latest arcade games. At the time of writing you can take out a free trial for a month, then it costs £4.99 a month to continue using the service.

To activate the service, tap 'arcade' on the panel along the bottom of the screen,

Tap 'try it free'. The confirm your purchase using touch id

You can browse through the games on the main page. Scroll down to the bottom of the page to see different categories of games you can play. Tap a category to select.

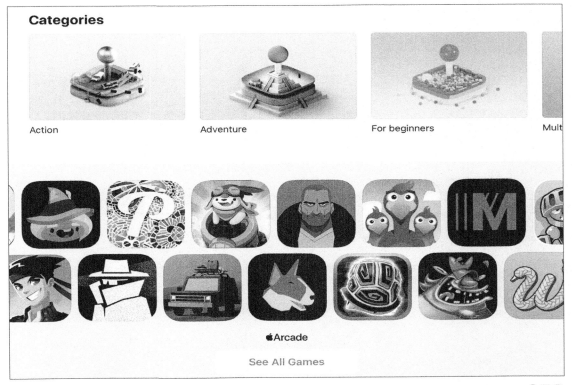

153

Chapter 4: Using Apps

Tap on the game icon to see more information...

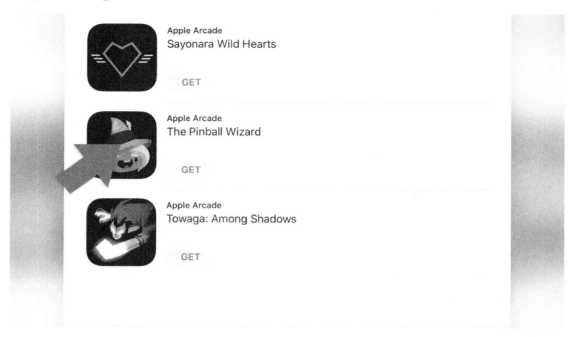

Tap 'get' to download the game, tap 'play' to start the game.

You'll find all your downloaded games on your home screen.

Chapter 4: Using Apps

Search the Store

To find an app, tap on 'search' on the bar at the bottom of your screen. Type into the search field on the main screen, as shown below. In this example, I'm going to search for one of my favourite games called 'worms'.

From the suggestions, tap on the closest match. Tap on the image to view more details about the app; here you'll see reviews, price, screen shots and other info.

To download the app, tap 'get' next to the app if it's free, or tap the price tag if it's paid.

155

Chapter 4: Using Apps

If it's a paid app, tap 'purchase' to confirm.

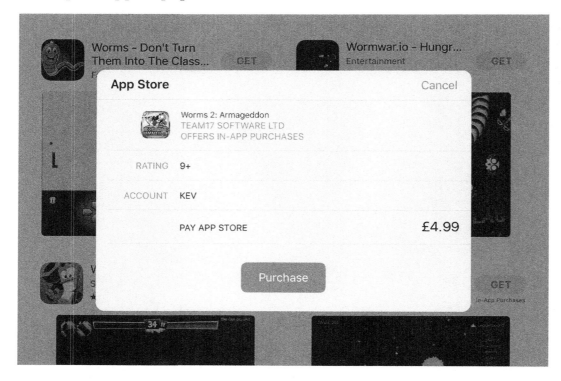

Authorise the purchase with your Apple ID password or if you have touch ID setup, with your thumb print.

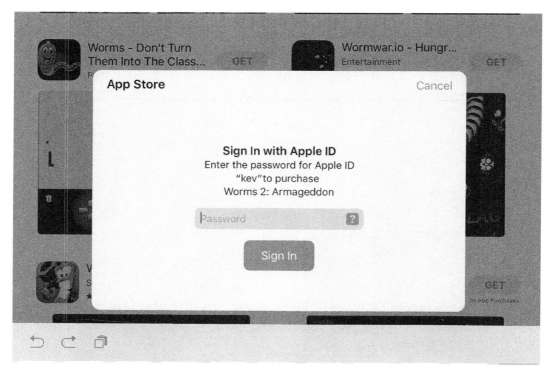

The app will appear on your home screen once it has downloaded and installed itself.

Chapter 4: Using Apps

Taking Notes

To start notes app, tap on the icon on the home screen.

When notes has loaded, you can view your saved notes along the left hand side - swipe from the left edge to reveal the sidebar.

Along the top of a note, you'll find some icons. You can add a tick box, scan documents, take pictures to insert into notes. You can handwrite notes using your pencil. You can also add lines and grid lines to help you write.

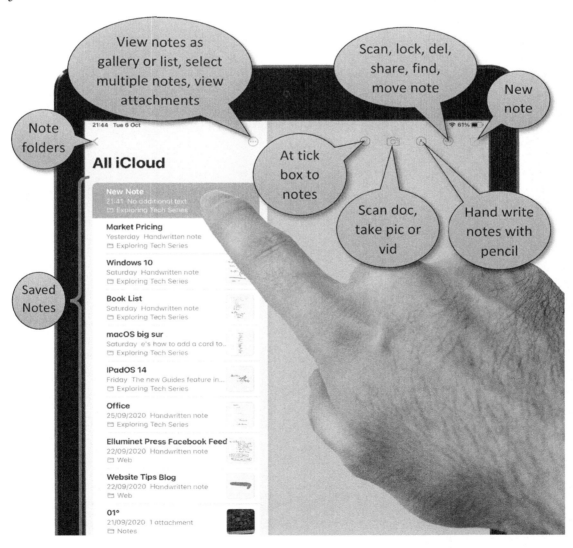

The last icon along the top creates a new blank note..

157

Chapter 4: Using Apps

Typing Notes

You can type your notes in as if it were a notepad, using the on screen keyboard.

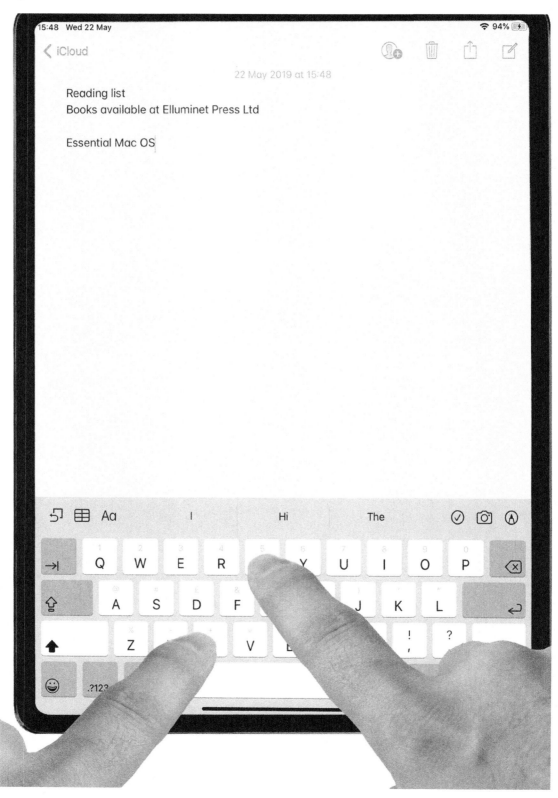

Chapter 4: Using Apps

Inserting Photos

You can use the camera on your iPad to scan documents, take photos or video, or choose a video from your Photos App. To do this, tap the camera icon on the top right of the screen. Select one of the options from the drop down. In this, I'm going to insert a photo.

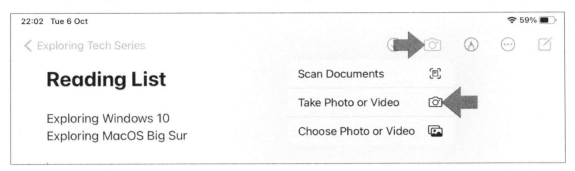

Take a photo of the object you want to add to the note. Tap 'use photo' on the bottom right. Tap 'retake' if you want to take the photo again.

Your photo will appear in your notes.

159

Chapter 4: Using Apps

Handwritten Notes

You can use your Apple Pencil to handwrite notes, draw diagrams, and annotate photos. To do this, open a new note, then tap the small pen icon on the top right of the screen.

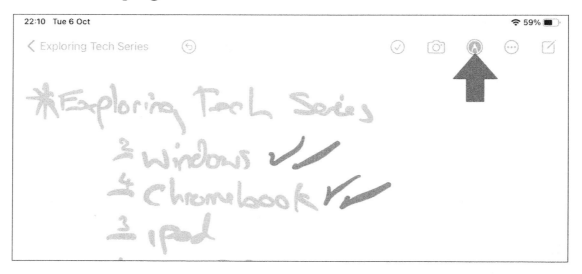

Your drawing tools will appear along the bottom of the screen. Here, you can choose from a marker pen, highlighter, pencil, eraser, or a lasso tool, as well as your colour pallet.

Tap on the pens to select. When you tap on a pen, you'll see a popup menu. Here, you can select pen thickness and opacity. If the pop up menu doesn't show, tap twice on the pen.

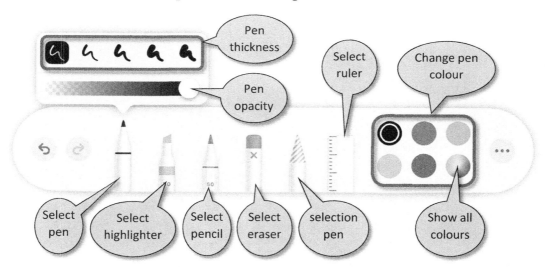

You can also use the selection pen to draw around an object to select it. This helps with copy and paste. There is also an on screen ruler that allows you to draw straight lines with your pen. On the right of the drawing tools you can choose a colour, tap the 'all colours' icon to choose show all colours.

160

Chapter 4: Using Apps

Paste Handwriting as Text

You can copy any handwritten text and paste into notes or another application as text.

Select your handwritten notes. Tap and hold your finger at the beginning of your writing then drag your finger over the writing to select.

From the popup menu, select 'copy as text'.

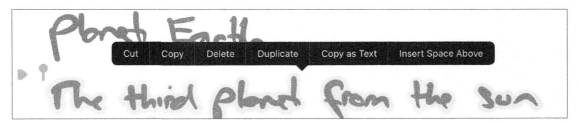

Go to your app, tap and hold your finger where you want to paste. Select 'paste'.

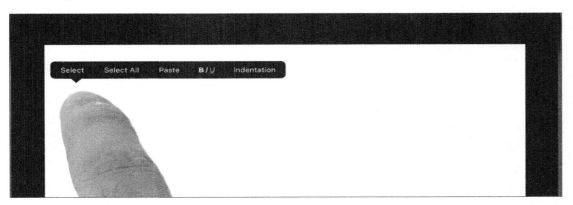

Chapter 4: Using Apps

Shape Recognition

You can create perfect shapes using your pen. Currently, you can draw any of these: line, curve, square, rectangle, circle, oval, heart, triangle, star, cloud, hexagon, thought bubble, outlined arrow, line with arrow endpoint, and curve with arrow endpoint.

To use this feature, draw an approximation of the shape, then hold your pencil on the glass for 1 second.

Your shape will convert into a perfect shape.

Chapter 4: Using Apps

Dictating Notes

Instead of typing, you can dictate notes using the voice dictation feature. To do this, tap the mic icon on the keyboard.

Record your notes using the voice recognition.

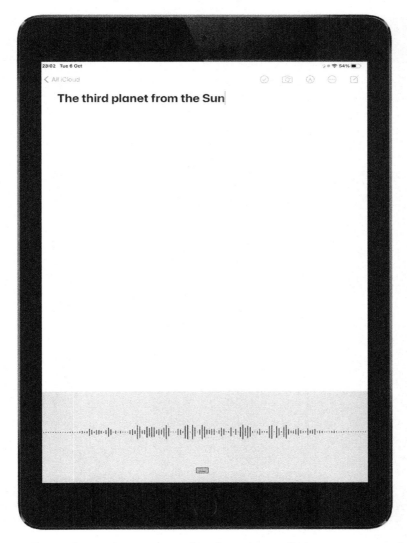

Tap the small keyboard icon at the bottom of the screen when you're finished.

Chapter 4: Using Apps

Quick Note

You can quickly open a new note using the control center.

You can also swipe diagonally from the bottom right hand corner of the screen.

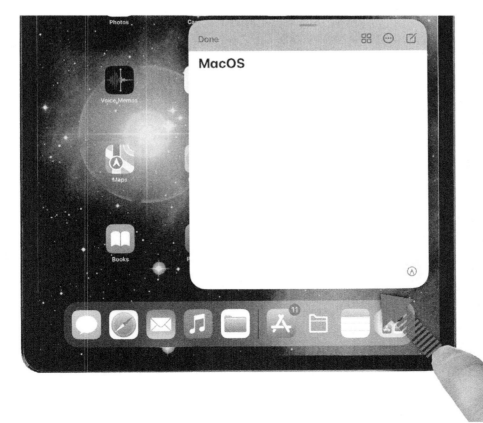

Chapter 4: Using Apps

Organising your Notes

You can create folders to organise your notes. To put a note into a folder, first open the note, then tap the three dots icon on the top right of the screen. From the drop down, tap 'move note'

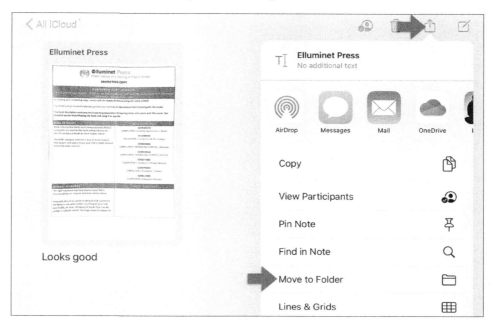

If the folder you want to add the note to exists (eg 'tips'), select it from the list. If the folder doesn't exist, tap 'new folder'.

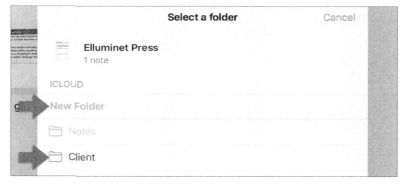

Swipe from the left edge of your screen to reveal the folders panel - you may need to swipe more than once to get back to the folders panel.

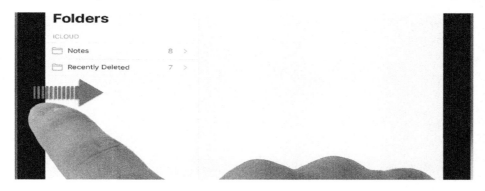

165

Chapter 4: Using Apps

Inviting other Users

You can invite other users to view and edit your notes. This can be useful in a meeting where people can add notes from their own iPad. To share a note, tap the invitation icon on the top right hand side of the screen.

Select 'share options'. From here, you can select whether you want people to be able to edit your note, or just view it. Tap 'add people' at the top of the drop down to return to the previous screen. Now, select how you want to send the invitation eg email.

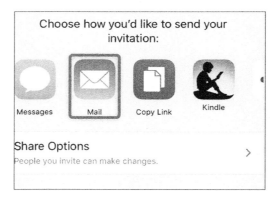

Enter the person's email address (or select from your contacts). You can also send via iMessage.

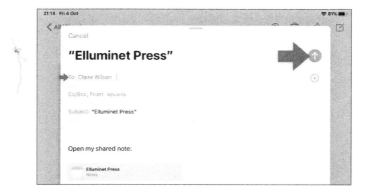

166

Chapter 4: Using Apps

When the other person checks their messages, they will find an email with a link they can click on, which will open the note in the notes app.

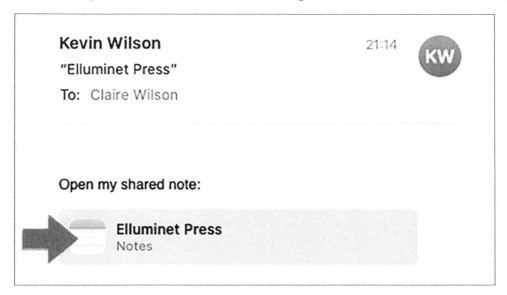

You can see in the demo below, the handwritten text at the top is from my iPad, and the handwritten side note in green on the right hand side is from Claire's iPad.

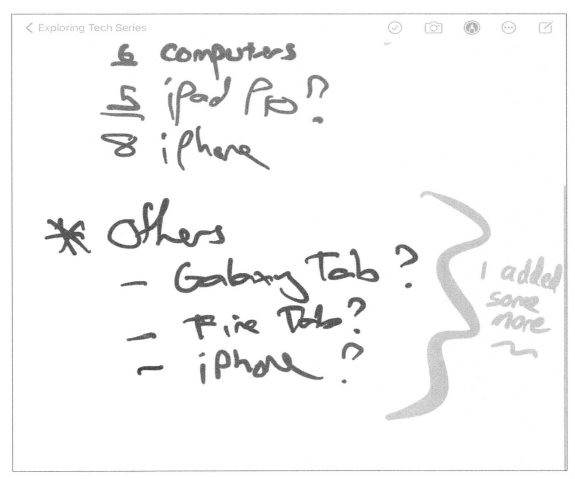

Chapter 4: Using Apps

Reminders

With reminders, you can create to do lists, and set alerts to remind you do to certain things.

To start reminders app, tap the icon on the home screen

Create a Reminder

Tap the list you want to add the reminder to, then tap 'new reminder' at the bottom of the screen.

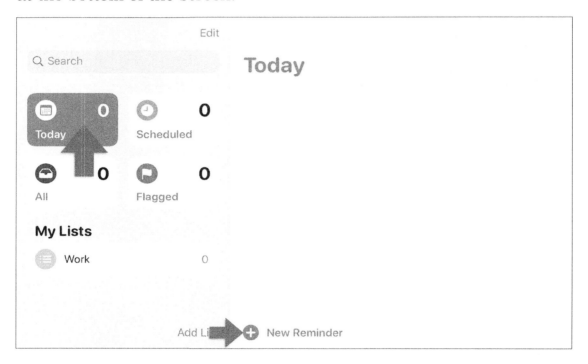

Type in your reminder. Tap 'done' on the top right when you're finished.

168

Chapter 4: Using Apps

Create a New List

Tap 'add list' at the bottom of the screen if you want to create a new one.

Enter a name for your list at the top, then select a colour and an icon to represent your list.

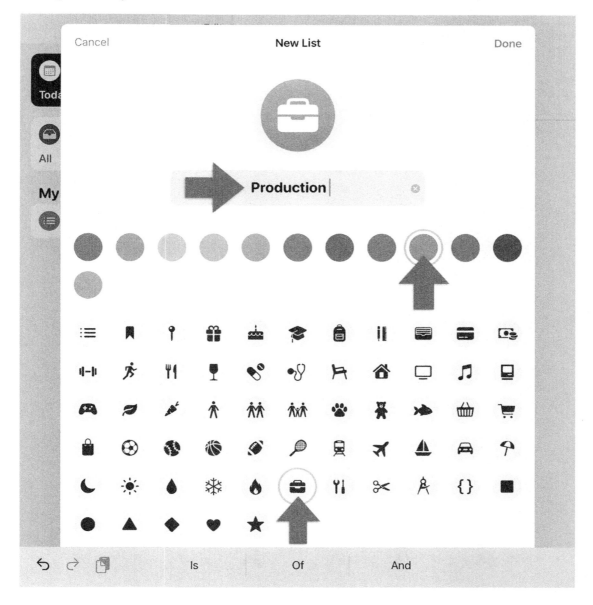

Tap 'done' on the top right when you're finished.

Your lists will appear under the 'my lists' section on the side panel of the reminders app.

169

Chapter 4: Using Apps

Schedule a Reminder

You can schedule a reminder to remind you of something on a particular day. To do this, tap the list you want to add the reminder to.

Tap 'new reminder' at the bottom of the screen.

Type in your reminder, then tap the 'i' icon on the right.

Tap 'remind me on a day', then on the next window tap 'remind me at a time'. Tap 'alarm', then select the date and time using the sliders.

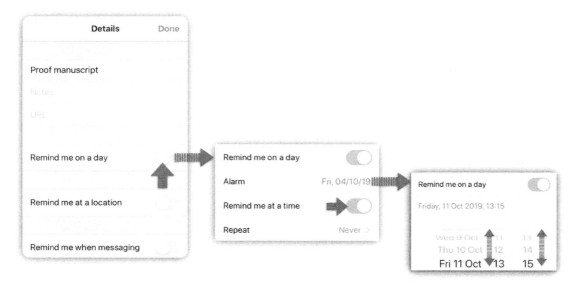

Tap 'done' when you're finished.

Chapter 4: Using Apps

Reminder When Messaging Someone

You can schedule a reminder to remind you of something when contacting a particular person on your contacts list. To do this, tap the list you want to add the reminder to.

Tap 'new reminder' at the bottom of the screen.

Type in your reminder, then tap the 'i' icon on the right.

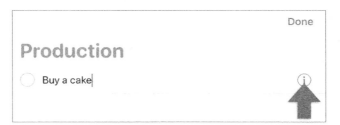

From the drop down, tap 'remind me when messaging' (you may need to scroll down a bit)

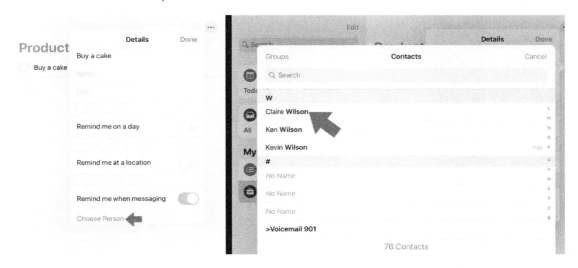

Select the person's name from your contacts list. Now the next time you contact this person, you'll get a reminder.

171

Chapter 4: Using Apps

Reminder at a Location

You can schedule a reminder to remind you of something when you are at a particular location. To do this, tap the list you want to add the reminder to.

Tap 'new reminder' at the bottom of the screen.

Type in your reminder, then tap the 'i' icon on the right. From the drop down, tap 'remind me at a location', then tap 'location'.

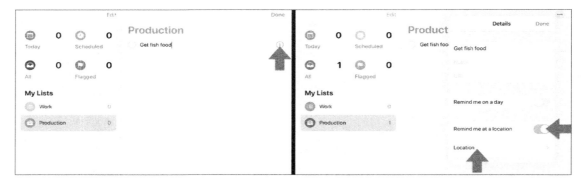

Type in the address, select the closest match from the suggestions.

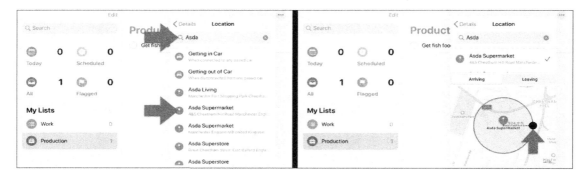

Tap 'arriving' to remind you when you arrive at the destination. Tap 'leaving' if you want to be reminded when you leave the destination. You can also set the distance from the location that triggers the reminder - in the example above, you'll be reminded when you're 524.9ft away. Tap the black circle on the location map and drag it bigger or smaller.

Tap 'details' to go back, then tap 'done'.

Chapter 4: Using Apps

Maps

Maps is an extremely useful app if you are trying to find out where a particular place is and need to find driving directions. It works like a SatNav/GPS giving you precise directions straight from door to door.

Using the panel on the left hand side, you can search for a location - just type in an address, or place name. Under that, you can add a 'home' location, and a 'work' location. This allows you to tap 'home' or 'work' to find that location and is useful if you want directions to that place, or traffic reports between 'home' and 'work'. You can also add favourite locations, ie locations you travel to regularly.

173

Chapter 4: Using Apps

You can view the map in three different types - tap the map icon on the top right of the screen to change this.

Select a map type from the options.

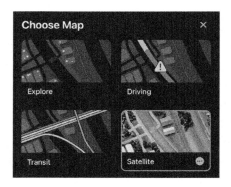

Here below, you can see the different maps: explore map, street map, transport map, and satellite map.

Explore maps are great for looking around a city or location. This map renders a location in a detailed 3D landscape.

Street maps are great if you are using the maps app as a GPS/Satnav while driving.

Transport maps give you public transport routes in a particular location for buses and trains. You'd be wise to check local public transport information for updates and changes.

Satellite maps are great if you are exploring a city or area of interest as well as planning a route. You can see these maps in 2D and 3D.

Chapter 4: Using Apps

Guides

The Guides feature is intended to provide expert recommendations for the best places to visit in a city, such as places to eat, shop, and places of interest to explore. Useful if you're visiting a city and want to find out where to eat, shop, or what to do. There are only a few cities such as Los Angeles, San Francisco, New York and Seattle that include this feature at the moment, but more will be added soon.

To view a guide on a city, type the city name into the search at the top left of the screen. Select the city name from the search results. If the city has guides you'll see them appear at the top of the info card for that city.

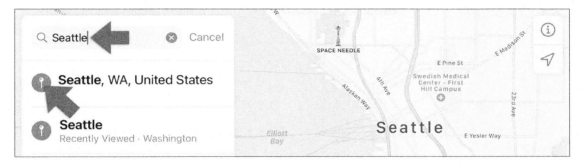

Tap 'see more' to see all the guides.

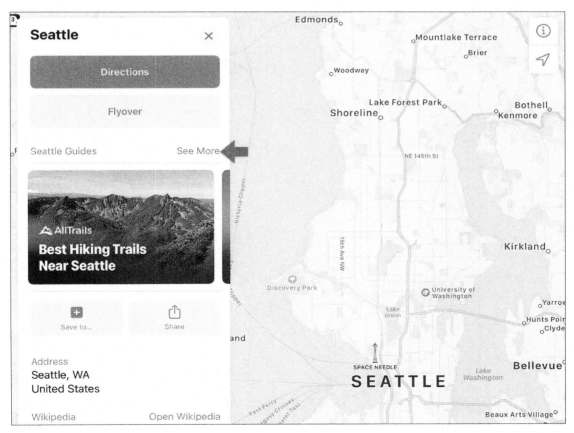

175

Chapter 4: Using Apps

Tap on any of the guides to view more information and see the location on the map. Select an attraction and you'll see the location appear on the map with an info card.

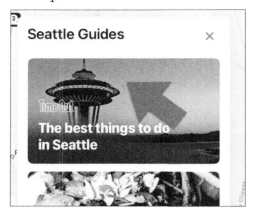

You'll see the location on the map and some details in the info card.

Tap 'directions' to get directions from your location. To explore the location, tap 'look around'. Drag the view around the explore.

Chapter 4: Using Apps

You can also create your own guides and share them with friends, family and colleagues.

To add a location to your own guide, tap the 'save to' icon in the info card.

Select the guide you want to add the location to. If you're creating a new guide, tap 'new guide'. Type in a name eg: 'Seattle Vacation'.

Share Location

To share a location tap the 'share' icon on the info card. Select the app you want to use to share your location.

Driving Directions

To find driving directions, type in your destination into the search field on the top left of the screen and select the destination from the list of suggestions.

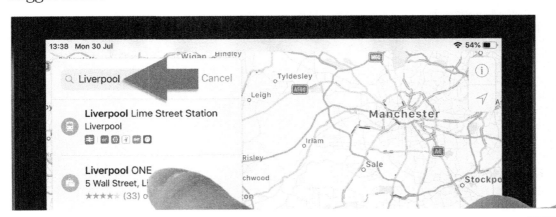

Chapter 4: Using Apps

Select 'directions' from the destination sidebar.

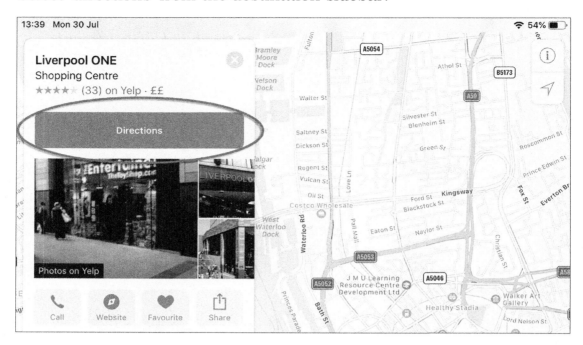

By default, the maps app will start the route from your current location - you can change this, just type in another location.

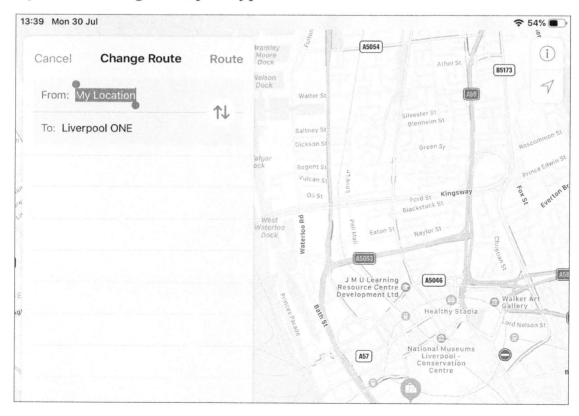

Tap on 'route' to calculate a route between your location and the destination you entered earlier.

Chapter 4: Using Apps

Along the bottom of the screen, you'll see 'drive', 'walk', and 'transport'. This allows you to get directions for driving, if you're walking, or if you're taking public transport. For this demo, we're looking for driving directions, so we'll keep the option set to 'drive'.

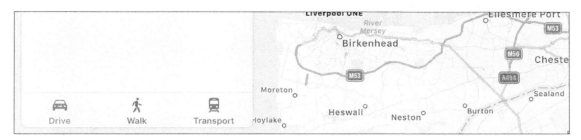

On the screen you'll see an overview of your route. You can zoom in and out or move around the map using your finger to see details or roads.

From options on the left hand side of the screen, select the best route if there is more than one route.

179

Chapter 4: Using Apps

Here you'll see the start of your route, with turn by turn directions that will automatically change as you drive along the route.

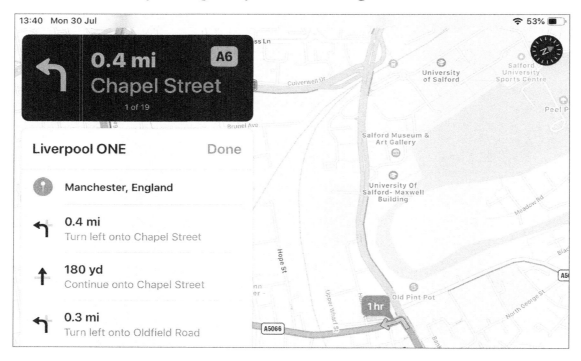

Drop a Pin

To drop a pin, tap and hold your finger on the location on the map.

180

Chapter 4: Using Apps

3D Maps

3D maps are a great way to explore landmarks, major cities and areas of interest. You can flyover a city and explore what it has to offer.

To do this, first change your map to a satellite map if you haven't already done so. Then tap the 3D icon on the right hand side to switch to 3D mode.

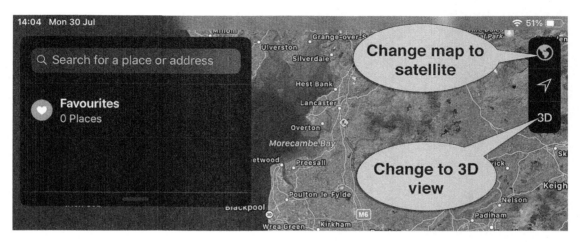

Type in a city name, place name or address into the search field on the top left of the screen.

You can zoom in and out of the 3D map and move around using your finger

To take a flyover tour, tap 'flyover' in the info side panel.

181

Chapter 4: Using Apps

Now move your iPad around, as you do this you'll notice the view move on your iPad. Use your finger to zoom in and out or move up and down the view.

Tap once anywhere on the screen to reveal the popup menu on the bottom left.

Tap 'start city tour' if available for that city to watch an animated 3D tour of the city.

Tap the x to close the flyover view.

Chapter 4: Using Apps

News App

The news app collects breaking stories from around the world and locally into one app, based on the topics you are interested in.

When you first start the app, you'll see a list of top stories, trending stories, and stories recommended for you. Scroll down the page, tap on a story to read the details.

183

Chapter 4: Using Apps

To open the side panel, tap the icon on the top left of the screen

From here you can select different news sources, magazines, newspapers and websites. Just tap the '+' next to the source to add.

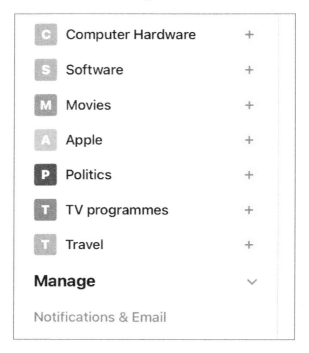

You can also search for specific channels. Tap the search field then type in your search.

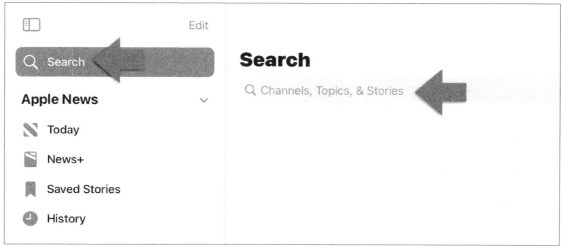

Chapter 4: Using Apps

To personalise your news, open the sidebar, then tap edit on the top left of the screen.

From the sidebar, scroll down to 'suggested by siri' and tap the '+'icon next to the channels you're interested in.

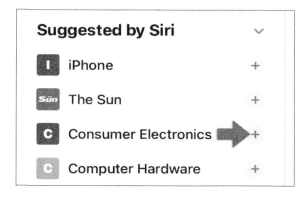

Scroll down to the bottom, then tap 'discover channels'.

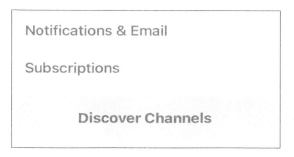

From here you can select different news sources, magazines, newspapers and websites. Tap the '+' icon to add a channel.

Tap 'done' at the bottom of the screen when you're finished.

185

Chapter 4: Using Apps

Apple Books App

Formerly known as iBooks, Apple Books is your electronic bookshelf and allows you to read ebooks. Tap the icon on your home screen.

You can download hundreds of different e-books that are available in the bookstore; from the latest novels, food, kids books or manuals.

Along the bottom of the screen you'll see some icons. Here you can see the books you are 'reading now', browse your library of books you've downloaded, browse the book store, look at audio books and search for a specific book title or author.

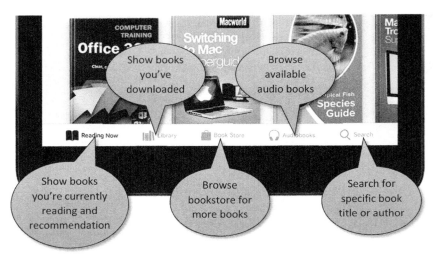

Just tap on the book cover to open the book.

Chapter 4: Using Apps

Browse the Store

You can also browse through the book store. To do this, tap 'bookstore' icon on the panel along the bottom of the screen.

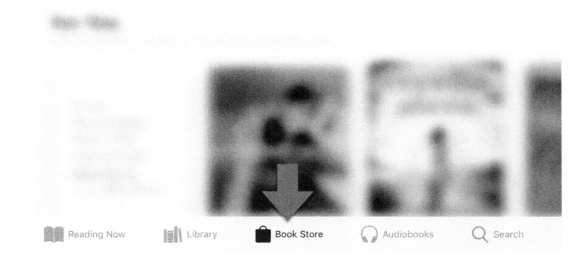

Click 'browse sections' to reveal the categories in the bookstore. Now select a category. Perhaps you're into 'crime thrillers', 'fiction', or 'education'. Just tap on a category to view the available books.

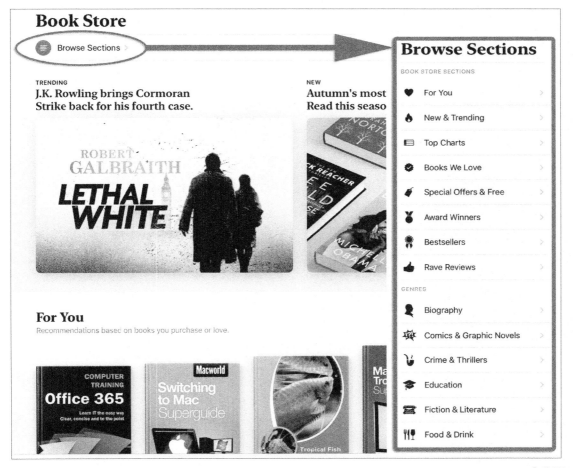

187

Chapter 4: Using Apps

Search the Store

You can also search for specific authors or titles. To do this tap on the 'search' icon on the panel along the bottom of the screen.

Then type what you're looking for in the search field at the top of the screen.

Tap on a book cover to see more details.

Chapter 4: Using Apps

From this page you'll be able to read a sample, the book's description, read any reviews, and buy/download the book.

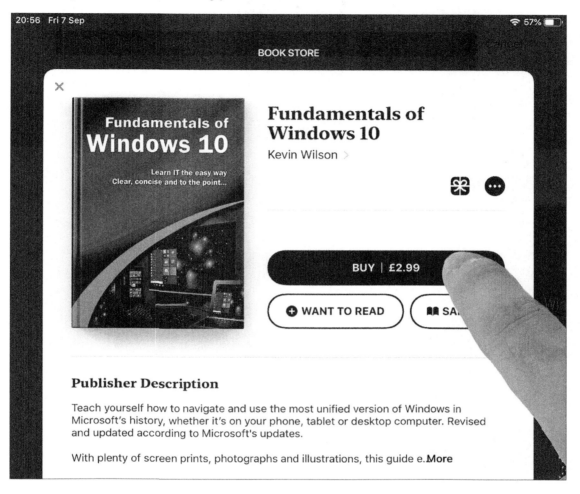

Tap 'get' if the book is free, or tap the price tag to download the book to your library. Once you've downloaded the book, you'll find it in your library. Tap the library icon on the panel along the bottom of the screen.

Chapter 4: Using Apps

Tap on the book cover to begin reading.

The book will open up full screen. Swipe left or right across the screen to turn the pages.

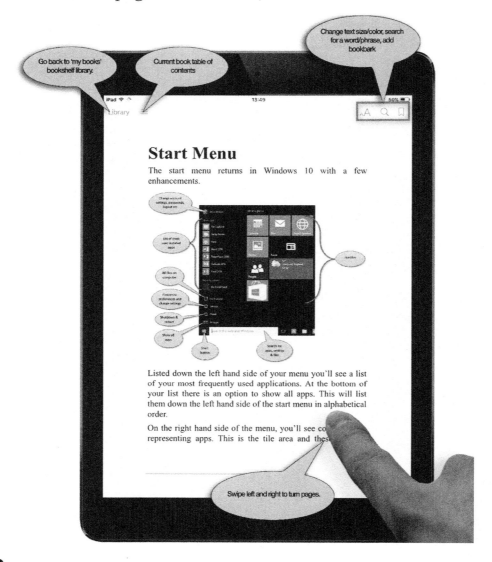

Chapter 4: Using Apps

Files App

The iCloud Drive App has been dropped and replaced with the Files App. You'll find the icon on your dock.

In the Files App, you'll find all your files that are stored on your iPad and iCloud Drive. The Files App works best if you hold your iPad horizontally.

When you first open the files app, you'll see your most recently opened documents. To see all your files tap 'browse' on the panel along the bottom of the screen.

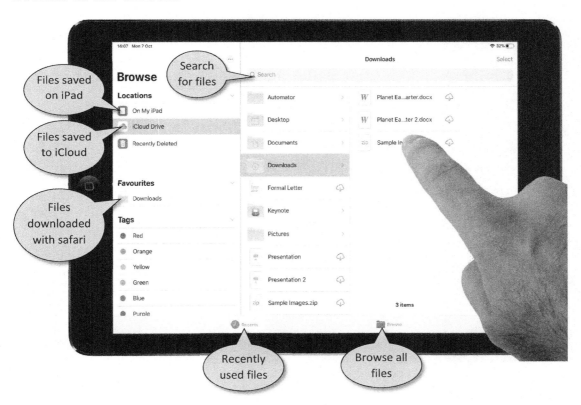

To see all the documents stored on iCloud, tap 'iCloud Drive' from the panel along the left hand side of the screen.

To see files saved physically on your iPad, tap 'on my iPad'.

To find any files downloaded with Safari web browser, tap 'downloads'.

Tap on any icon to open the folder or file.

Chapter 4: Using Apps

Create New Folders

You can also create your own folders. To create a new folder, tap on the location you want the new folder to appear in, eg 'pictures' folder on iCloud drive.

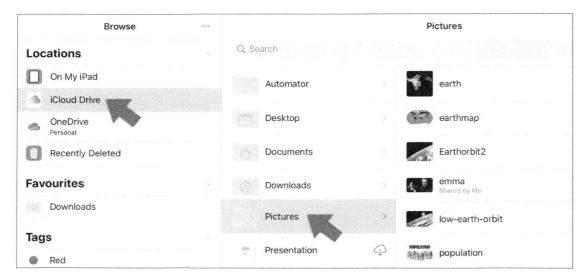

Tap and hold your finger on the blank space at the bottom of the file list. Tap 'new folder' from the popup.

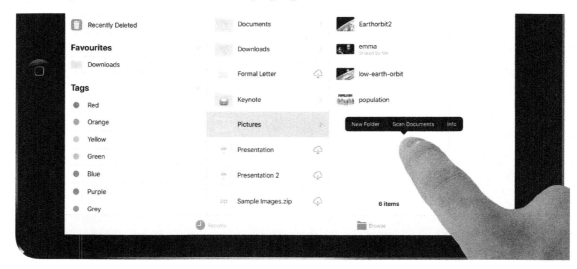

Enter a name for your folder. Tap 'done' on the top right.

Chapter 4: Using Apps

Drag Files into Folders

You can drag and drop files into these folders. Tap and hold your finger on the file, then drag your finger across the glass to the folder you want to put the file into. In this example, I'm going to drag and drop a photo into the 'Summer' folder.

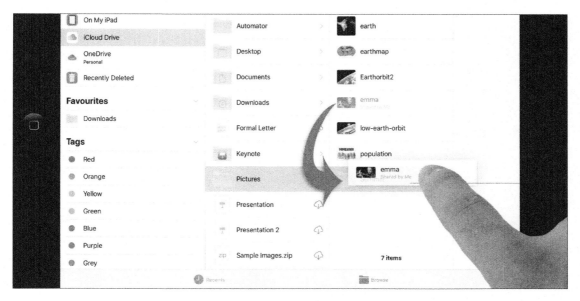

Tap on the folders to open them, tap on the file thumbnails to open the files.

Delete Files or Folders

You can also delete files. Tap 'select' on the top right of the screen.

Tap on the files you want to delete.

Tap the delete icon on the toolbar along the bottom of the screen.

193

Chapter 4: Using Apps

Share a File

Tap 'select' on the top right of the screen.

Tap the file you want to share, then tap the share icon on the toolbar along the bottom of the screen.

Select your sharing method from the options. You can share with iMessage, email, or airdrop.

You can also share folders with friends, family and colleagues using iCloud Drive.

External Drive Support

You can access files on a USB drive, SD card or hard drive. To plug in an external drive into an iPad Air, iPad, or iPad Mini, you'll need a Lightning to Micro USB Adapter. *If you're using an iPad Pro, USB-C devices will plug directly into the docking port on the bottom of the iPad Pro, for any other devices you'll need a USB-C to USB adapter.*

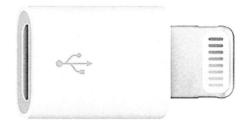

Plug the adapter in the docking port on the bottom of your iPad. With this, you can plug in a standard USB external drive, SD card reader, or USB drive.

Chapter 4: Using Apps

Your drive will appear under 'locations' on the side panel of your files app. Tap on the device to view files and folders stored on the drive.

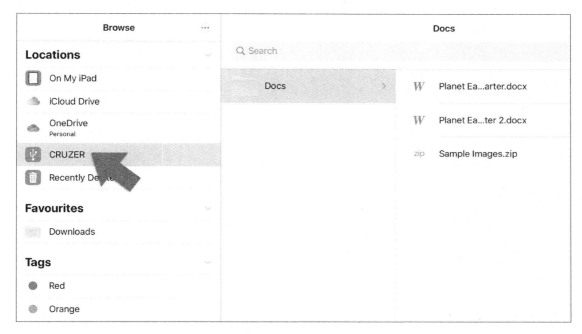

You can drag and drop files onto the USB device.

Rename Files or Folders

Tap and hold your finger on a file or folder, then select 'rename' from the pop up menu.

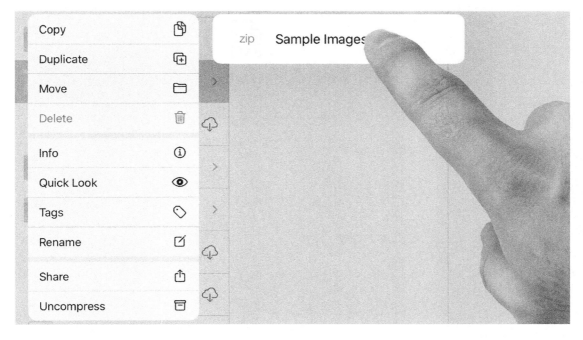

Type in the new name for the folder or file.

195

Chapter 4: Using Apps

File Servers

You can connect to a file server at work or a home PC using the SMB protocol. To connect to a server, tap the 3 dots icon on the top right of the left hand pane. From the drop down, tap 'connect to server'.

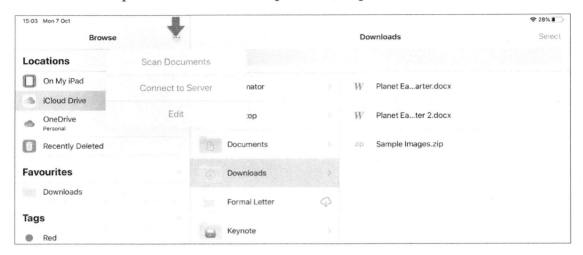

Enter the server's address.

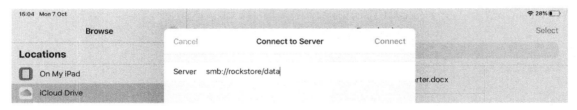

For example, if I wanted to connect to my file server on the network, I'd enter the server name followed by the shared folder name.

```
smb://rockstore/data
```

Enter the shared folder's username and password when prompted.

Once connected, your folder will appear on the 'shared' section on the left hand pane.

196

Chapter 4: Using Apps

Voice Memos

You can record audio using your iPad's built in mic or a bluetooth external mic. You can record voice memos, meetings and lectures.

You'll find the voice memo app on your home screen.

Lets take a look at the main screen. Here you can see your previous recordings listed down the left hand side. Any recording you select here will appear in the white panel on the right hand side of the screen.

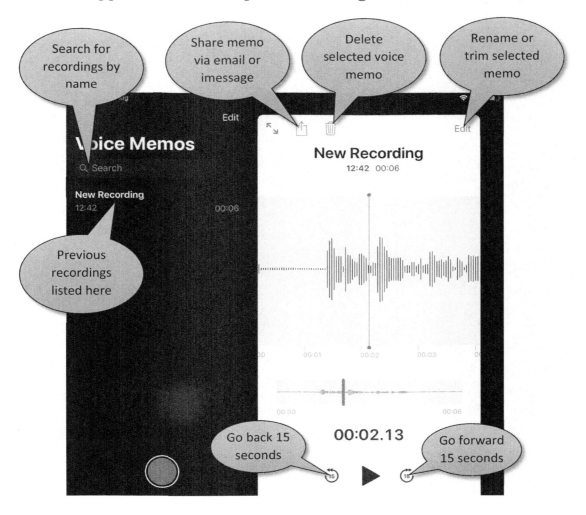

Tap the play button in the grey panel on the right to playback the recording.

197

Chapter 4: Using Apps

Recording Memos

To record a memo, simply tap the red record button on the bottom left of the screen.

The memo app will start recording. You'll see a wave form appear in the middle of the screen to indicate the app is picking up audio.

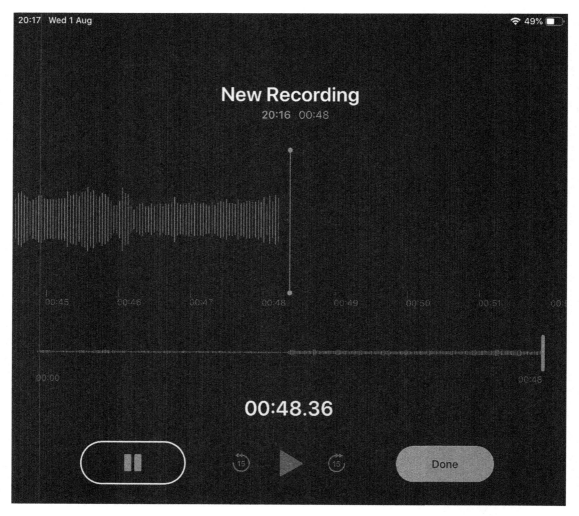

To pause a recording temporarily, tap the pause icon on the left. To stop the recording, tap 'done'.

Your memo will appear in the list on the left hand side of the main screen.

Chapter 4: Using Apps

Renaming Memos

The first thing you should do with a new voice memo recording is give it a meaningful name. The last thing you want is every memo called 'new recording.

To demonstrate this, we'll rename the voice memo we just recorded. Select the voice memo from the list on the left hand side. Then tap and hold your finger on the name in the right hand panel, until the keyboard pops up.

Delete the default text, then type in a meaningful name for the recording. Tap enter on the on-screen keyboard to confirm the name.

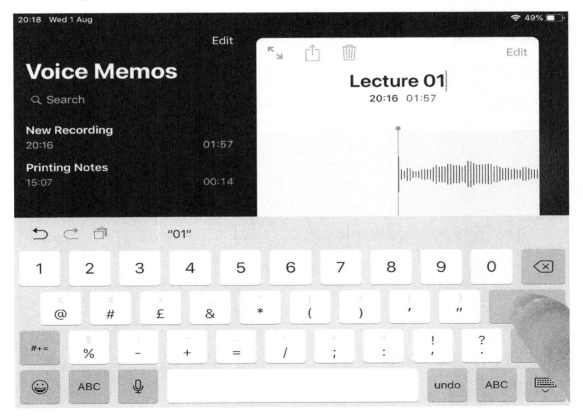

199

Chapter 4: Using Apps

Trim a Memo

You can trim the beginning and the ends of the memo voice recording. To do this, select the recording you want to trim from the list on the left hand side of the main screen. Then tap edit on the top right of the grey panel on the right hand side.

Tap the trim icon on the top right

Now to trim the beginning and ends of the clip, drag the yellow handles along the track until you get to the start and end points you want.

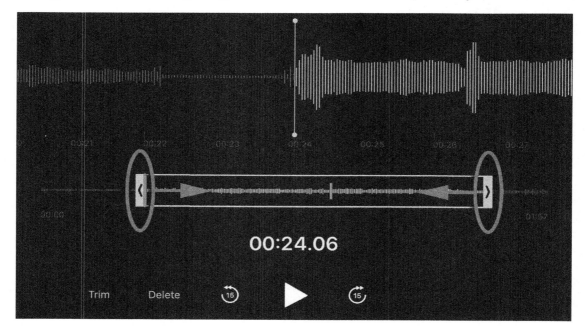

Tap 'trim' when you're done.

Chapter 4: Using Apps

Clock App

You can use the clock app to set alarms, timers, as a stop watch, and create time zone clocks so you can see the time in other countries.

You'll find the clock app on your home screen.

World Clock

With world clock, you can create clocks for any city or country in the world. This is useful if you have friends or family in another country, so you know what time it is there and don't call them in the middle of the night. It's also useful if you're travelling.

To see the world clock, tap 'world clock' on the panel along the bottom of the screen.

To add a clock, tap the + sign on the top right of the screen.

Type in the name of the city or country you want to add

Tap the name of the city/country in the list of suggestions.

201

Chapter 4: Using Apps

Now you'll see the clock appear on the map.

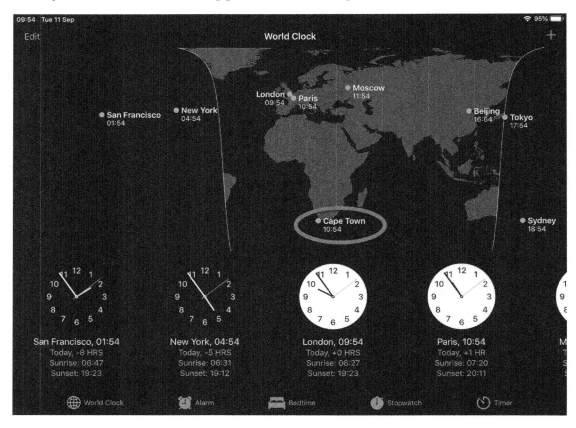

To remove a clock, just tap 'edit' on the top left and you'll see a small red sign appear on the top left of each clock. Tap the red sign to remove it.

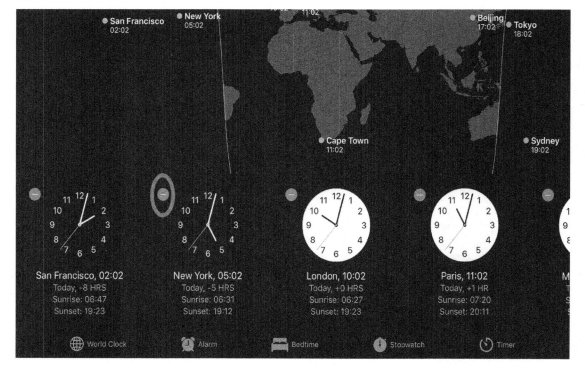

Chapter 4: Using Apps

Alarm

You can also set multiple alarms. Eg one for wake up. To do this, select 'alarm' from the panel along the bottom of the screen.

This will display all the alarms you have set.

To set a new alarm, tap the + sign on the top right.

Set the alarm to the time you want the alarm to go off. Tap 'repeat' to set what days you want the alarm, eg 'weekdays'. Tap 'label' to name the alarm, eg 'wakeup'. Tap 'sound' to choose what your alarm sounds like - you can select a sound or a song from your music library. Tap 'save' on the top right when you're done.

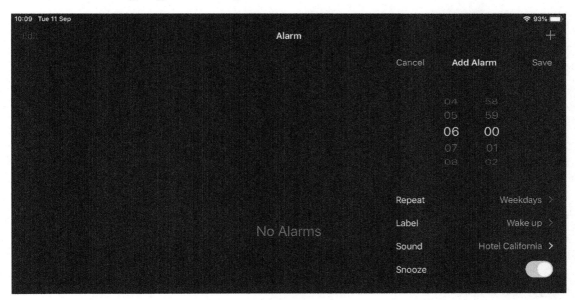

You'll see the alarms you've added. Tap the green slider on the alarm to turn it on and off.

203

Chapter 4: Using Apps

Bed Time

Bed time allows you to create a sleep routine, allowing you to set a time to go to bed and a time to wake up, and the clock app will remind you.

Select 'bed time' from the panel along the bottom of the screen.

The first time you run this feature, you'll need to go through the setup. To do this tap 'get started'. Select the time you want to wake up using the sliders on the screen. Tap 'next'

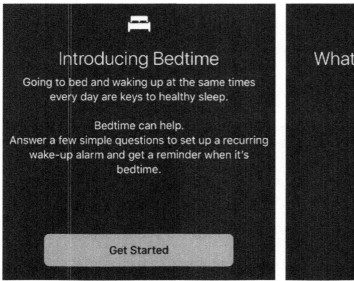
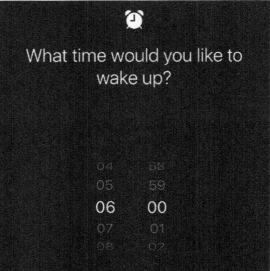

Select the days of the week, then select the number of hours sleep you need. Usually 8 hours. Tap 'next'.

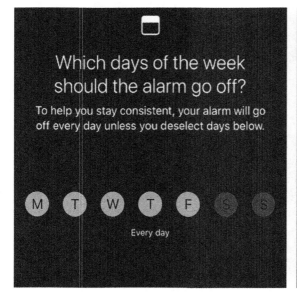
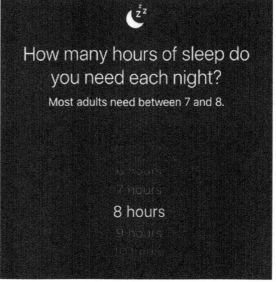

204

Chapter 4: Using Apps

Set the days of the week you want your routine to be in force. Tap 'next'.

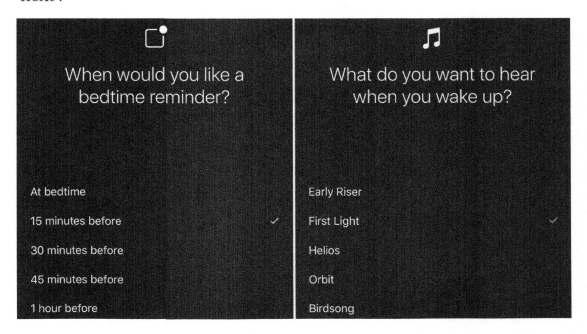

Once you've completed the setup, you can see your bedtime on the main screen. To adjust the bedtime time, drag the sleep marker around the clock. Similarly to adjust your wakeup time, drag the wake marker around the clock.

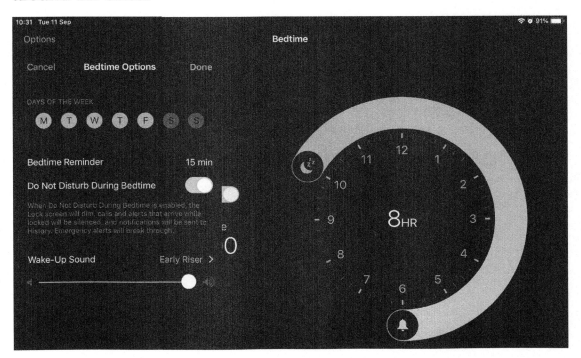

To change your options, tap 'options' on the top left of the screen. Here you can change the days of the week, set a reminder and set a wake up sound.

205

Chapter 4: Using Apps

Stop Watch

Use the stopwatch to time events. Eg an athletics event. Select 'stopwatch' from the panel along the bottom of the screen.

Tap 'start/stop' to start and stop the timer.

Tap 'lap' to count the number of laps if you are timing a sporting event such as athletics or racing.

Timer

Use the timer to set a count down timer. Select 'timer' from the panel along the bottom of the screen. Use the sliders to select the length of time in hours, minutes and seconds. For example, if you're playing a game or timing an egg, just set the amount of time allowed.

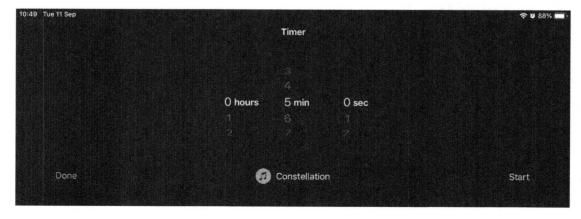

Tap 'start' to start the count down. Tap the iTunes icon next to where it says 'constellation' to change the sound the timer makes when the time runs out.

Chapter 4: Using Apps

Shortcuts

You'll find the shortcuts app on the dock, or in the applications folder in finder.

Shortcuts

Lets take a look at the shortcuts app...

On the sidebar at the top, you'll see the gallery, which is a library of shortcuts, grouped into sections based on their functionality. You'll also see links to other shortcuts you've created.

Creating Shortcuts

Select 'all shortcuts' from the sidebar on the left, then click the + icon on the top of the screen.

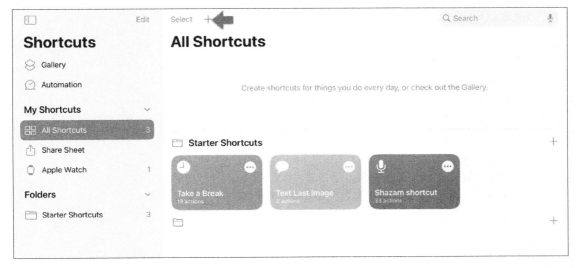

207

Chapter 4: Using Apps

Using the search bar on the top right, type in the action/app you want to use to execute your shortcut. You can also select one from the list on the right. In this demo, I want to create a shortcut that will send an email to my production team, so I can send files and updates to them without having to add the email addresses each time. In this case, I would select 'send email' from the actions. Click and drag the action onto the canvas

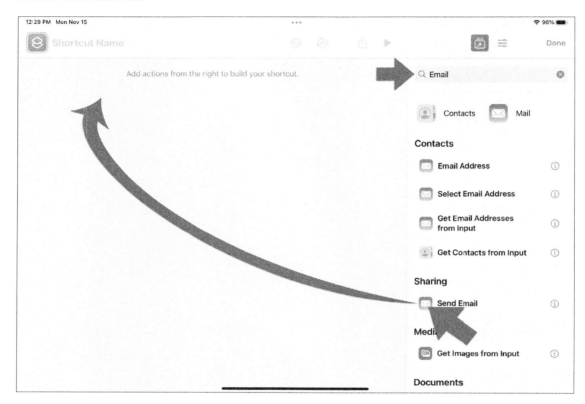

Now we need to add all the email addresses.

Rename the shortcut. Give the shortcut a meaningful name.

208

Chapter 4: Using Apps

Select the settings icon on the right hand side. Now add the shortcut to the menus you want. Add it to the home screen, or the share sheet, etc.

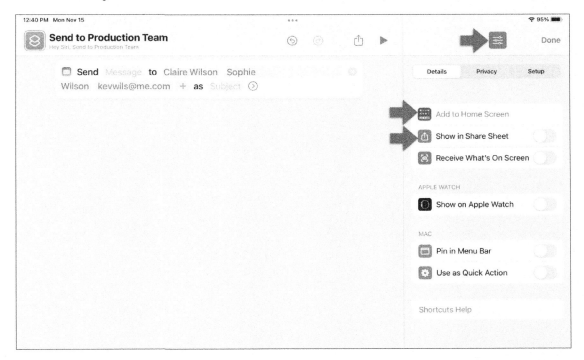

Shortcut Gallery

The shortcut gallery contains pre-built shortcuts you can use and customise to your needs. To view the gallery, select 'gallery' from the sidebar on the left hand side.

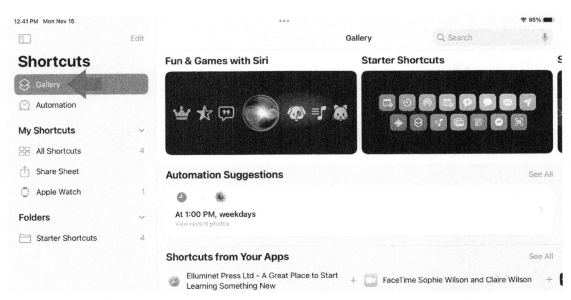

You'll find basic shortcuts for creating a note, reminder, or sending a photo to someone. As well as shortcuts for sharing files on mail, or social media, and ones that work with Siri.

209

Chapter 4: Using Apps

First use the search field on the top right window to find a shortcut, or select one from the categories on screen.

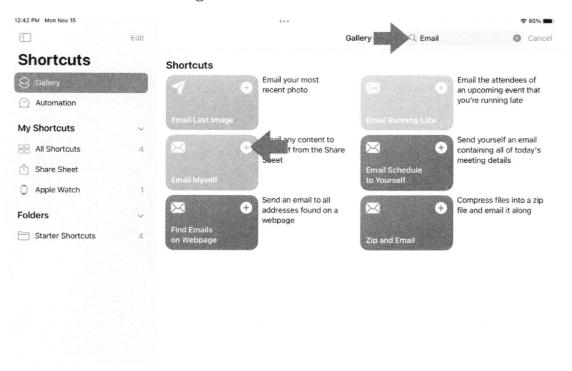

Click the '+' icon on the top right of the shortcut to open it up.

Customise any settings if prompted. In this example, I need to supply an email address. Click on 'add shortcut'.

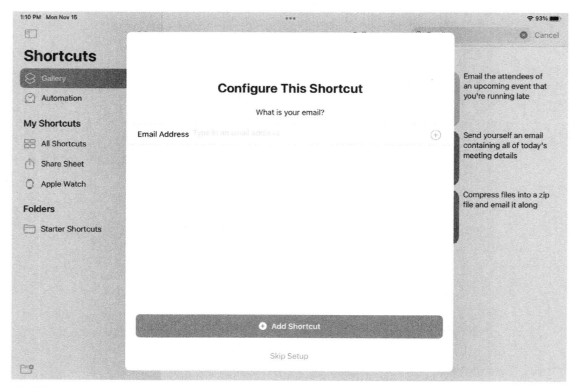

Chapter 4: Using Apps

Now, select 'all shortcuts' from the side panel on the left. You'll see the shortcut you've just created. Tap the three dots icon on the top right of the shortcut.

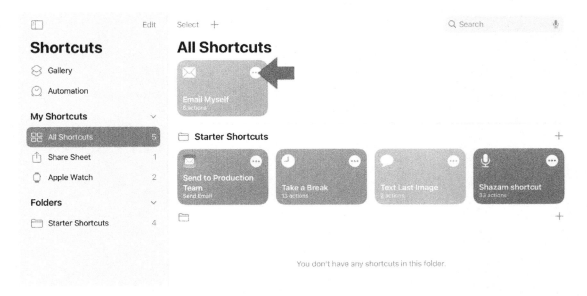

In the left hand pane, you'll see all the steps the shortcut will go through when executed. Check the steps. In this case we're sending an email, so make sure the email address is correct. Over on the right hand side, click the 'settings' icon.

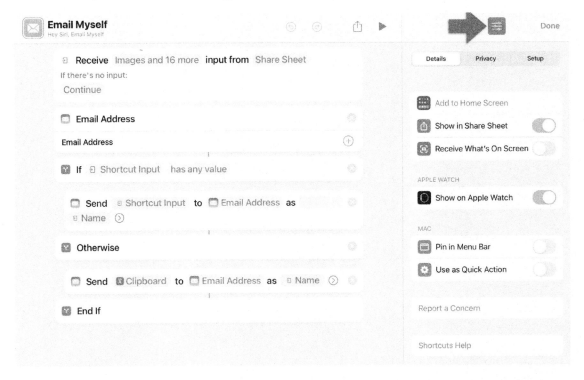

Pin the shortcut to the home screen. You can also add the action to the share sheet.

211

Chapter 4: Using Apps

Running Shortcuts

To run your shortcuts, tap on 'all shortcuts' from the side bar.

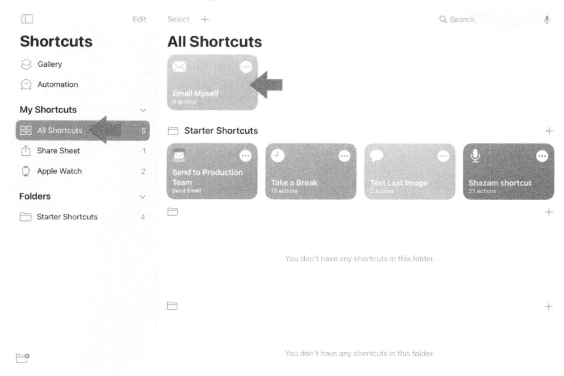

If you added the shortcut to your home screen, tap on the icon on the home screen.

Chapter 4: Using Apps

Pages Word Processing

To launch Pages, tap the icon on your home screen.

Once Pages has opened, tap 'continue' on the welcome page. You'll see your most recently opened documents, you'll also be able to browse through your documents, and create new blank documents or one from a template. Tap 'browse' on the bottom right of the screen.

Tap 'create new document'.

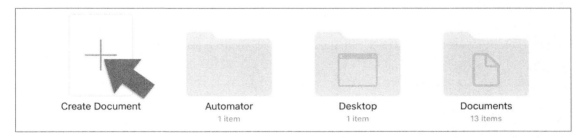

Select a template, or tap 'blank' to start a new document.

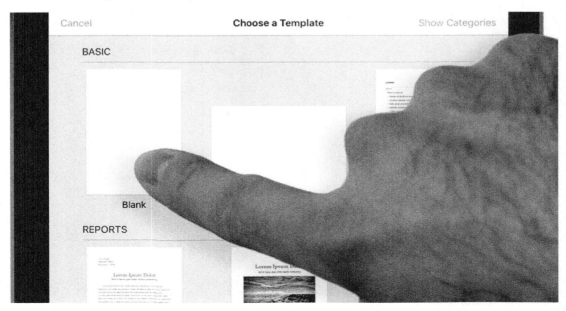

Chapter 4: Using Apps

Once you have selected the template to use you will see the main work screen. Let's take a closer look at the main editing screen.

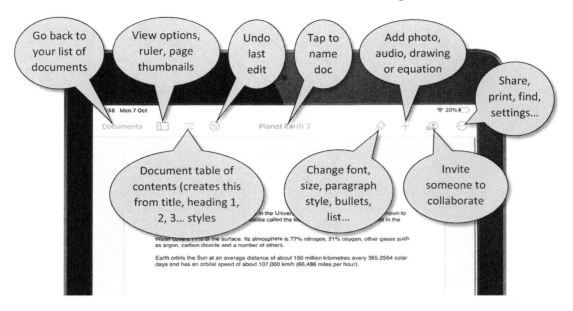

You'll find your toolbar across the top of the screen where you'll find your tools for formatting your text.

Along the bottom, you'll see your on-screen keyboard. Along the top of your keyboard there are some icons. From the left you have, tabs, indents, change font, predictive text suggestions, font size, text align, and an icon to add comments, page breaks, contents page etc.

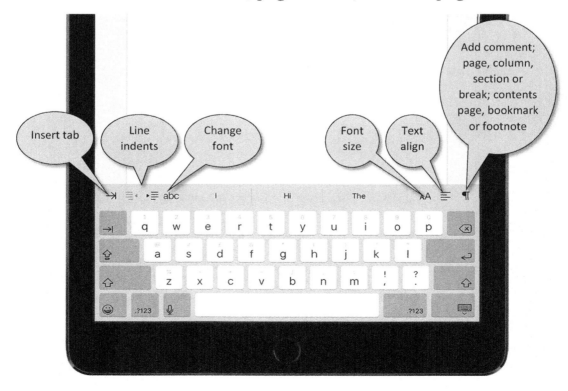

Chapter 4: Using Apps

Formatting Text

Begin typing in your text into the main window as shown above.

The text we entered needs formatting. To add a heading, type it in above the block of text.

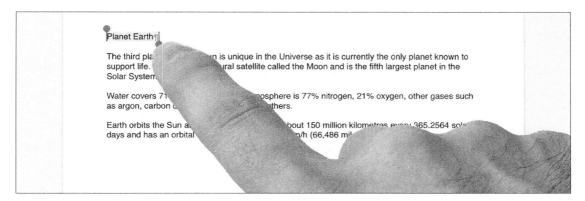

Highlight your text with your finger as shown above by dragging the blue dots over the text, then tap the paint brush from the toolbar.

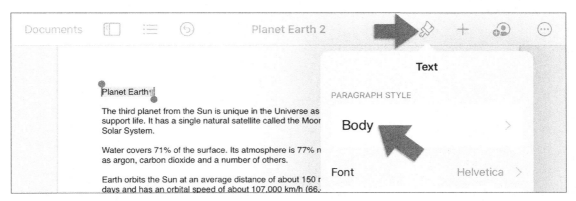

Tap 'title' to change the title style of the selected text.

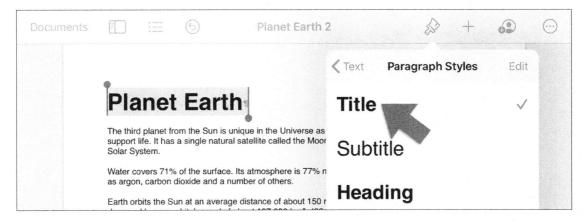

Make sure you use the correct heading styles for different parts of your document, so Pages can automatically generate a table of contents.

Chapter 4: Using Apps

Using this menu, you can also change the font, font size, font colour, text alignment (left, center, right), line spacing, bullet lists, and columns.

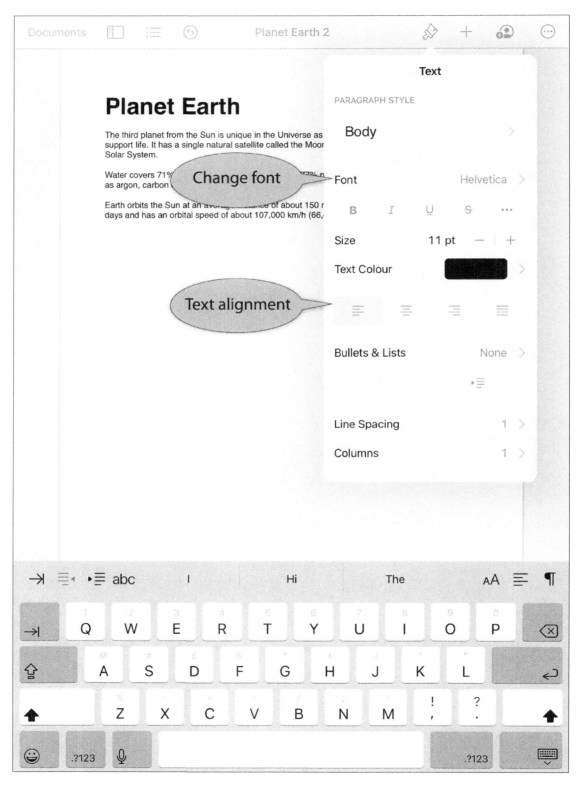

Just select the icon from the drop down menu.

Chapter 4: Using Apps

Adding a Picture

The easiest way to add a picture is to tap the plus sign on the right hand side of the toolbar. Then from the dropdown, tap the image icon on the right. Select one of your albums if you want to insert a photo you took with your camera or tap 'insert from' if you have an image on your iCloud drive. Tap your pictures folder and select an image.

You can resize your image by clicking the resize handles, circled below, and dragging them.

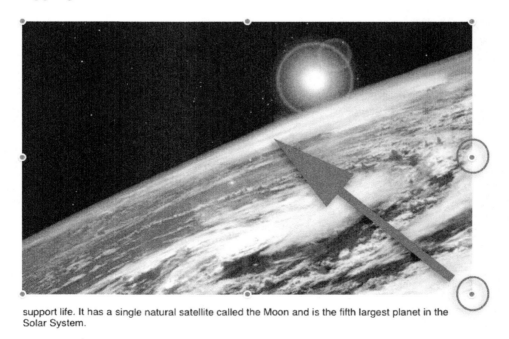

You can change the styles by adding borders and shadows by tapping on the paint brush icon on the top right of your toolbar.

217

Chapter 4: Using Apps

Collaboration

You can invite people to collaborate with you on your document. This works well for group projects where more than one person can edit a document at the same time. To invite people, open your document then tap the 'people' icon on the top right.

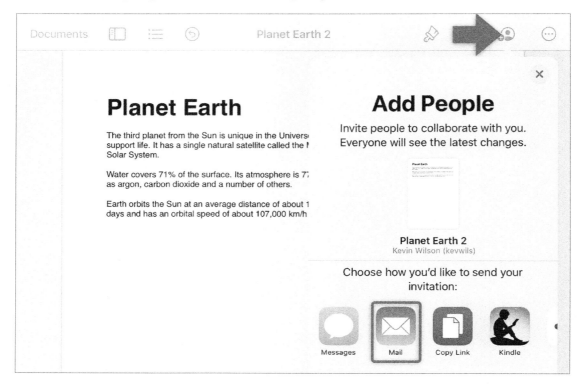

From the 'add people' sheet, select how you want to send the invite - use either email or messages. Add the person's email address and tap send.

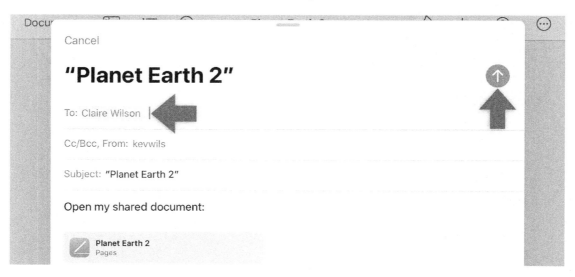

When the other person accepts the invitation, they can edit your document

Chapter 4: Using Apps

Keynote Presentations

Keynote allows you to create multimedia presentations. To launch keynote, go to your home screen and tap keynote.

Tap continue if you're running keynote for the first time. You'll see your most recently opened presentations, you'll also be able to browse through your presentations, and create new blank ones or one from a template. Tap 'browse' on the bottom right of the screen.

Tap 'create presentation'.

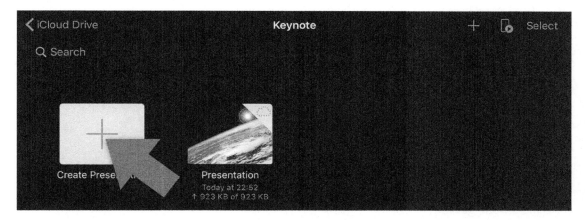

From here you can select from a variety of pre-designed templates with different themes, fonts and colours.

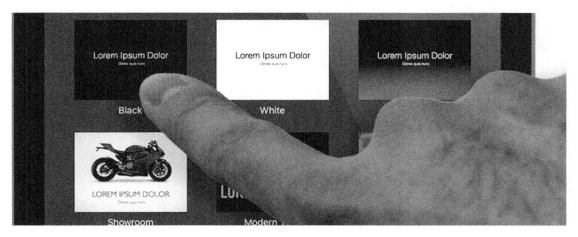

219

Chapter 4: Using Apps

Once you have selected a template you will see the main screen as shown below. This is where you can start building your presentation.

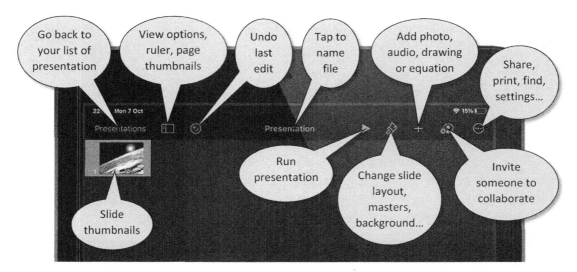

Editing a Slide

Double tap in the heading field shown below and enter a heading eg 'Planet Earth'. You can tap and drag the heading wherever you like.

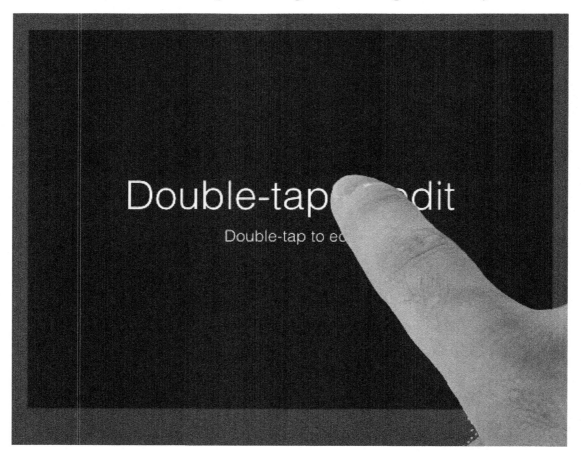

Chapter 4: Using Apps

Adding a New Slide

Tap the new slide button located on the bottom left of the screen, then tap a slide layout from the options that appear.

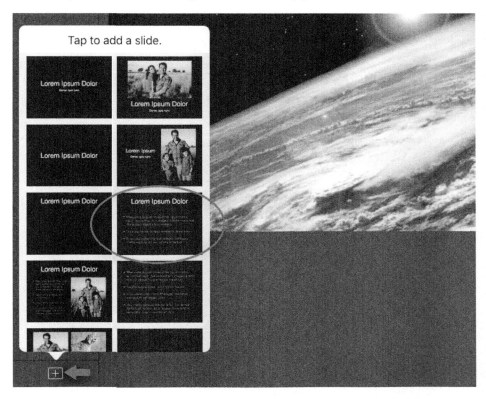

Add some text by double clicking on the text box that appears in the slide.

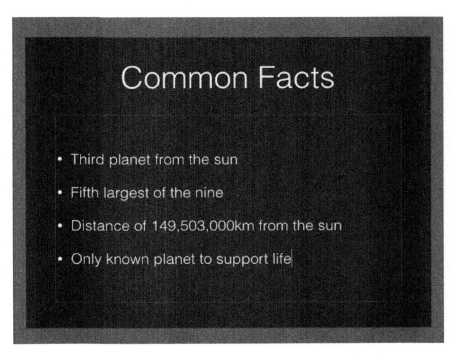

221

Chapter 4: Using Apps

Adding Media

To add images and media to your slide, tap the plus sign on your tool bar at the top right of your screen. Then tap the image icon on the right.

If you want to add one of your photographs from your photo library, tap on one of your albums and select 'photo or video'. If you want to insert a picture from your iCloud, tap 'insert from...'. If you want to take a new picture, tap camera, if you want to add audio, tap 'record audio'...

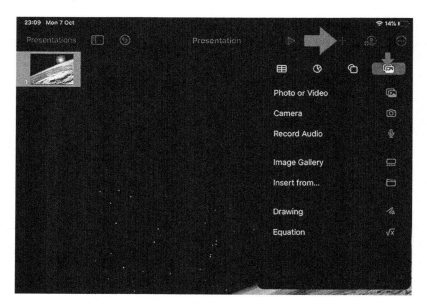

From your iCloud drive, select pictures. Tap on a picture.

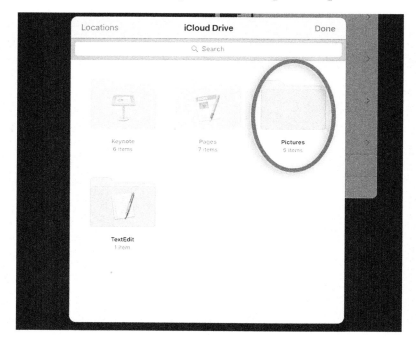

Chapter 4: Using Apps

Animations

Animations allow you to make objects such as text or photographs appear...

Tap on your text box and select the animate icon located on the top right corner of your screen

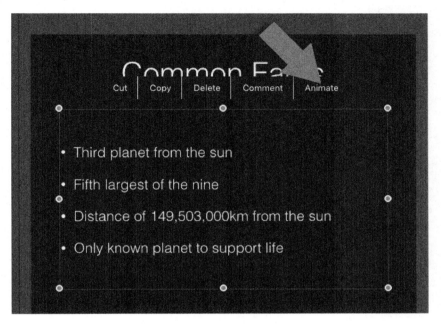

Then tap 'add build in'

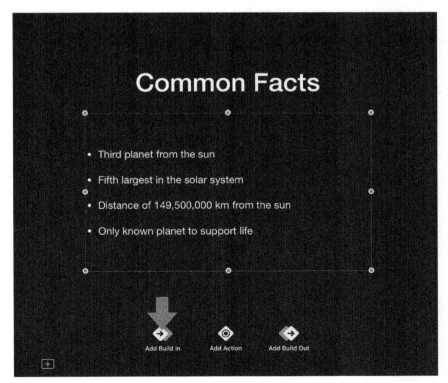

223

Chapter 4: Using Apps

Then select an effect you want, eg 'appear'.

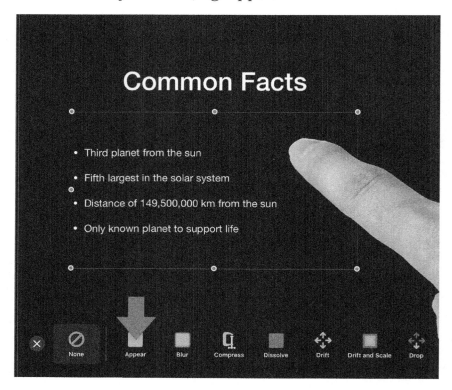

Tap on your slide, then tap 'appear' again to specify that you want the bullet points to appear one by one. Tap 'delivery' and select 'by bullet'.

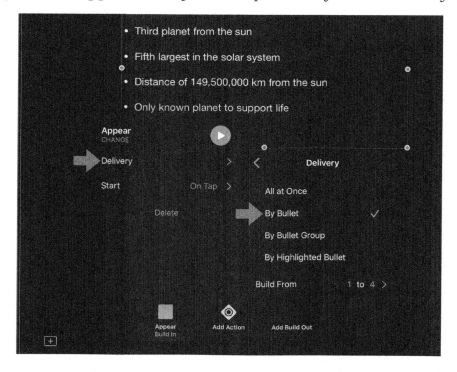

To see what the effect looks like, tap the play button on the top right of your screen.

Chapter 4: Using Apps

Formatting Text Boxes

Tap on a text box you want to format. You can add borders to your text boxes, reflection effects or background colours.

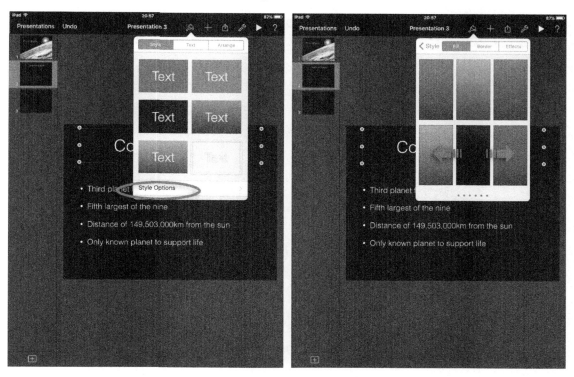

To format the border and fill your text box, tap your text box and tap the paint brush icon, on the top right of the screen.

Tap fill to change the background colour of the text box. Then swipe your finger across the selections of effects and tap on one to select it. In this example, I am going for a nice blue gradient fill.

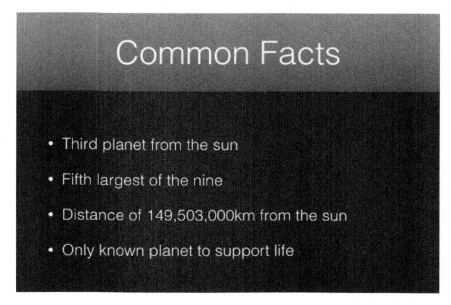

225

Chapter 4: Using Apps

Formatting Text Inside Textboxes

To change the formatting of the text, for example to change the colour of the text or make it bold.

First select your text in the text box you want to change. Tap on the text three times to select it all. Then tap the paint brush icon on the top right of your toolbar.

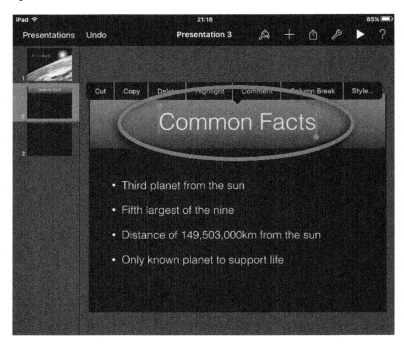

From here you can change the font, the font colour, size etc.

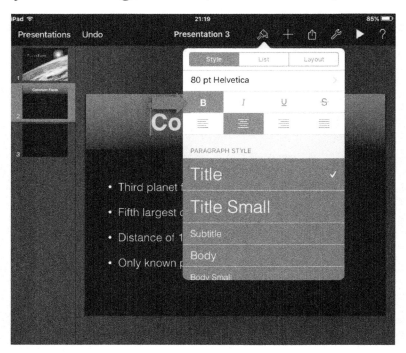

Chapter 4: Using Apps

As an example I have changed the colour to light blue and made it bold.

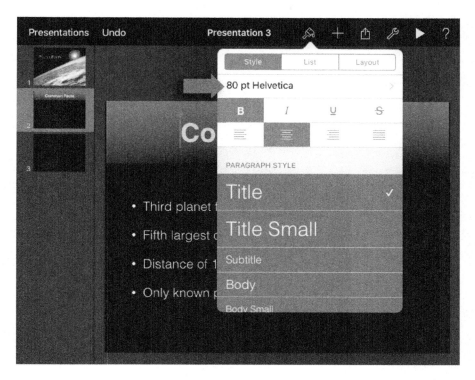

Tap on the font name, illustrated with the red arrow in the image above. Then from here you can change the size, the colour and the typeface.

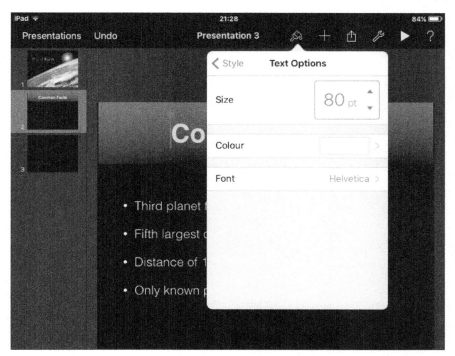

Tap the colour and select a colour. Do the same for 'font' - tap font and select a font.

Chapter 4: Using Apps

Numbers Spreadsheets

Numbers is a spreadsheet program that allows you analyse and present information. To launch Numbers, go to your home screen and tap 'numbers'.

Tap continue if you're running keynote for the first time. You'll see your most recently opened presentations, you'll also be able to browse through your spreadsheets, and create new blank ones or one from a template. Tap 'browse' on the bottom right of the screen.

Tap 'create spreadsheet'.

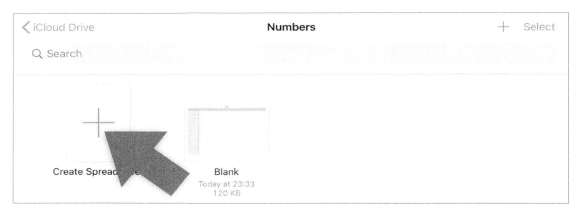

From here you can select from a variety of pre-designed templates with different themes, fonts and colours.

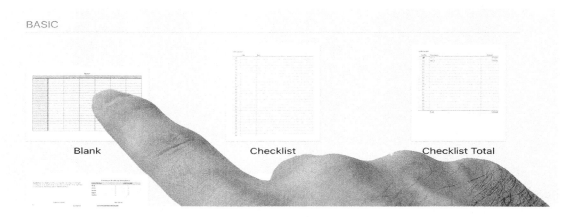

Chapter 4: Using Apps

Once you have selected a template you will see the main screen as shown below. This is where you can start building your spreadsheet.

Let's take a closer look at the different tools available on the numbers main screen.

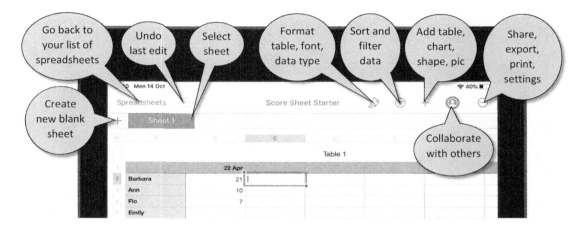

Entering Data

In the example, we are going to create a basic scoring sheet. When you tap inside a cell on your spreadsheet, you'll see the on-screen keyboard show up. This will allow you to enter data.

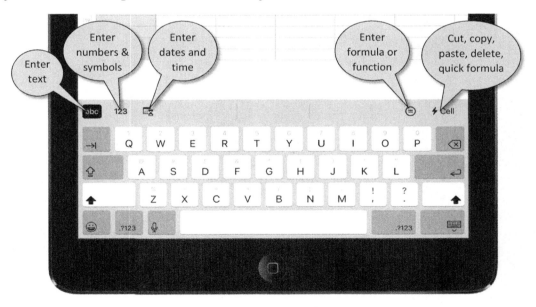

Along the top of the on-screen keyboard, you'll see an icon for entering text, numbers or symbols, dates and times. On the other side, you will find tools to enter formulas as well as copy and paste tools.

Just tap in a cell, select the type of data you want to enter from the bar along the top of the keyboard, then type it in using the on-screen keyboard.

229

Chapter 4: Using Apps

Simple Text Formatting

Sometimes it improves the readability of your spreadsheet to format the data in the cells.

For example, let's make the total column bold. To do this tap and hold your finger on the first cell, then drag your finger across the rest of the cells to select them.

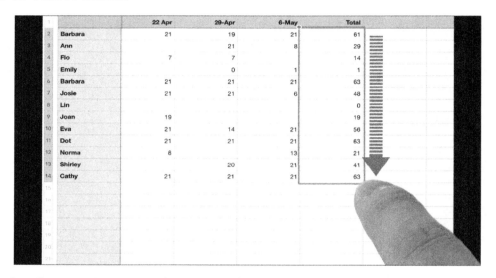

Tap the format icon on the top right

Select the 'cell' tab. Tap the bold icon. You can also change the text colour, size and font, as well as alignment, and wrap

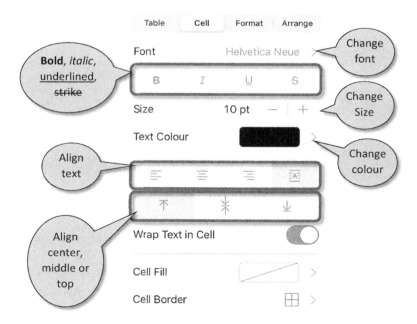

Chapter 4: Using Apps

Resizing Rows and Columns

You can resize a column or row by clicking and dragging the column or row handle. To resize, tap on a column, you'll see a small handle appear.

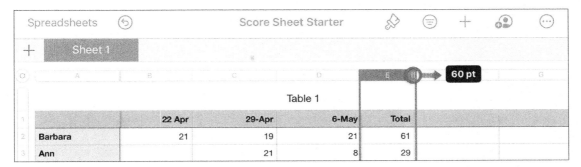

Do the same for resizing rows.

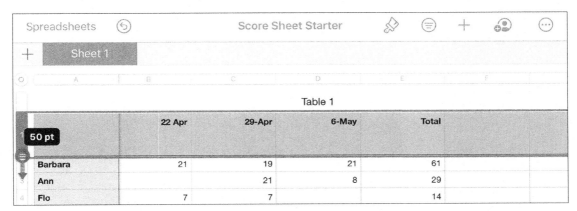

Inserting Rows & Columns

To insert a row between Flo and Emily, tap the row 'flo' is in, then tap the green 'row' icon on the bottom right of your screen.

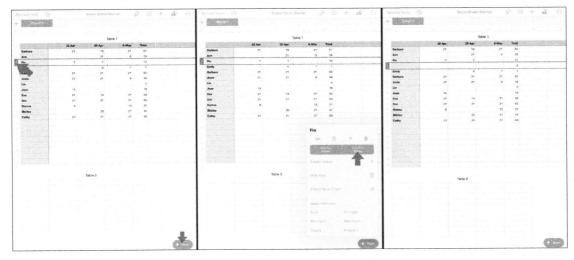

Tap 'add row below'. Use the same procedure for columns.

231

Chapter 4: Using Apps

Formulas

You can add formulas to manipulate data. For example, if I had two numbers and wanted to find the difference, I could subtract one number from the other.

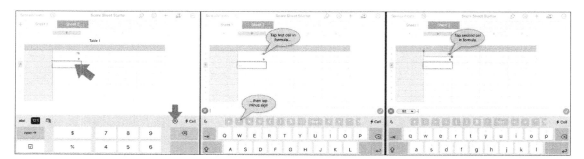

First, tap in the cell you want the solution to appear in, then tap the '=' sign on the top right of the on-screen keyboard. This will bring up the formula bar. Tap the first cell in the formula, tap an operator from the bar along the top of the on-screen keyboard (the minus sign in this example), then tap the second cell in the formula. Tap the green tick icon on the right when you're finished.

Functions

A function is a predefined formula that you can use to perform calculations and manipulate your data. For example, on our scoring sheet I can create another column and use a function to add up the scores. To insert a function, tap the cell you want the solution to appear in, then tap the '=' sign on the top right of the on-screen keyboard, then tap the 'fx' icon on the left hand side.

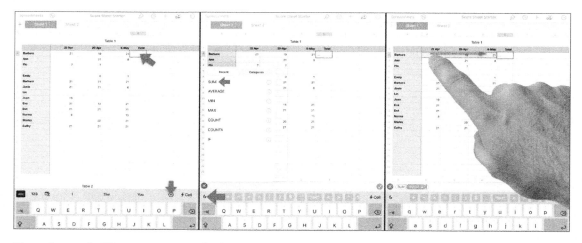

Tap 'sum'. Now, tap and drag your finger over the values you want to apply the function to. Tap the green tick on the right to finish.

You can also find other functions, just tap 'categories' and browse through the functions.

232

Chapter 4: Using Apps

Fonts

Apple has added a feature allowing users to install third party fonts in iPadOS. First, you'll need to download a font management app from the app store. To do this, open your app store, select 'search' and search for 'ifont'. There are others available but most are rubbish. I found ifont easiest to use and the app is free.

Tap 'get' to download the app.

The app will appear on your home screen once installed. Tap on the icon to start the app. Let's take a look at the app

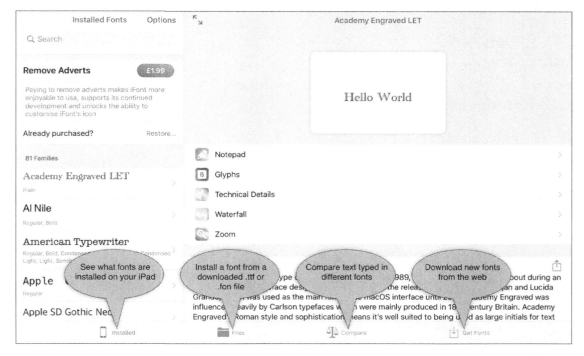

Using the menu bar along the bottom you can install fonts and download fonts.

233

Chapter 4: Using Apps

Downloading

To download new fonts, tap 'get fonts', then tap a site to download the fonts from. Eg 'Dafont'

Tap in the search field on the top right of the screen and enter the font name you want to download.

Tap 'import to iFont' on the popup.

Now tap 'files' on the menu bar along the bottom of the screen. Tap 'install' next to the font you just downloaded. Tap 'allow', 'close', then 'done' on the popups.

Now, open your settings app, select 'general', then tap 'profile'.

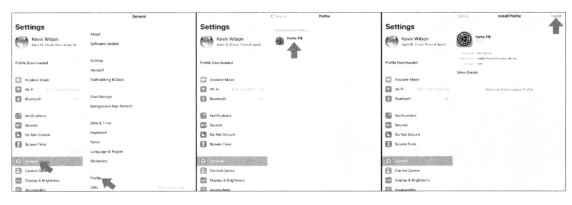

Tap 'install' on the top right of the screen.

234

Chapter 4: Using Apps

Installing from File

If you've downloaded a font file from Safari, open the ifont app select 'get fonts' from the menu bar along the bottom of the screen.

Select 'open files' on the top left. Navigate to your downloads folder and select the font file you want to install.

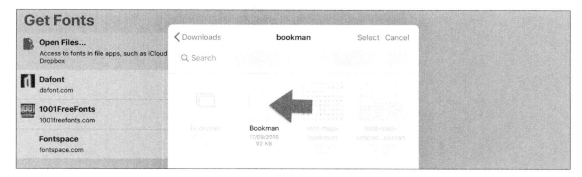

Select 'files' from the menu bar along the bottom of the screen.

Tap 'download' next to the font you just installed.

Tap 'allow', 'close', then 'done' on the popups.

Now, open your settings app, select 'general', then tap 'profile'.

Tap 'install' on the top right of the screen.

235

Chapter 4: Using Apps

Printing Documents

To print documents from an iPad you'll need a printer that is compatible with Air Print. Most modern printers will have this feature included.

Air Print

If your printer is Air Print enabled, then your printer will show up in the print dialog box automatically.

To print a document, select the share icon, then tap 'print'. If you're using the Pages App, select the '...' icon and tap 'print'.

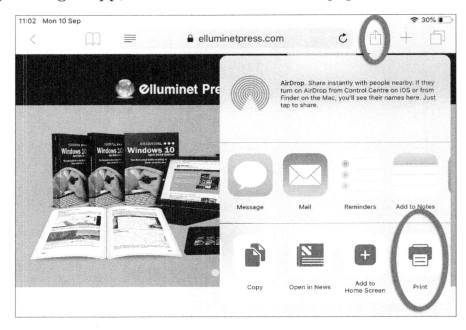

Select your printer from the printer field, enter the number of copies you want, and select the page range you want to print (eg pages 2-4), or leave it on 'all pages', if you want the whole document.

Tap 'print' on the top right when you're done.

Chapter 4: Using Apps

Older Printers

If your printer doesn't have the Air Print feature, you can download an app from the App Store for your printer.

- **HP Printers** download **HP Smart**
- **Samsung Printers** download **Samsung Mobile Print**
- **Epson Printers** download **Epson iPrint**
- **Canon Printers** download **Canon Print**

Open the app on your iPad and select the document you want to print.

Select print.

237

5 Internet, Email & Comms

Your iPad has a lot of features that allow you to connect to the internet, browse the web, send and receive emails, share pictures with friends, store addresses and contacts, have video chat conversations with friends and family. To do this, Apple have provided some built in apps: Safari for web browsing, Mail for email and Face Time for video chat.

In this chapter, we'll take a look at

- Using Safari
- Using Email
- Contacts App
- Calendar App
- FaceTime
- Group FaceTime
- Messages
- Digital Touch in Message
- Sending Payments with Messages
- Emojis
- AirDrop

Lets start by taking a look at Safari web browser. Take a look at the video resources.

elluminetpress.com/ipad-comms

Chapter 5: Internet, Email & Communication

Using Safari

To launch safari, tap on the safari icon located on your dock.

Start Page

The start page appears whenever you open a new tab. Along the top you'll see your favourite websites. Underneath you'll see a privacy report, reading list, Siri suggestions, iCloud tabs and so on.

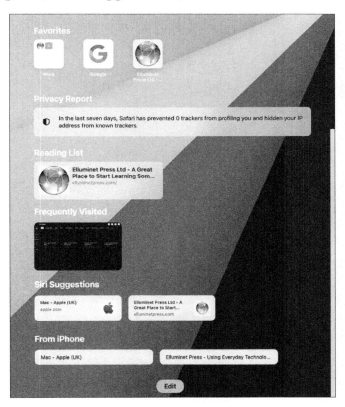

To customise the start page, tap on 'edit' at the bottom of the page. Here, you can sync your start page across all your devices. This means you'll get the same start page on your Mac, iPhone as well as your iPad, depending on what Apple Devices you have.

Chapter 5: Internet, Email & Communication

Further down you can add sections to your start page such as favourites, frequently visited websites, privacy reports, siri suggested content, your reading list and iCloud tabs that sync open tabs in Safari across all your devices.

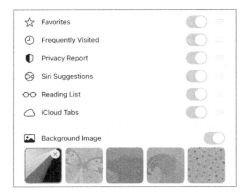

You can also select a background, just click on an image from the selections.

The Toolbar

Lets take a look at the toolbar along the top of the main screen.

Tap in the website address field, to enter the website's address, or Google search keyword.

The Sidebar

The first icon on the left hand side of the toolbar opens the sidebar. This allows you to access your tab groups, favourite or bookmarked sites, reading list, and browsing history.

240

Chapter 5: Internet, Email & Communication

Share Menu

The share menu allows you to share the current website link via text message, email or social media. Just tap on the icon to share the site on twitter or facebook, email the link or send it via text.

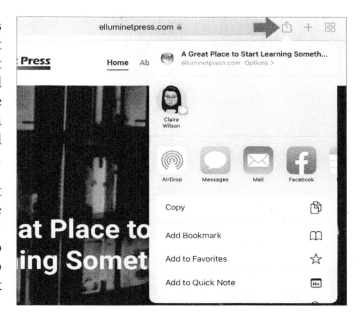

Along the bottom of that menu, you can add the current site to bookmarks/favourites. To do this tap bookmark. You can also add the site to a quick note.

Browsing Tabs

You can open sites in multiple tabs, this helps to keep track of open sites.

Tab Bar

The tab bar appears along the top of the screen when you open more than one tab. You can show these tabs in separate view or compact view.

Compact view reduces the tab bar to the address bar.

To change this, open the settings app, select 'safari' from the list on the left hand side of the screen.

On the right, scroll down to tabs. Select 'separate tab view' or 'compact tab bar' for compact view.

241

Chapter 5: Internet, Email & Communication

New Tab

Hit the + sign to add a new tab where you can open another website, Google search, favourite and so on.

Show All Tabs

The final icon on the right hand side, allows you to see all the tabs you currently have open.

Safari will display your open tabs/websites as thumbnail previews, you can tap on to open up.

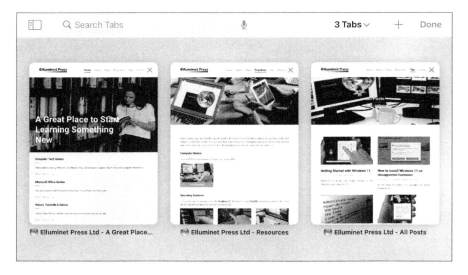

Tab Groups

Introduced in iPadOS 15 are tab groups. With tab groups, you can organize your tabs and keep them together in groups according to interest. You can also drag your tab groups into an email, note or message.

If you're doing web research, it can involve visiting several websites meaning you can have multiple sites open in tabs at the same time If you're researching multiple things, this can quickly become difficult to track.

Chapter 5: Internet, Email & Communication

This is where group tabs come in. Group tabs allow you to save groups of these tabs together. For example, if you are planning a holiday (or vacation), you could be visiting multiple sites to compare prices for flights and hotels, as well as checking weather forecasts and local activities. You can save all these sites as tabs into a tab group, so you can return to the sites later.

New Tab Group

To save your open tabs into a new tab group, click the sidebar icon.

From the sidebar panel tap the tab groups icon at the top. Select 'new empty tab group.

If you already have a load of tabs open, that you want to add to the group, select 'new tab group from...'

Give the tab group a meaningful name.

243

Chapter 5: Internet, Email & Communication

You'll see the tab name appear on the top left. Now, when you open more tabs, they will be added to this tab group.

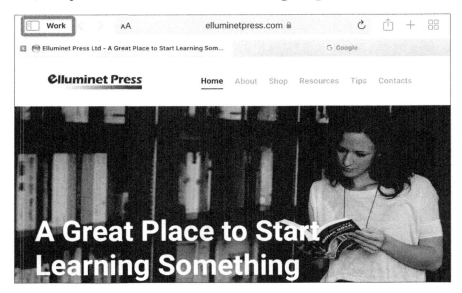

Use this group for one task. Create more tab groups for other tasks such as research, vacation/holiday, and so on. Then open the tabs to do with this task. This helps to keep your website tabs organised.

Reopen Tab Group

Open the sidebar.

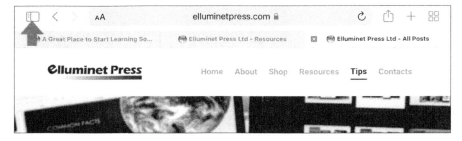

Halfway down the panel, you'll see your tab groups. Tap on the group to reopen.

Chapter 5: Internet, Email & Communication

You'll see the group name appear on the top left, with all your tabs open in the tab bar underneath.

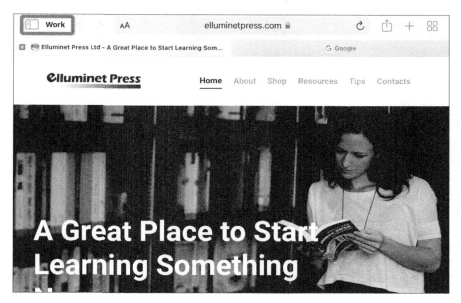

Bookmarking a Site

Bookmarking sites makes it easier to find websites that you visit most often, without having to search for them or remember the web address. To bookmark the site you're on, tap the sharing icon on the top left of the toolbar.

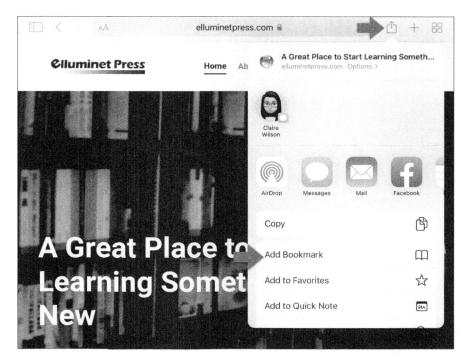

From the popup menu, tap 'add bookmark'.

245

Chapter 5: Internet, Email & Communication

Enter a meaningful name if required as indicated below, then tap 'save'.

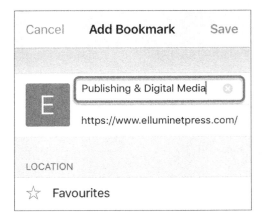

Tap 'favourites' under 'location' to select a folder to save your bookmark into. Select 'bookmarks'.

Selecting 'bookmarks' adds the website to the bookmarks section of the side bar, selecting 'favourites' adds the website to the favourites section of the start page.

Revisiting a Bookmarked Site

You'll find all your bookmarked sites on the sidebar. To access this menu, tap the icon on the toolbar along the top left of the screen.

Select the bookmarks link.

Chapter 5: Internet, Email & Communication

You'll see a list of sites you have bookmarked. Tap bookmark to revisit site.

To edit a bookmark, tap and hold your finger on the bookmark in the list.

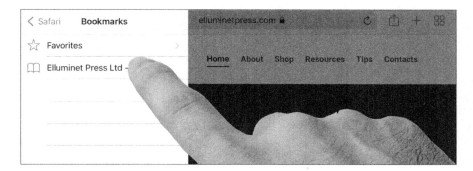

Select 'edit' from the popup menu. You can enter a new name, or change the web address.

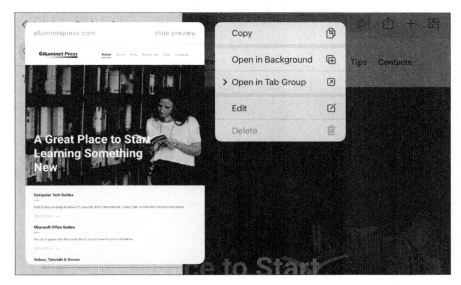

You can also open the bookmarked site in a the background or open it in a new tab group

To Delete: Swipe right to left across the bookmark, and tap delete, to remove a bookmark.

Chapter 5: Internet, Email & Communication

Browsing History

Safari keeps a list of all the websites you have visited in the browser history. To view the history, open the side, then select the 'history' link from the list..

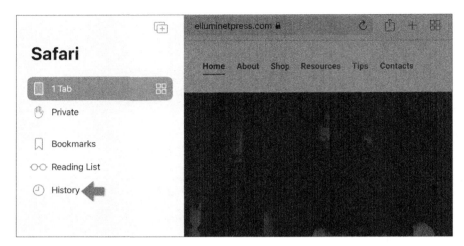

Scroll down the list, tap on a site to revisit.

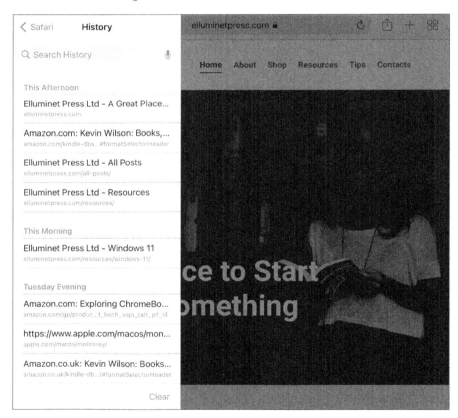

Swipe right to left over the site in the list and tap delete, to remove the site from the history.

Tap 'clear all' on the bottom right to clear the entire history.

Chapter 5: Internet, Email & Communication

Reader View

Reader view makes it easier to read web pages without all the unnecessary background clutter that usually comes with a website.

Reader view is not available on all web pages but is on most. To enable reader view, tap the 'AA' icon on the left hand side of the web address search field. From the menu, select 'show reader view'.

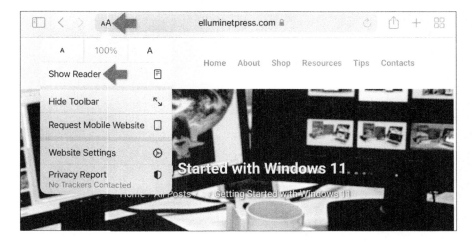

When you're in reader view, tap the AA icon again. Here you can change the font size of the text, the type face, and the background colour.

To go back to normal view, tap the 'hide reader'.

Chapter 5: Internet, Email & Communication

Page Zoom

You can quickly zoom in and out on a website's text. To zoom in, spread your thumb and forefinger apart across the glass. To zoom out, pinch your thumb and forefinger together.

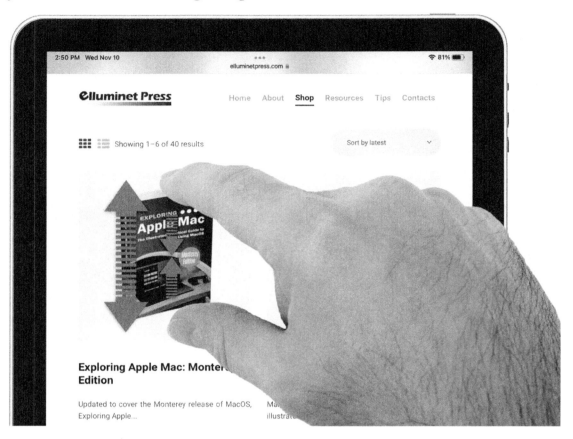

You can also control the text size and zoom using the 'AA' icon on the top left of the address field.

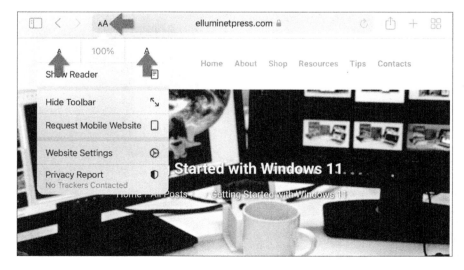

Tap the 'A' icons to decrease or increase the size.

Chapter 5: Internet, Email & Communication

Download Manager

When you download a file in Safari, a new icon will appear on the toolbar. Tap this icon to see your downloads.

You'll see the status of files you're downloading, as well as files you've downloaded. You can tap on the filename to open the file, or tap the magnifying glass icon to open your downloads folder

You'll also find your downloads folder in the files app. Here you'll find all the files you've downloaded.

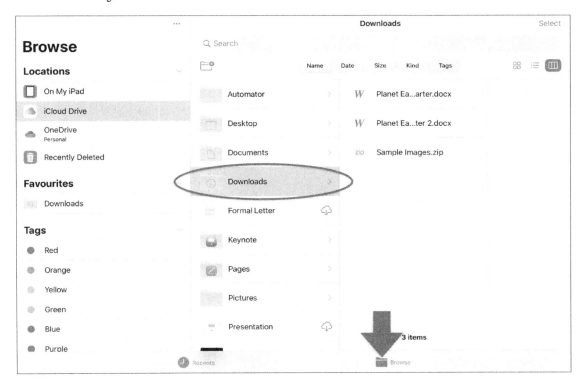

251

Chapter 5: Internet, Email & Communication

Generate Automatic Strong Passwords

Tap Safari and go to a website where you need to sign up for an account. In this example I'm creating a new Gmail email account.

Input a username or email address into the first field.

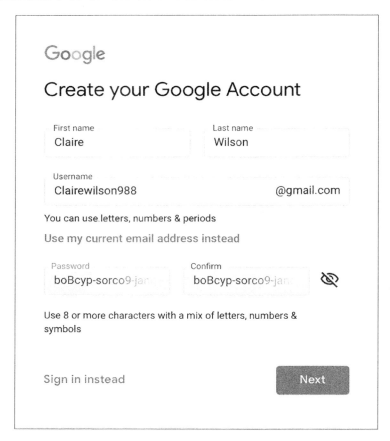

Tap on the password field. Safari will generate an automatic strong password for you.

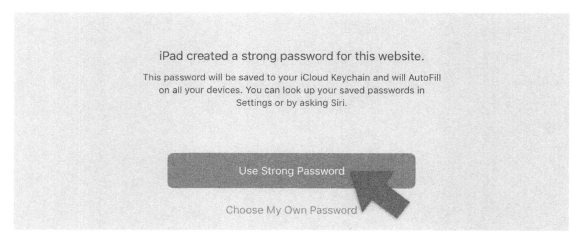

Tap 'Use Strong Password' to store it in your keychain.

Chapter 5: Internet, Email & Communication

Autofill Passwords on Websites

Tap Safari and go to a site that you already have an account with. Eg the Gmail account we created earlier. Select the text input field for the username or email address associated with the account.

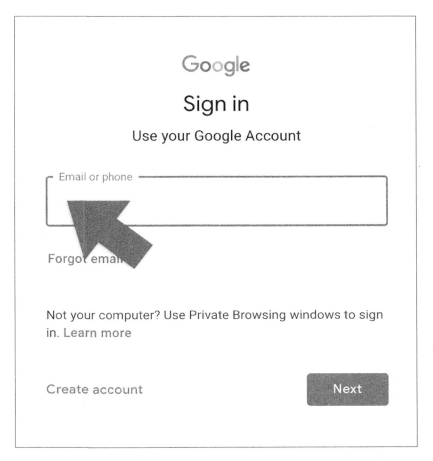

In the suggestions on the keyboard below, select "for this website". Authenticate the action with your Touch ID, Face ID, or passcode when prompted.

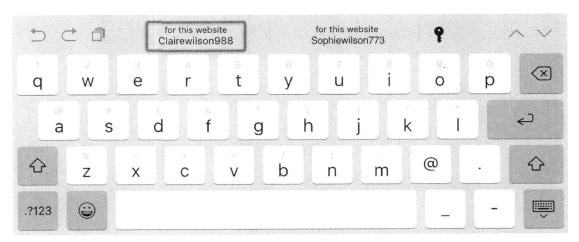

253

Chapter 5: Internet, Email & Communication

Automatically add Password to Keychain

When you sign into a website or for the first time, you will receive a prompt asking you whether you want to save your login details to keychain.

Tap Safari and navigate to the website you want to sign into. In this example, I'm signing into a facebook account.

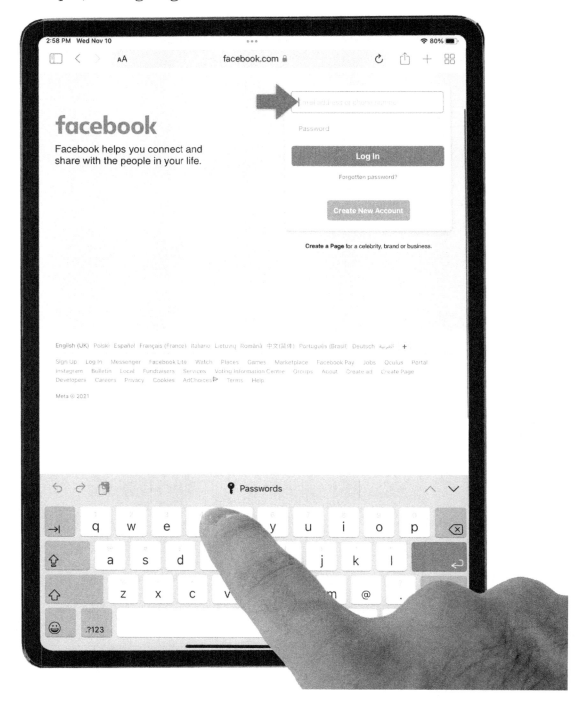

Sign in with your username and password, in the normal way.

Chapter 5: Internet, Email & Communication

Once you sign in successfully, Safari will prompt you to save the password to your keychain. Tap 'save password'.

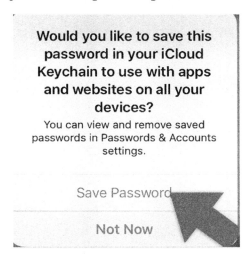

This will save your password so you don't have to type it in each time. To sign in the next time, just click in the username or password field.

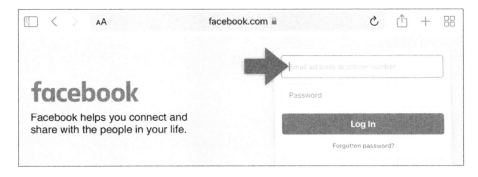

Select the password from the suggestions along the top of your keyboard

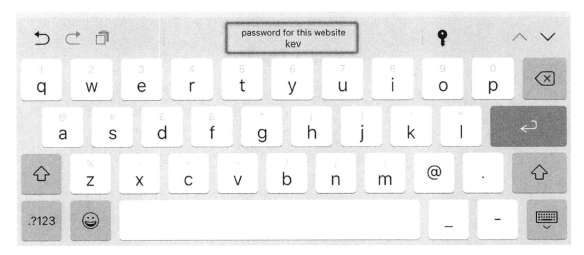

Tap the password suggestion from the options on the top of your keyboard. If your password isn't there, tap the key icon then select the password from the list.

255

Chapter 5: Internet, Email & Communication

Forms Autofill

You can get safari to automatically fill in a form for you using your contact information.

Add Contact Info

To set it up make sure you have filled in your contact information correctly in the contacts app. Open the contacts app.

Select the contact card with your name on it (it will have 'me' written next to it). Enter your contact details.

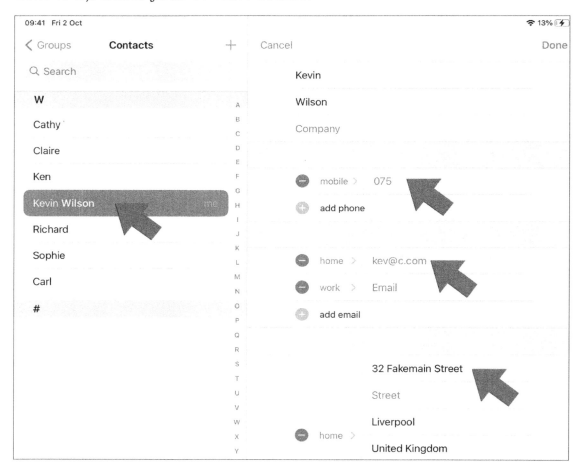

Add all the details you want to show up in the forms you fill in online. Name, phone number, email address, street address, and so on.

Click 'done' on the top right when you're finished.

256

Chapter 5: Internet, Email & Communication

Now, open the settings app, select 'safari' from the list on the left hand side. Then select 'autofill'.

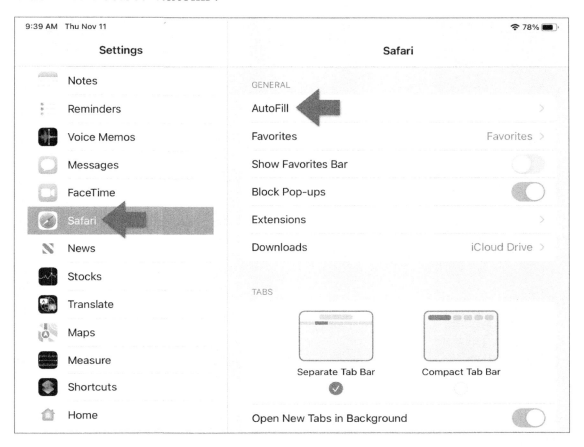

Under 'my info' select your contact card.

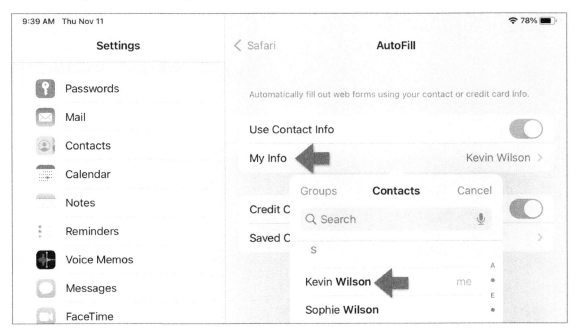

Close the settings app.

257

Chapter 5: Internet, Email & Communication

Adding Credit Cards

Open the settings app, select 'safari' from the list on the left hand side. Select 'autofill'.

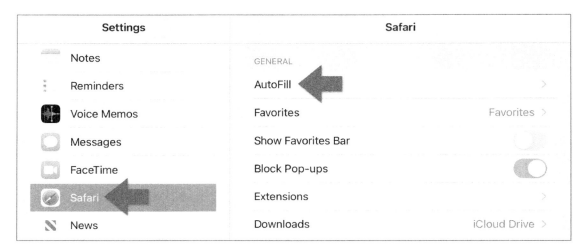

Select 'saved credit cards'.

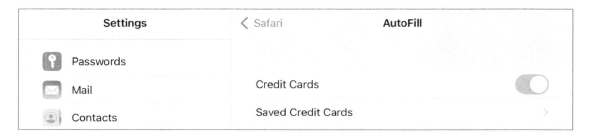

Enter your credit card info, or tap 'use camera' to scan the card.

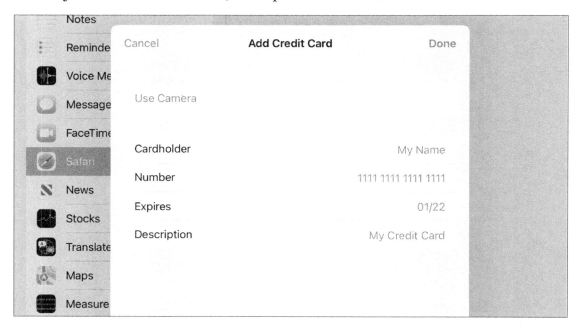

Tap 'done' when you're finished.

Chapter 5: Internet, Email & Communication

Using Autofill to Fill in a Form in Safari

In safari, tap in a field on the form. For example, here I'm filling in my contact details on an online store.

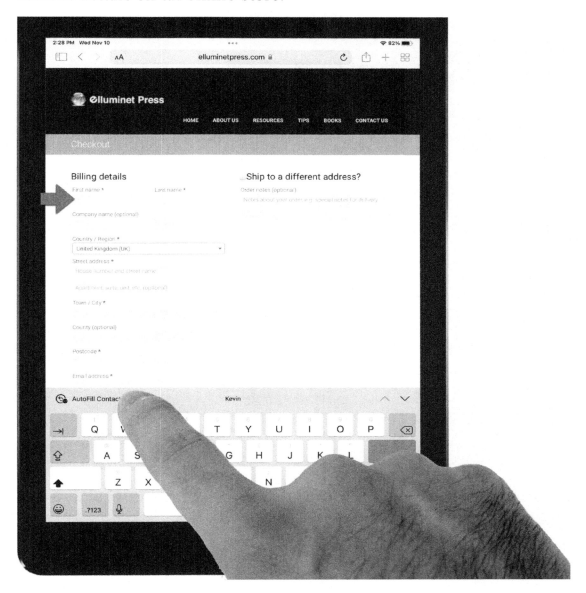

Select the contact info from the popup, or tap 'customise' to select the information to autofill.

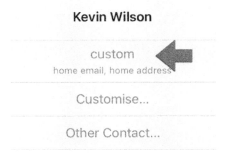

259

Chapter 5: Internet, Email & Communication

Using Autofill to Fill in Payment Details in Safari

In safari, tap in a field on the form. For example, here I'm filling in my contact details on an online store.

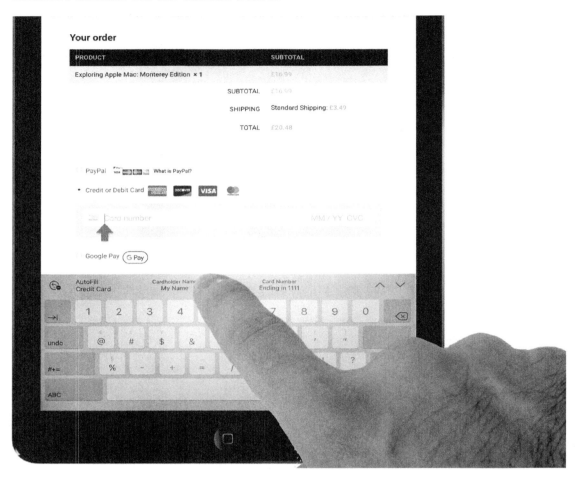

You your Face ID or Touch ID to authorise the payment. You'll see the card details appear in the fields.

Enter the CVC code on your card.

Chapter 5: Internet, Email & Communication

Password Monitoring

Safari monitors passwords you've saved to your keychain, keeping an eye out for passwords that may have been involved in a data breach or passwords that have been repeated or are considered easy to guess. If Safari discovers a breach, it will alert you and help you generate a new secure password.

You can see any password alerts in the settings app. Open the settings app and select 'passwords'. You'll a 'security recommendations' section where you can see passwords that have been compromised or are weak.

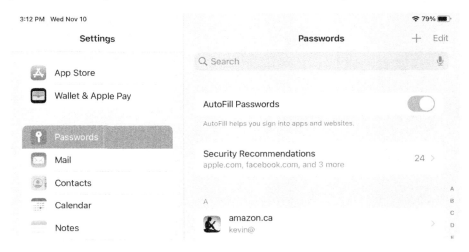

Underneath, you'll see a list of sites Safari has saved a password for. Tap on one of these to view details.

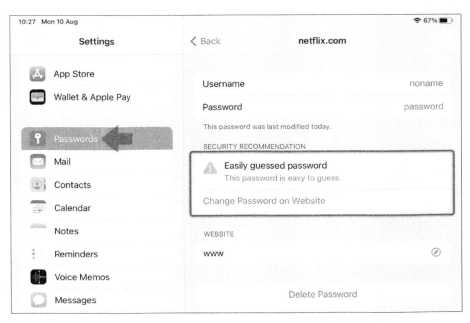

Tap 'change password on website'. To delete the site from your passwords list, tap 'delete password'.

261

Chapter 5: Internet, Email & Communication

This will take you to the website and allow you to log in. Then you'll need to go to the 'change password' section in your account with that website and follow the 'change password' steps.

Website Privacy Report

Safari uses it's Intelligent Tracking Prevention to identify and block trackers advertisers use to track your web activity.

On the toolbar tap the 'AA' icon. Select 'privacy report'.

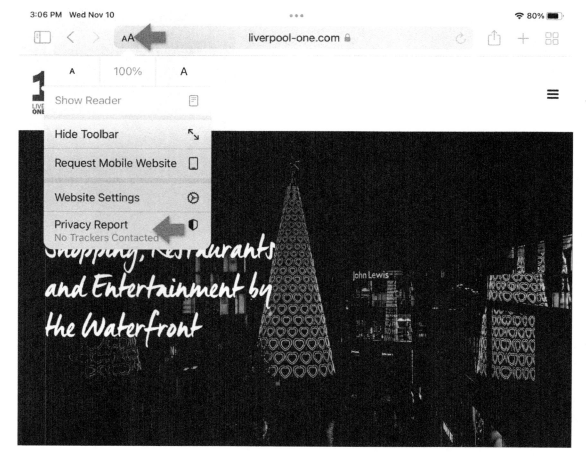

Chapter 5: Internet, Email & Communication

You'll see some stats. Tap the 'websites' tab to see all the websites where trackers have been blocked. Select the 'trackers' tab to see a list of all the trackers that have been blocked and who they belong to.

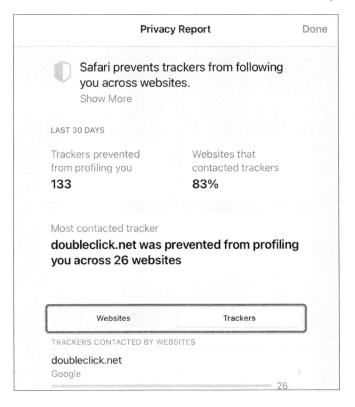

Tap on the site in the list to view details

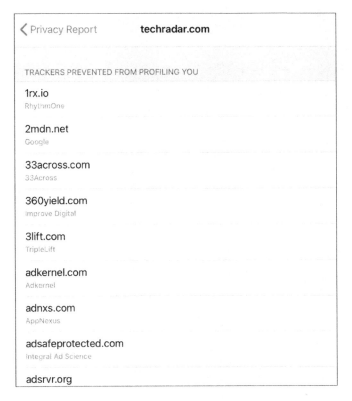

Chapter 5: Internet, Email & Communication

Using Email

To start the mail app, tap 'mail' on the dock at the bottom of the screen.

Once your email is setup it will open on the main screen. The email app works best if you use your iPad in horizontal orientation. On the left hand side, is a list of all your emails. Just tap on one to view.

Reply to or Forward a Message

To reply to an email, select the email you want from your inbox, then tap the 'reply to sender' icon on the bottom right.

From the popup, tap 'reply' to reply to the sender, tap 'reply all' to reply to sender plus any other recipients who were copied in, tap 'forward' to send the message to someone else. Tap 'delete' to delete the email.

Chapter 5: Internet, Email & Communication

Email Threads

An email conversation that spreads across dozens of messages in your inbox is called a thread. Apple Mail organises your email messages by thread. Here in the demo below is an email conversation between Claire and me.

You can see in my inbox below, my email conversation with Claire. To make things easier to understand, I've marked the messages I've sent in blue, and the message I've received from Claire in green. Notice the latest email is at the bottom of the thread.

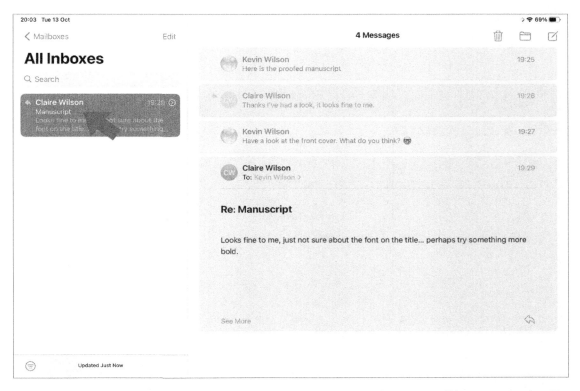

When you select the email conversation in the inbox, you'll automatically see the latest message appear, just scroll up to see the history. To reply to the message, tap the reply icon on the bottom right of the thread.

Select 'reply' from the popup menu.

265

Chapter 5: Internet, Email & Communication

You can turn this feature off, if you'd rather list all your emails in your inbox as they arrive. To do this, open your settings app. Select 'mail' from the list on the left hand side.

Under the 'threading' section, de-select 'organise by thread'.

Add a Signature

Open your settings app. Select 'mail' from the list on the left hand side. Scroll down to the bottom, tap 'signature'

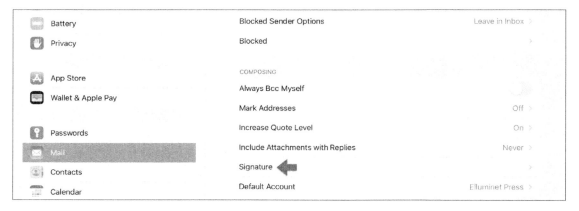

Select 'all accounts' to add signature to all your email accounts. Select 'per account' to add a different signature to each account you have. Enter the signature you want.

Chapter 5: Internet, Email & Communication

New Message

To send a new message, click the 'compose new email' icon on the top right. This will bring up a new email. Tap in the 'To:' field to enter an email address. If you are replying to a message, the email address of the person that sent you the message will appear here automatically.

Tap in the subject field and add some text.

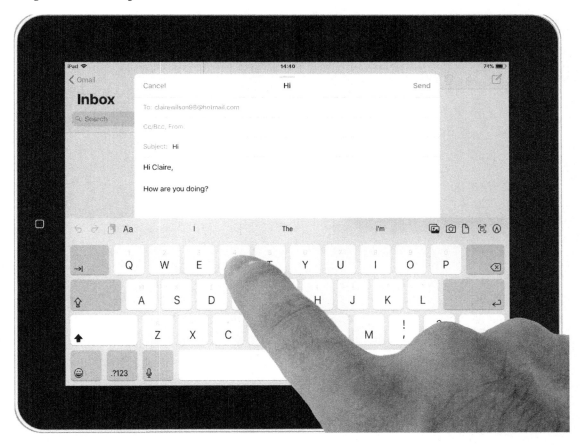

Tap in the message body underneath and type your message using the pop up on screen keyboard.

If you look on the top of the on screen keyboard you'll see some icons.

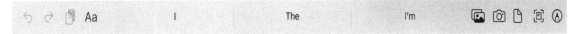

On the left, you can undo/redo text - undo is a good one if you make a mistake with your typing. You can also paste some text or an image you have copied from somewhere else. Next is the format icon, you can change your text to bold, italic or underlined. In the centre you have some text predictions - this shows up words you're most likely to type while writing your email - tap word to insert into message. You can insert a photo directly from your photos app, camera, and add an attachment, scan or markup.

Chapter 5: Internet, Email & Communication

Formatting Messages

A new menu adds comprehensive text formatting tools to help you compose better looking emails.

To use the formatting tools, tap the 'AA' icon on the top left of the on-screen keyboard to open the menu.

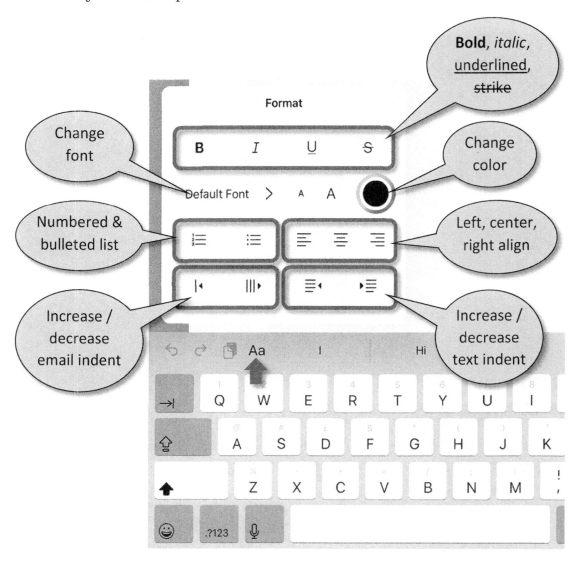

Select the formatting tool you want, then type your text.

Formatting includes new font style, size and colour selections, strikethrough, alignment, numbered and bulleted lists, and indenting options.

If you want to indent text, use the 'increase/decrease text indent' icons. Increase/decrease email indent is for indenting parts of an email from someone you're replying to.

Chapter 5: Internet, Email & Communication

Attachments

To add an attachment such as a document, tap the document icon on the top right of the on-screen keyboard.

From the popup dialog box, select the document you want to attach to your email.

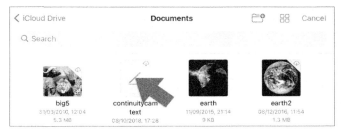

To take a photo, click the camera icon on the top right of the on-screen keyboard. Take your photo using the camera app.

To add a photo from your photos app, select the photos icon. Choose a photo from the popup.

To scan a document tap the scan icon. Use your cam to take a pic of the doc.

To insert a drawing, tap the markup icon.

Chapter 5: Internet, Email & Communication

Flagging Messages

You can choose from a variety of colours when you flag an email message. Coloured flags are synced with iCloud to the Mail app on all your Apple devices.

To flag a message, open it up and tap the reply icon on the bottom right, then tap 'flag'. You'll see a small panel open up with different colours. Select one.

Create a Mailbox Folder

To create a mailbox, swipe inwards from the left hand edge to open the side panel.

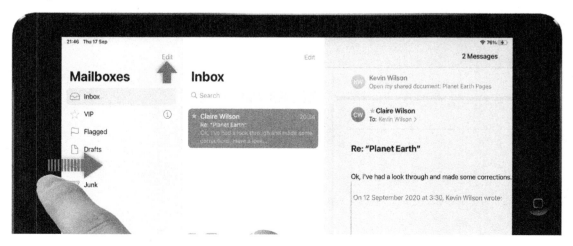

Tap 'edit' on the top right of the panel.

Chapter 5: Internet, Email & Communication

Tap 'new mailbox' on the bottom right of the panel. Type in a meaningful name...

Select 'iCloud' or your email account in 'mailbox location'. Click 'save'.

Move Message

To move a message to another folder. Open the message, tap the 'reply' icon on the bottom right, then tap 'move message'.

Select the mailbox to move the message to eg 'Work'

Block Sender

You can have email from a specified sender blocked and put directly to the trash. Blocking a sender works across all your Apple devices. First, open the message, tap the sender's email address at the top. Select 'Block This Contact' from the drop down.

271

Chapter 5: Internet, Email & Communication

Contacts

The Contacts App is your address book. It contains all the names, email addresses, phone numbers and addresses of the people you correspond with.

To launch your contacts app, tap the icon on the home screen.

This is the main screen. You can browse contacts, or add new ones.

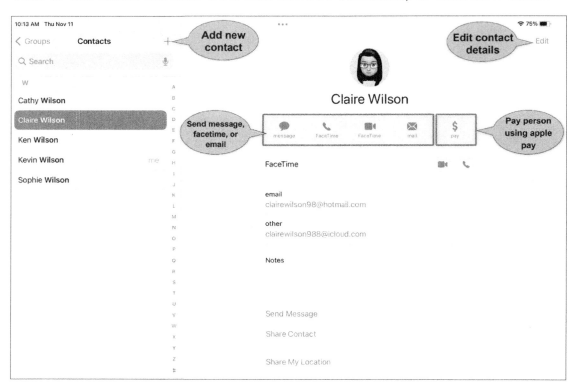

Tap on a contact in the list down the left hand side to view a contact's details.

Tap the + sign on the top right of the left hand panel to add a new contact.

If you're viewing the contacts app in portrait mode, swipe inwards from the left hand side of the screen to reveal the side panel.

Tap 'edit' on the top right to edit the contact's details.

Chapter 5: Internet, Email & Communication

View Contact Details

To view a contact's details, tap on the name in the contacts list on the left hand side.

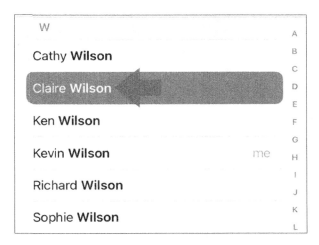

From here you can edit their details, send a message, email, FaceTime them if they have an iPhone, or give them a call.

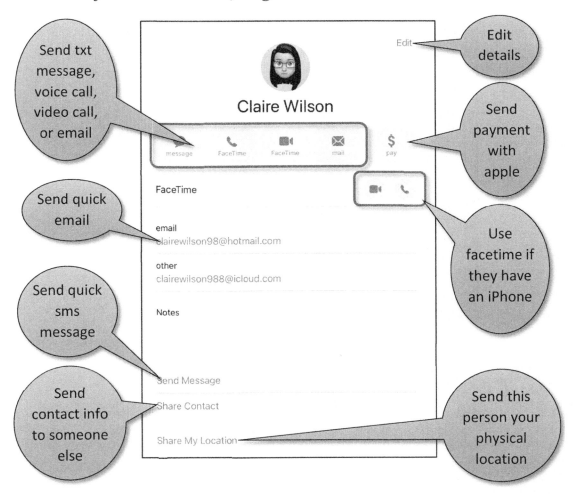

273

Chapter 5: Internet, Email & Communication

New Contact

Tap on the + sign on the top right of the main page to add a new contact.

On the screen that appears, enter the person's name and contact details in the fields.

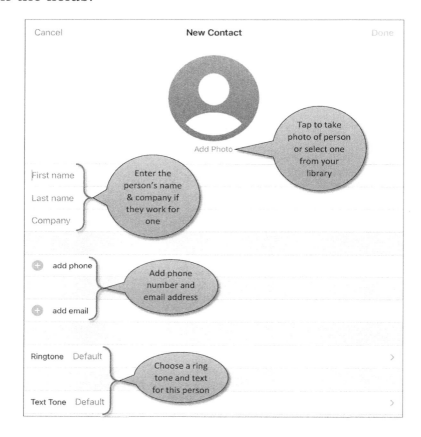

Add a profile photo. This photo appears on your phone screen when the person calls. To take a photo tap 'take photo', you can either take one with your camera or select one from your photo library.

Add their phone number, and email addresses in the relevant fields.

Choose a specific ring and text tone for this person. This is the sound you'll hear when this person sends you a message or calls you.

Tap 'done' on the top right when you're finished.

Chapter 5: Internet, Email & Communication

New Contact from a Message

You can also add a contact from an email message. Open the email message in the Mail App. Tap the top line of the email to reveal the links.

Tap the link on person's name at the top of the email. From the drop down, tap 'create new contact'.

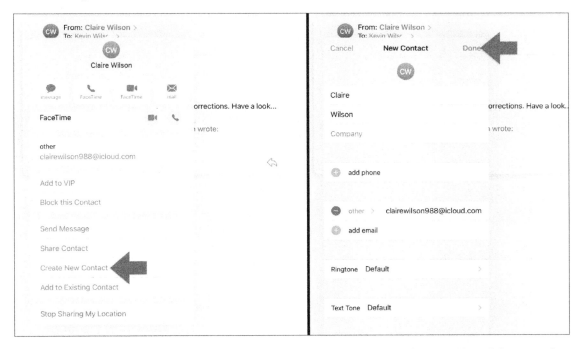

Your iPad will automatically add the names and email address the message was sent from.

Add any other details if necessary. Tap 'done' when you're finished.

You can do the same with text messages in Message. Tap on the message, then tap 'details', tap the 'i' icon (top right), tap 'create new contact'. Enter their name and details in the screen that appears.

275

Chapter 5: Internet, Email & Communication

Delete a Contact

To delete a contact, open your contacts app and select the person's name in the list on the left hand side.

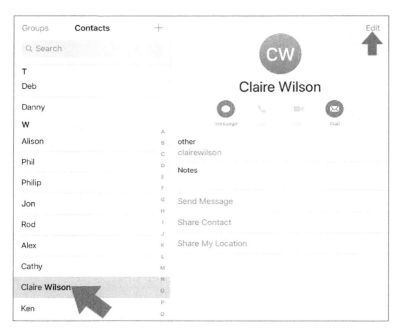

Scroll down to the bottom of the page, then click 'delete contact'

Chapter 5: Internet, Email & Communication

Calendar App

To start calendar app, tap the icon on the home screen

This will bring up the calendar main screen. I found it easiest to view the calendar in month or week view. Below is in month view.

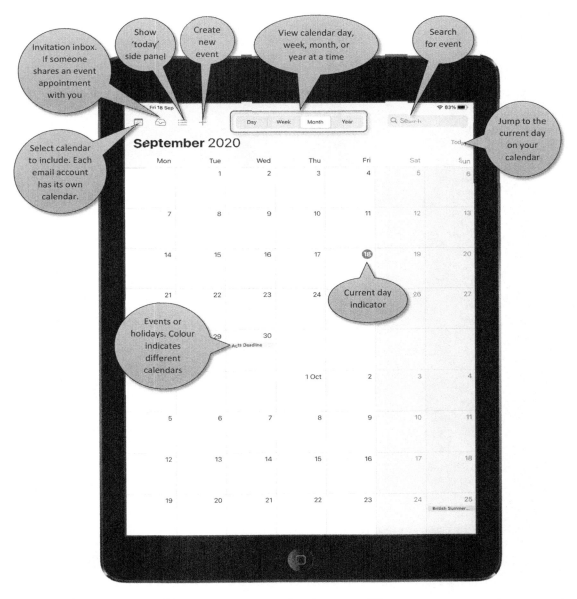

Along the top you'll see your main icons. Here you can view your calendars, invitations, show 'today' side panel, create a new event, display calendar as day/year/moth view and search for event or appointment.

277

Chapter 5: Internet, Email & Communication

Adding an Appointment

To add an event to the calendar, go to month view, then tap and hold your finger on the day the event or appointment falls on.

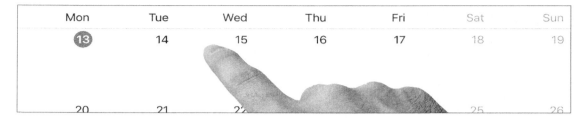

In the popup that appears. Tap 'title', then type a name for the appointment or event.

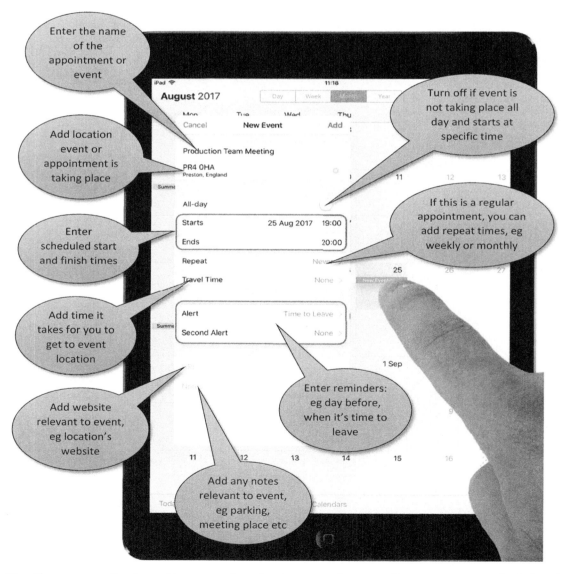

Do the same for location, and select your times. Once you are finished tap done.

278

Chapter 5: Internet, Email & Communication

Add a Recurring Appointment

To add a recurring event to the calendar, tap and hold your finger on the first day the event falls on.

In the popup that appears. Tap 'title', then type a title (what the event or appointment is).

Do the same for location, and select your times.

Now to create a recurring event, tap 'repeat' in the 'new event' window. Here you can set the event to recur once a week, once a month, every two weeks and so on. All you have to do is tap on the one you want.

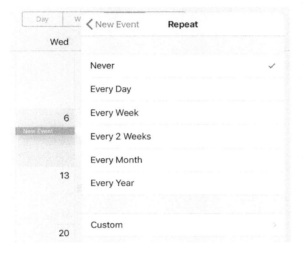

You can also set a custom option, tap 'custom'. Say the event occurs every three weeks. Set the frequency to 'weekly'. Then tap 'every' and select the number of weeks. In this example, three weeks, so slide the number to '3'.

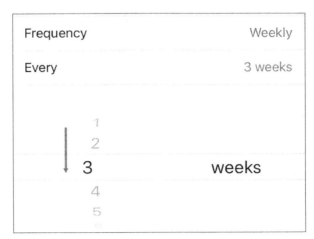

Once you are finished, tap 'repeat' on the top left of the repeat window to go back. Tap 'add' to add the event to your calendar.

Chapter 5: Internet, Email & Communication

Adding an Appointment from a Message

Apple Mail, Message and FaceTime will scan your message for phrases that look like dates and times and will create a link in the email for you. To add the event from the email or text message, tap on this link. From the popup box tap 'create event'.

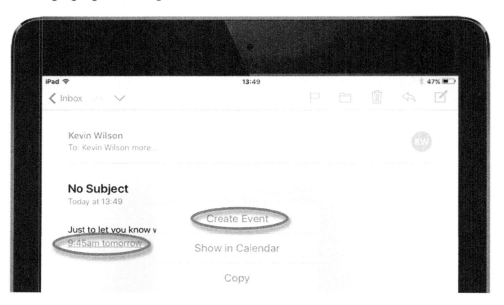

Enter a title and location if calendar didn't pick one up from the email. You can also tweak the information and add additional information if required.

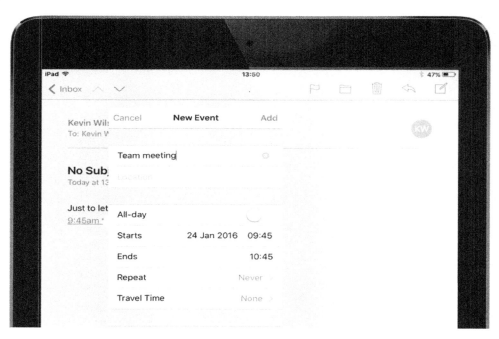

Once you have done that, tap 'add' to enter the appointment into your calendar.

280

Chapter 5: Internet, Email & Communication

FaceTime

To use FaceTime, tap the icon on the home screen. You will need your Apple ID and a wifi/data connection to the internet.

When you open FaceTime, you will be prompted to sign in if you haven't already done so.

Once FaceTime has opened, you'll see in the main window a preview of your camera. On the left hand side you'll see a darkened panel where you'll find your contacts, history of calls and a search for you to search for people

Chapter 5: Internet, Email & Communication

Making a New Call

In this demonstration, Claire is going to FaceTime Sophie from her iPad. To make a new call, tap the green 'New FaceTime' icon on the top left of the screen.

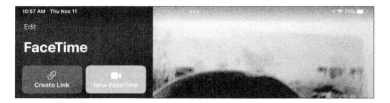

Start typing the person's name you want to FaceTime into the 'to' field on the top left of the screen. If the name is in your contacts, then it will appear underneath. Tap the person's Apple ID email address, phone number or name. Or select one of the suggestions.

Wait for the other person to answer...

Chapter 5: Internet, Email & Communication

Claire's iPad is on the left in the demo below. She is placing a FaceTime call to Sophie who's using the iPad on the right.

In the background of your screen (iPad on the left in the demo), you'll see a preview of your camera - so make sure you're squarely in the frame so when the call is answered, the other person can see you clearly.

You can see on Sophie's iPad on the right, it's telling her who is calling with the caller id at the top of the screen.

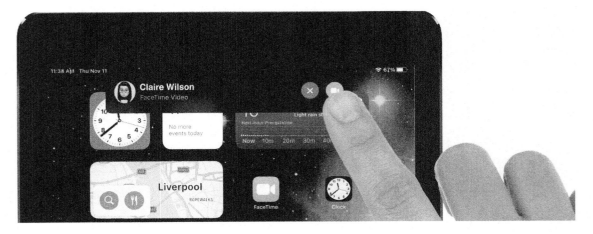

To answer the call just tap the green button. The red button declines the call.

283

Chapter 5: Internet, Email & Communication

The call will go full screen. Tap the green button to answer. Tap the red button to decline.

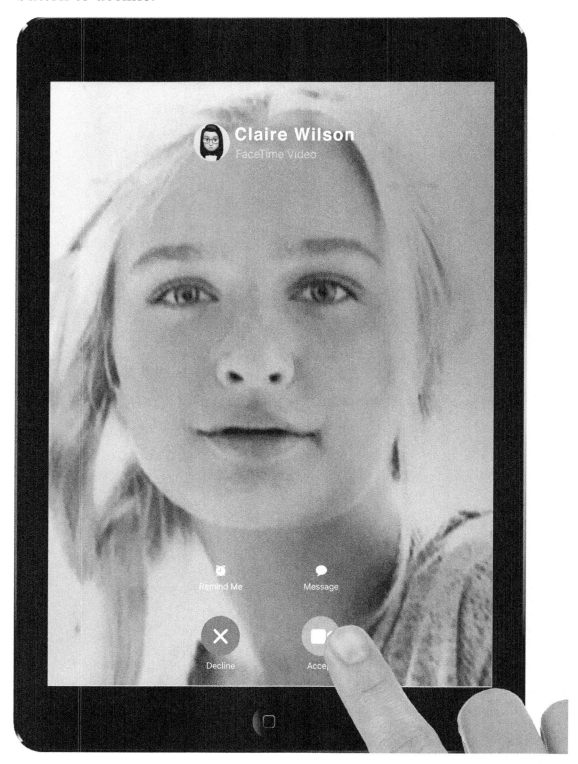

You'll also see two other icons above these two. Tap 'remind me' to set a reminder to call back. If you can't talk, tap 'message' to send a quick message such as 'on my way', 'can I call you later', or 'cant talk now'.

Chapter 5: Internet, Email & Communication

Once the other person answers, you can now have a video conversation. The onboard microphone on your iPhone/iPad will pick up your voice, so just talk naturally.

You'll see an image of the person calling in the centre of your screen with a thumbnail view of your own camera on the bottom right. Here's the view of Claire's call from her iPad.

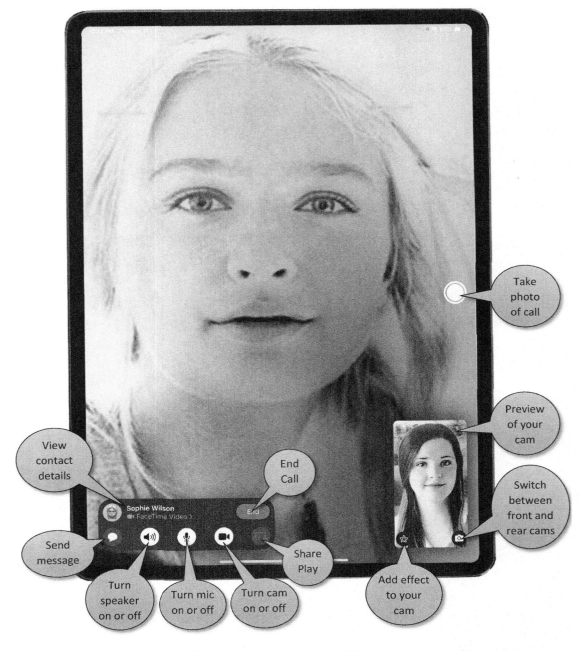

Along the bottom, you'll see some icons. If these icons disappear, tap the screen once and they'll re-appear.

It's a great tool to keep in touch with family, see the kids if you're away, and so they can see you too.

285

Chapter 5: Internet, Email & Communication

Adding Effects

During a call, you can add all sorts of effects to your image. To do this, tap the effects icon on the bottom left of your camera preview in the bottom right corner.

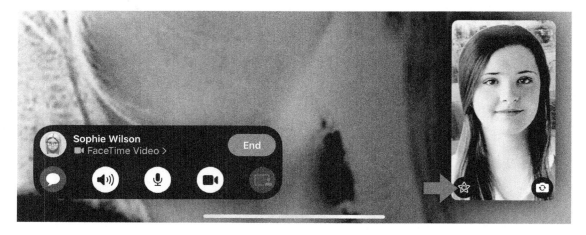

Add a Memoji, to do this tap the effects icon on your camera preview.

You can select from multiple memojis. If you have an iPad Pro with a true depth camera, you can map the memoji to your facial expressions.

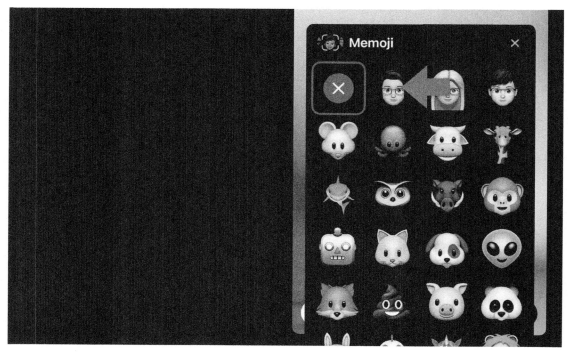

Chapter 5: Internet, Email & Communication

Smile, the memoji copies your facial expressions.

Lets add a text effect. Tap the effects icon on your camera preview.

Tap the text icon, select an effect,

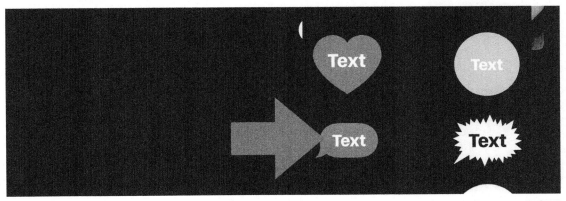

287

Chapter 5: Internet, Email & Communication

Then type in some text, tap anywhere on the screen to accept, then drag the effect into place.

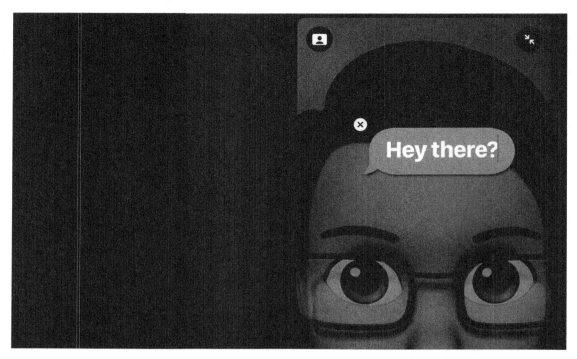

Lets have a look at what the effect will look like. This is what the other person you're talking to will see.

Try some of the other effects and filters on the panel. Try adding a shape or an icon and see what happens.

Chapter 5: Internet, Email & Communication

Group FaceTime

Group FaceTime allows you to set up groups and chat to up to 32 people at a time. To use Group FaceTime, all participants must have iOS 12 or later, otherwise you won't be able to add them to the group.

To place a group call, tap the green 'New FaceTime' icon on the top left of the screen.

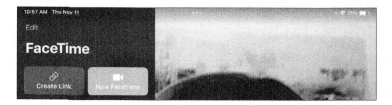

Type the names of the people you want to place a group call to in the 'to' field, or tap the + icon and add them from your contacts list.

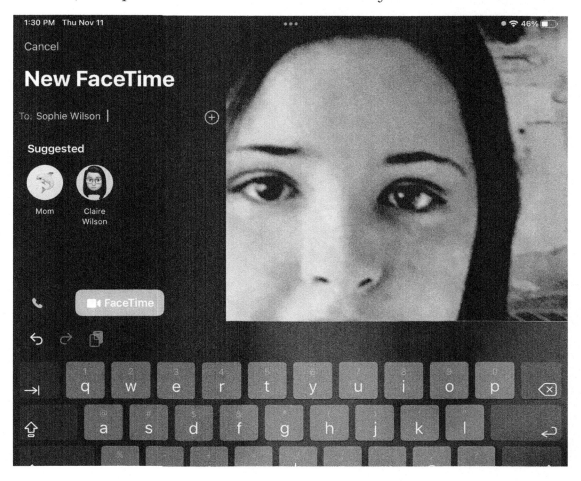

If they all have iOS 12 or later installed on their devices, you'll see two green buttons appear along the bottom of the side panel.

Tap on 'facetime' to place a group video call.

289

Chapter 5: Internet, Email & Communication

When your contacts answer, you'll see a thumbnail of each of them on your main display. Tap 'grid' on the top right if you want to change to grid view.

You'll see a thumbnail of your own camera in the bottom right of the screen. The other contacts in your group will show up in a thumbnail window in the main area of the screen.

With spacial audio, you'll hear each contact from a different position making it sound like the people are in the same room as you.

FaceTime is useful for keeping in touch with family and friends who don't live near by, or live in another country.

Chapter 5: Internet, Email & Communication

Share Screen

If you want to share your screen, within a FaceTime call, tap the share icon on the bottom right

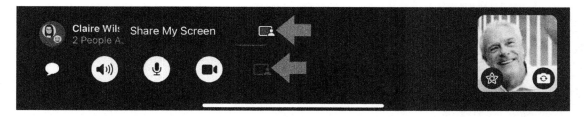

Now you can open another app and show your screen.

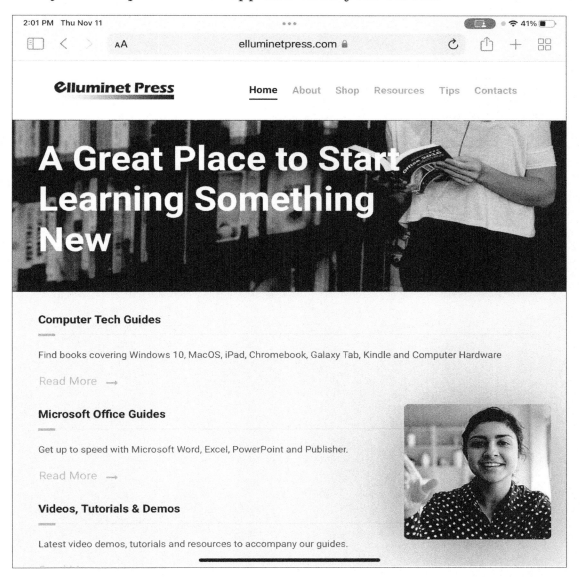

Tap back on the thumbnail on the bottom right to return to FaceTime

Tap the icon share again to stop sharing

Chapter 5: Internet, Email & Communication

SharePlay

Within a FaceTime call, swipe up from the bottom edge of the FaceTime call, then open an app that supports SharePlay such as the TV app. Tap the app library if it isn't on the dock.

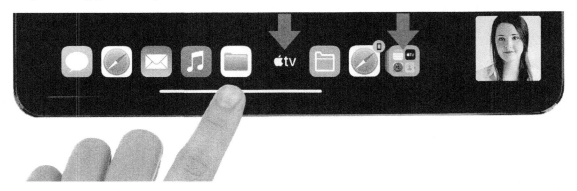

Choose a movie or TV show, and press play.

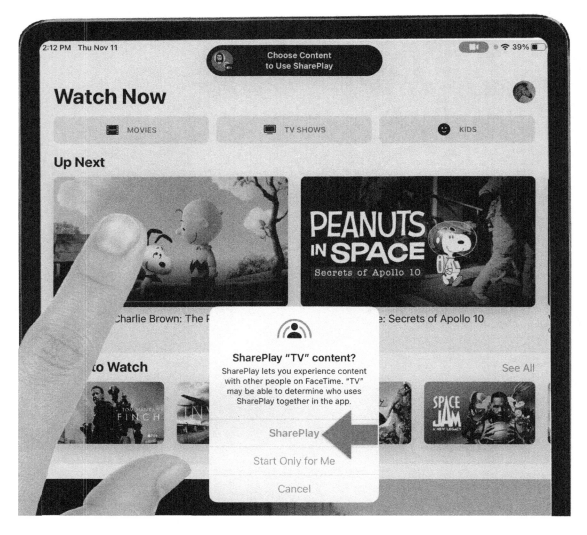

Tap SharePlay.

Chapter 5: Internet, Email & Communication

Now you can watch together... You'll still be table to hear everyone.

Tap on the FaceTime preview on the bottom right to switch back to the chat. Here, the girls are enjoying Charlie Brown & Snoopy together.

293

Chapter 5: Internet, Email & Communication

Messages

You can send photos and videos and also voice messages to anyone with an Apple device. To start Message, tap the icon on the dock on your home screen.

When you open Message, you will see a list of all your received messages. Tap on a message to read and reply. Tap the new message icon on the top of the messages list on the left hand pane.

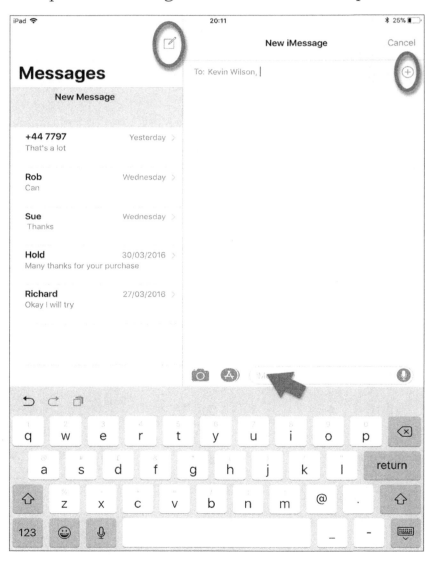

Tap the + sign to add an address or phone number from your contacts.

Type your message in the box indicated with the red arrow.

Chapter 5: Internet, Email & Communication

You can send a voice message by tapping and holding your finger on the mic icon. Record your message, then release your finger to stop.

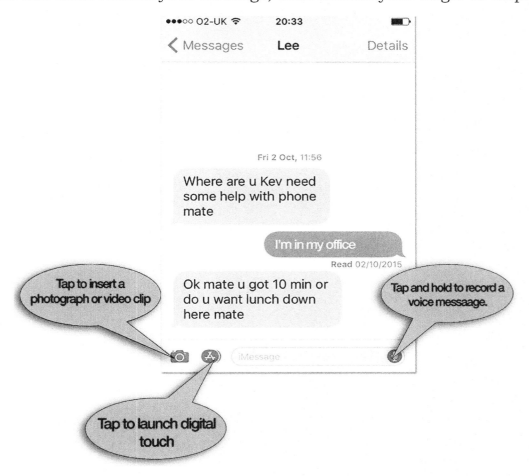

From the options that appear, select from the icons below.

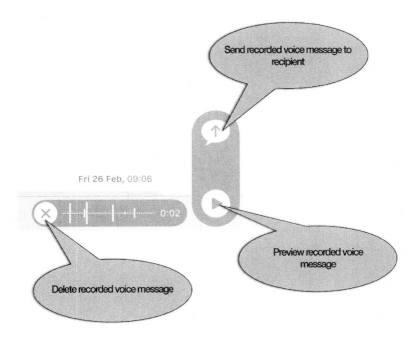

295

Chapter 5: Internet, Email & Communication

Sending Photos from Photos App

To send a photograph or video you've taken previously, tap the small app icon on the bottom left of your message window.

Tap the 'photos' icon.

Select the photo you want to send from your photos. Tap 'all photos' to see more.

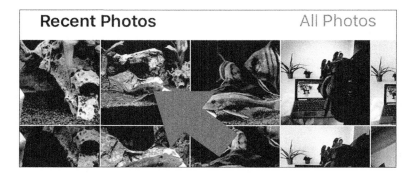

Type in a message where it says 'add comment or send'.

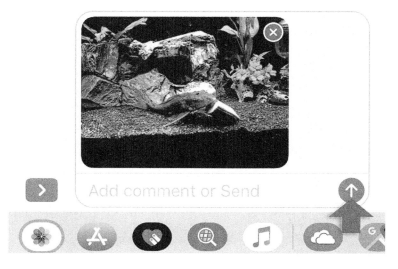

Tap the blue icon on the right hand side to send the image.

Chapter 5: Internet, Email & Communication

Sending Photos from Camera

To send a photograph or video, tap the small camera icon on the bottom left of your message window.

Your camera app will open up. Select 'photo' from the list on the bottom right, then tap on the white circle to take the picture.

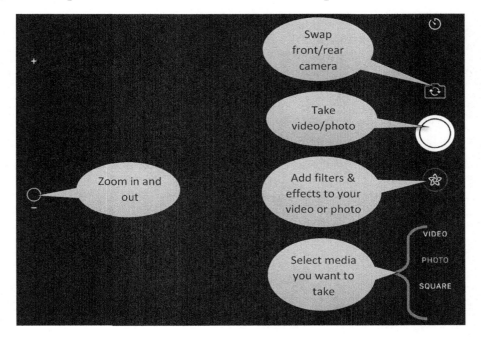

Once you've taken your photo, you can add effects and annotate the image before you send it. Just tap the markup icon on the right hand side of the screen. Tap 'save' on the top right, then tap the blue arrow to send.

Chapter 5: Internet, Email & Communication

Adding Effects

You can also add effects to a photo or video. To do this, select 'photo' from the list on the bottom right, then tap on the white/red circle to take the picture.

Once you've taken your picture, select the effects icon from the panel on the right hand side. Then select an effect from the panel that appears along the bottom.

 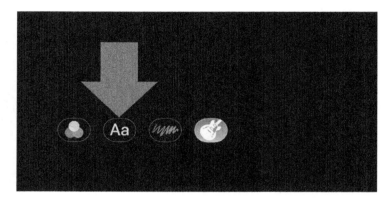

Add some text and effects to your image. Tap and drag the effect into place.

Try a few of the other effects.

Chapter 5: Internet, Email & Communication

Tap the blue arrow on the right hand side to send immediately, or tap 'done' on the top right of the screen to return to the message window.

If you returned to the message window, enter a message in the text field, tap the blue arrow to the right of the text field to send.

Chapter 5: Internet, Email & Communication

Digital Touch in Message

In digital touch mode, you can draw with your finger and send animations.

Tap the store icon to the left side of the text field to reveal additional options. Then tap the digital touch icon.

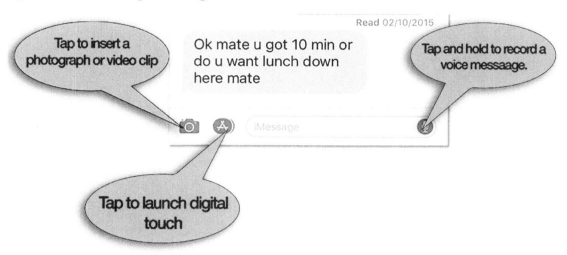

This opens up the digital touch interface. Make sure you select the digital touch icon on the bottom left. Tap the red circle on the left hand side.

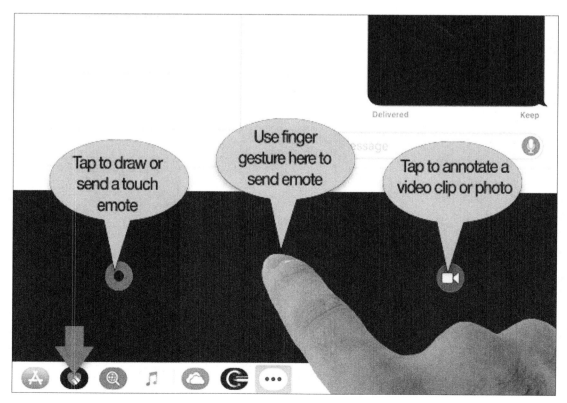

300

Chapter 5: Internet, Email & Communication

This will allow you to use certain finger gestures to send different emotes. For example, you can use one finger to draw or write something, press with one finger to send a fireball effect, tap with two fingers to send a kiss and so on. Here's a list of a few of the good ones…

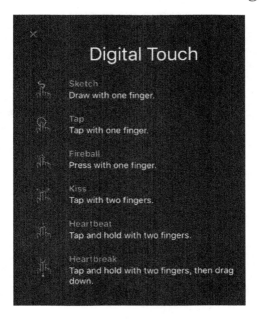

You can also draw using your finger, tap on a colour along the left hand side, then draw a diagram on the black screen in the centre. Press on a colour to open up the colour wheel if the colour you want isn't listed.

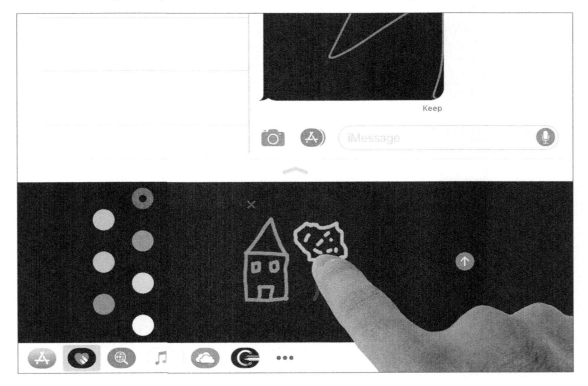

Tap on the blue arrow to the right to send.

Chapter 5: Internet, Email & Communication

You can also annotate a video or photograph using digital touch. To do this, from digital touch interface, tap the camera icon.

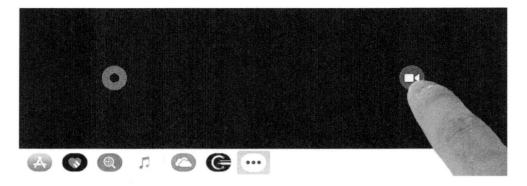

Tap the red button to start recording. While the video is recording, use the digital touch tools to draw on it. Tap a colour, then draw or write on the image with your finger.

The white button at the bottom left takes a photo, while the red button in the centre records a video.

302

Chapter 5: Internet, Email & Communication

Try a few 'tap and holds' with two fingers to add a few hearts. Or tap with two fingers to send a kiss.

Tap the record button again to stop recording. Tap the blue arrow at the bottom right to send your finished piece.

Chapter 5: Internet, Email & Communication

You can also share gifs which are short animations. Select the digital touch icon circled below. Then along the bottom of the screen, select the 'search gif' icon. Tap on a gif to add it to your message or type in to the 'find images' field to search for something specific.

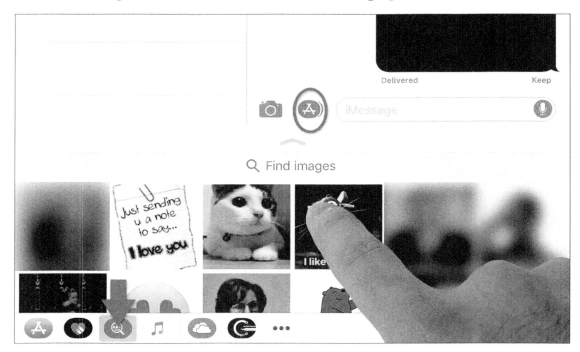

You can also share what music you are listening to on iTunes. Select the digital touch icon circled below. Then along the bottom of the screen, select the 'iTunes' icon.

You'll see all the music you have been listening to or currently listening to on your iPad. Tap on a track to share.

Chapter 5: Internet, Email & Communication

Sending Payments with Message

You can send payments to contacts on Message using Apple Pay. This only works between Apple devices at the moment, so you can't send payments to users of other phones or tablets.

Tap the store icon to the left side of the text field to reveal additional options. Then tap the Apple Pay icon.

If you have Apple Pay set up on your iPad, you'll see this icon at the bottom.

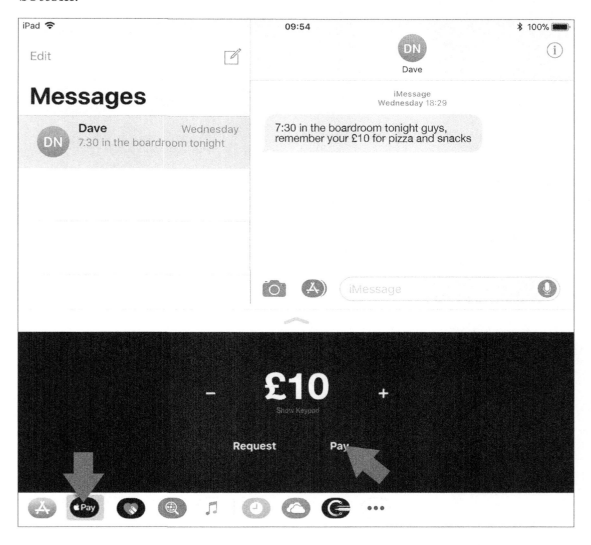

Enter the amount. Either use the + and - buttons to increase/decrease the amount, or tap 'show keypad' to tap in the amount. Once you're done hit 'pay'.

If people are owing you money, you can enter the amount as above and tap 'request' to send them an invite to pay you the amount.

Chapter 5: Internet, Email & Communication

Emojis

Also known as emoticons, emojis are little ideograms used to express emotion in a text based world. These ideograms could be facial expressions such as smilies, common objects, places, and animals. You can use them in Message, text messaging, and email.

Using Emojis

You'll find the emoji panel on your on screen keyboard. To open the panel, tap the small 'smiley' icon on the bottom left.

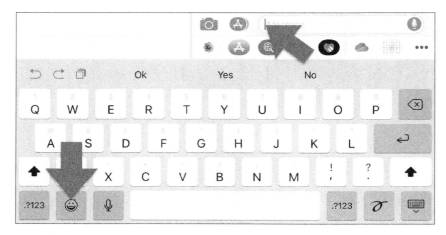

Swipe left to scroll through the list of emojis. You can also tap the grey icons along the bottom to jump to different categories, eg food, places, sports, and so on.

Tap on the emoji you want to insert.

Tap 'abc' on the left hand side to close the emoji panel.

Chapter 5: Internet, Email & Communication

AirDrop

AirDrop allows you to transfer files from one device to another using bluetooth wireless technology.

To use AirDrop you will need a compatible device, such as the iPhone 5 or later, fourth-generation iPad, iPad mini, and fifth-generation iPod touch, and have both Bluetooth and Wi-Fi enabled.

Swipe your finger downwards from the top right edge of your screen to open control center. Tap the icons to yurn on Wi-Fi and Bluetooth.

To enable AirDrop open Control Centre and press the AirDrop icon. Make yourself discoverable to just those in your contacts.

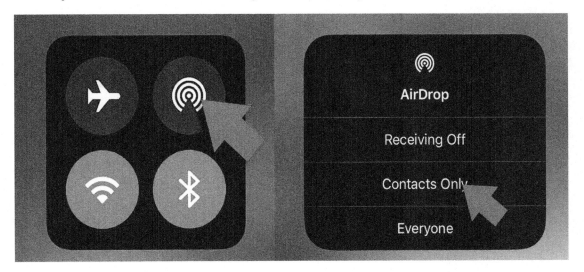

Be careful if you select 'everyone' as this means anyone in your vicinity that has an airdrop enabled device can connect to and send files to your device, which could be a possible security risk.

307

Chapter 5: Internet, Email & Communication

To Send a file to Someone using AirDrop

You can send a file from your iPad to another Mac, iPhone or iPad. In this example, I am going to send a photo. So launch Photos app. You can also files AirDrop from other apps too.

Tap the image or video you want to share from your albums. Tap on the 'share' icon.

Select 'airdrop' from the share sheet.

AirDrop will detect other devices in the vicinity. In this example, AirDrop has detected an iPhone. This is the one I want to share with.

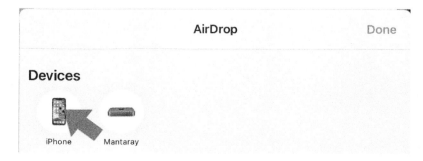

Tap the icon of the person/device you want to send to.

Chapter 5: Internet, Email & Communication

Now when you send the photo, the other person will see the photo appear in their photos app. Tap 'accept' if prompted.

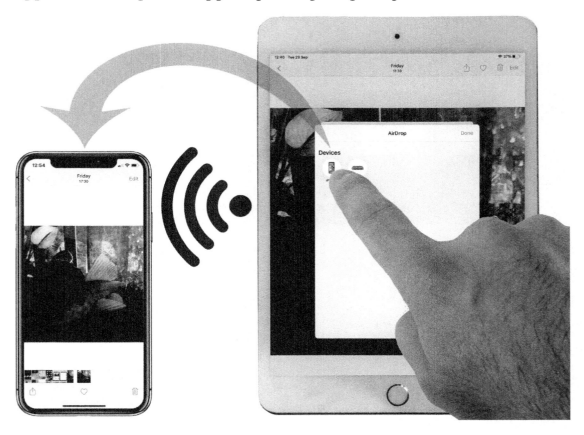

The image/video will be added to your photo library. The photo sent has appeared in photos app on the iPhone.

This works the same for other files to such as documents, music, videos etc. Files will appear in the relevant apps. Music will go to Music App and files will be stored in Files App. If iOS doesn't recognise the file type, then it will ask you what app you want to open the file with.

309

Chapter 5: Internet, Email & Communication

To Receive a File from Someone using AirDrop

Make sure your AirDrop is enabled on your device. Open the control center.

Tap on the airdrop icon.

Change the setting to 'contacts only' to receive airdrops from people on your contacts list, or select 'everyone' to receive airdrops from any device in range.

AirDrop will try to negotiate the connection with near by devices.

Chapter 5: Internet, Email & Communication

More often than not, the file will automatically download. If you get a prompt, tap on 'accept' when the photo comes through

Go into your photos app and the photo will be stored in there.

6
Using Multimedia

Your iPad is a multimedia rich device, meaning you can take photos and record videos. You can even edit and enhance your photos, correct colour and brightness.

You can post your photographs to your favourite social media account for the world to see. You can create slide shows, edit your videos, download and watch TV programmes and films. You can download and play any kind of music you can think of, all from your iPad.

In this chapter, we'll take a look at:

- Photos App & iMovie
- Camera App
- Music & Podcasts App
- Apple Music
- iTunes Store
- Apple TV App
- Airplay
- Apple Pencil
- Scribble
- Document & QR Code Scanner

Take a look at the video resources

elluminetpress.com/ipad-mm

Chapter 6: Using Multimedia

Photos

Using the photos app, you can import photos from a memory card or digital camera, edit and share photos taken with the on board cameras on your iPad.

Import Photos

There are two adapters available to accomplish this: the Lightning to SD Card Reader, or the Lightning to USB Adapter.

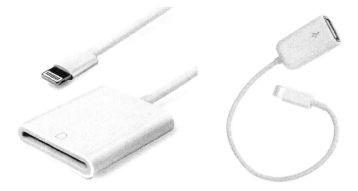

The card reader enables you to insert the SD card from your camera and copy images from it. The card reader plugs into the docking port on the bottom of the iPad. Launch the iPhoto app. Tap on camera or card.

313

Chapter 6: Using Multimedia

You can also connect your camera directly using a lightning to USB connector. (USB C on iPad Pro and new iPad Air).

Plug the connector into the bottom of your iPad, then plug the USB cable that came with your camera into the other end of the lightning to USB adapter.

When iPad detects your media or camera, it will show up as a device on the side bar. Tap the device to select it. Tap the photographs you want to import, then tap 'import' or 'import all' to copy the photos across.

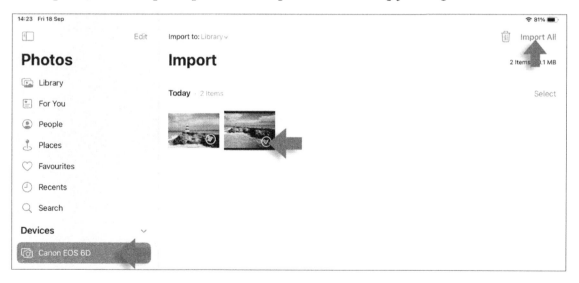

Once the photos have been imported, you will see a prompt asking you whether to keep the images or delete them. If you select keep, this leaves all the photos intact on the memory card. If you select delete, this deletes the photos you just imported off the memory card.

Once all the photos have been imported it is safe to delete the photos off the card/camera.

Chapter 6: Using Multimedia

Browsing Through your Photos

View your photos app in horizontal orientation as shown below. This will allow you to clearly see the sidebar as well as all your photographs.

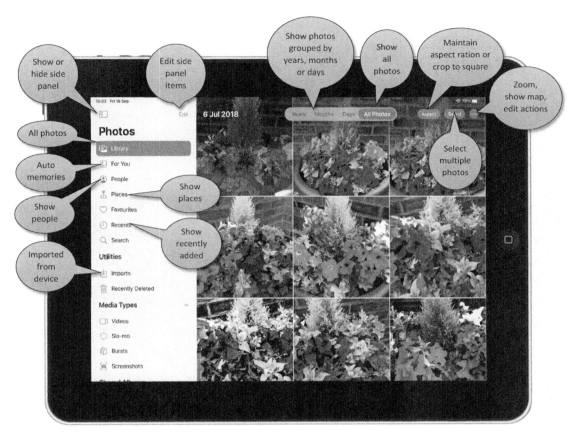

Down the left hand side you'll see your sidebar. Swipe inwards from the left edge if you don't see it. From the sidebar you can select photos, devices, view media types by photograph, video etc.

Scroll up and down to scroll through photographs and videos you have taken.

Use your thumb and forefinger to make the photo thumbnails bigger or smaller. Tap on a photo to view it in full.

Chapter 6: Using Multimedia

Editing Photos

You can do some basic editing on your iPad. You can lighten up dark images, crop and rotate your photos.

To do this, select 'library' from the side panel.

Tap on the photo you want to adjust.

When your photo opens up, tap 'edit' on the top right of the screen.

When the adjustment screen appears, you'll see three icons on the left hand side. On the right, you'll see some adjustment dials.

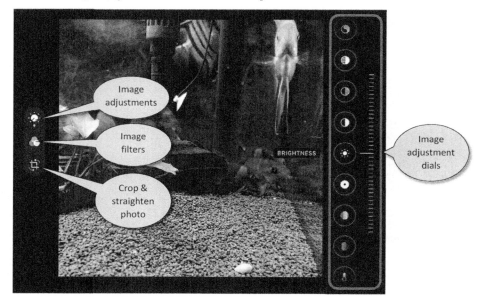

Chapter 6: Using Multimedia

Adjusting Images

To adjust images, tap the image adjustment icon from the three on the left hand side. The image adjustment dials will appear down the right hand side. Let's take a look at what each icon does.

- Auto
- Exposure
- Brilliance
- Highlights (bright or white parts of image)
- Shadows (dark or black parts of image)
- Contrast
- Brightness
- Black Point (brightness of the black parts of image)
- Color saturation (intensity of the colors)
- Color vibrance
- Warmth (white balance - bluish or orange tint to photo)
- Tint
- Sharpness
- Photo definition
- Noise reduction (removes noise from photo)

To adjust the image, select one of the tools on the panel. For example, to brighten up the whole image, select brightness. You can drag the panel upwards with your finger to see all the icons. Tap the icon you want, then drag the dial up or down to adjust.

Select another icon to adjust, or tap 'done' on the top right when you're finished.

317

Chapter 6: Using Multimedia

Crop an Image

To crop an image, tap the 'crop and rotate' icon from the three on the left hand side. The image crop dials will appear down the right hand side.

Around the edges of your image you'll see some crop handles. Tap and drag these around the part of the image you want to keep.

You can also use the two lower icons on the right hand side to remove distortion from your image.

Tap and drag the dial up and down to adjust the image.

Chapter 6: Using Multimedia

Rotate an Image

To rotate an image, tap the 'crop and rotate' icon from the three on the left hand side.

Tap the rotate icon on the right hand side.

Tap and drag the dial up and down to rotate the image.

Tap 'done' on the top right when you're finished.

319

Chapter 6: Using Multimedia

Creating Albums

You can create albums to organise your photos. To do this, from the side panel, select 'library'.

Tap 'select' on the top right

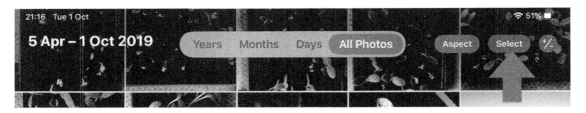

Tap the photos you want to add to your album.

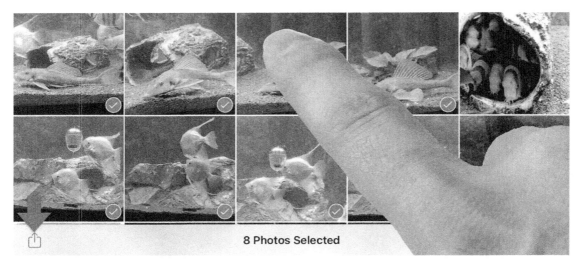

Tap the share icon on the bottom left.

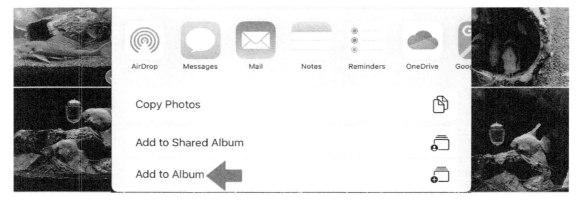

Scroll down, select 'add to album'

Chapter 6: Using Multimedia

Now if you want to create a new album, tap 'new album' and type in a name. If you want to add the photos to an existing album, tap the name of the album under 'my albums'.

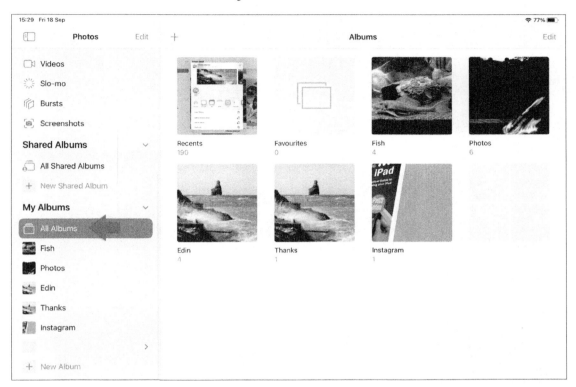

You'll find your albums in the 'albums' section of the side panel.

Search for Photos

The photos app automatically scans your photos for recognisable objects, animals, places and people. To search, tap 'search' on the sidebar.

Type in your keywords in the search field at the top of the screen.

321

Chapter 6: Using Multimedia

Sharing Photos

To share a photo with a friend, or on social media, first tap 'library' on the sidebar.

Select the photo you want to share.

Once the photo opens up, tap the share icon in the top right corner.

322

Chapter 6: Using Multimedia

Select the app you want to use to share your photo. You can share the photo via email, messages, or social media (if you have the app installed). For example, select 'Facebook' from the list of icons to post on Facebook.

Chapter 6: Using Multimedia

Type a message in your post, then hit 'next' then 'post'.

You can use the same procedure for Twitter, email, iMessage and any other social media you use. Just select the icon from the icons list.

Chapter 6: Using Multimedia

iMovie

iMovie is a video editing app you can use to edit videos on your iPad. You can drag in videos you've taken with your camera and edit them together into a movie. Useful if you want to create little movies to share with people on social media.

You'll find iMovie on your home screen. *If it isn't there, open the app store, search for iMovie, then install it.*

Creating a New Project & Adding Media

Once the app starts, tap 'create project' on the top left of the screen.

Select the type of project you want to create. To create a movie from your videos, select 'movie'. If you want to use a pre-designed template, tap 'trailer'. In this demo, I'm going to select 'movie'.

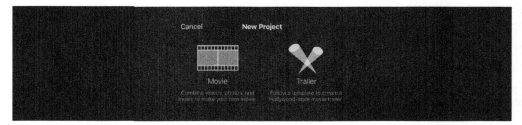

On the left hand side of the screen, you'll see options for different types of media that are imported from the photos app. You can select photos, or videos. The videos you've taken with your iPad/iPhone will be in 'videos'.

325

Chapter 6: Using Multimedia

Tap recently added to view your latest videos.

Tap and drag your finger across the thumbnails to preview the video clips.

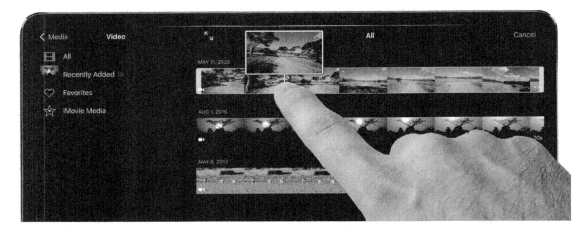

Tap a video clip, you'll see two yellow markers at each end of the preview. These are used to trim the clip.

Tap and drag the marker on the left to the position in the clip you want it to start from.

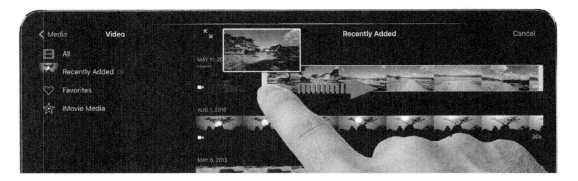

Do the same with the right hand marker - drag it to the position in the clip you want it to end.

Chapter 6: Using Multimedia

When you're done, tap the tick icon to select the clip.

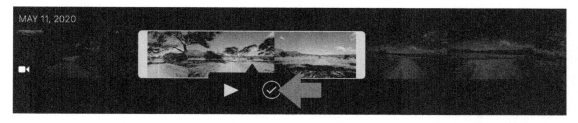

Select and trim any other clips you want to add if any. Tap 'Create Movie' at the bottom of the screen

Editing your Movie

When the new project opens, you'll see your main editor. At the top, you'll see a preview screen that allows you to preview your movie.

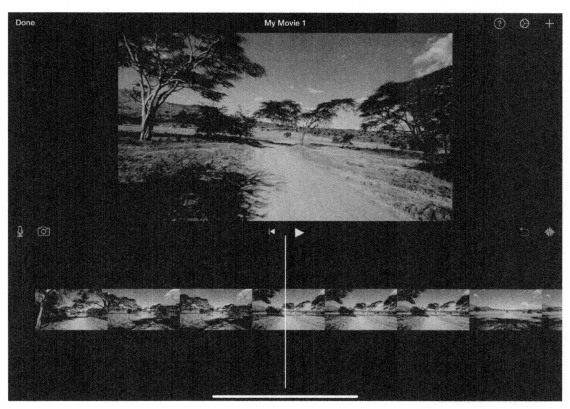

Along the bottom, you'll see your movie timeline. This is where video clips, photos and other media will be added to build your movie.

You drag the timeline left and right to view your movie.

327

Chapter 6: Using Multimedia

Reorder & Trim

As you scroll along the timeline, you'll see any clips you've already added. If you want to reorder the clips, just tap and drag them into position

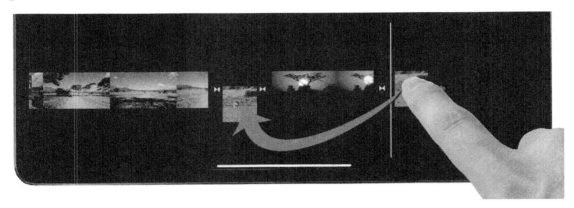

If you want to trim a clip, tap on it, them move the yellow markers. Tap and drag the marker on the left to the position in the clip you want it to start from. Do the same with the right hand marker - drag it to the position in the clip you want it to end

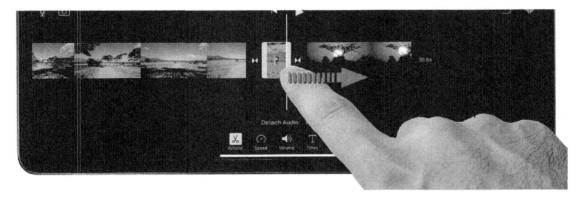

Add Text to a Clip

Move the play bar to the position in the clip where you want the titles to appear.

Chapter 6: Using Multimedia

Tap on the clip, the select the titles icon. Select a title style.

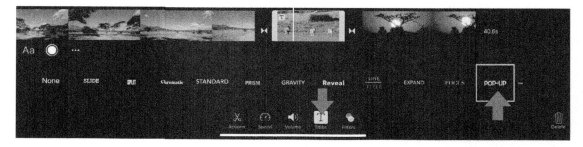

You'll see a text placeholder appear over the video, tap on 'edit' to change the text.

Enter the text you want, then tap the enter key. Drag the text into position.

Tap the 'Aa' icon on the left hand side to change the font, tap the colour icon to change the colour.

Chapter 6: Using Multimedia

Transitions

In between each clip you'll see a transition marker. You can add a dissolve between the two clips, or a slide. Tap on the transition marker, then select a duration and a style (dissolve, slide, wipe or fade).

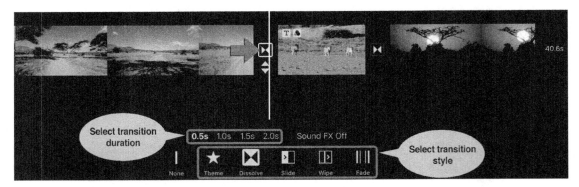

Add Additional Media

You can add more photos, video clips or backgrounds to your project. To do this tap the '+' icon on the top right of the screen.

Select 'media' from the two tabs at the bottom. Select a media type, eg backgrounds. I'm going to use this as a title page for my video

Select an object, then tap the '+' icon to add.

Drag the media into position on the timeline.

Chapter 6: Using Multimedia

Add Audio

You can add music to your movie. To do this, tap the '+' icon on the top right.

Select 'audio' from the tabs on the bottom. Here, you can add a soundtrack from the library, add your own music from the music app, or add sound effects. Tap 'soundtracks' to select a track from the library.

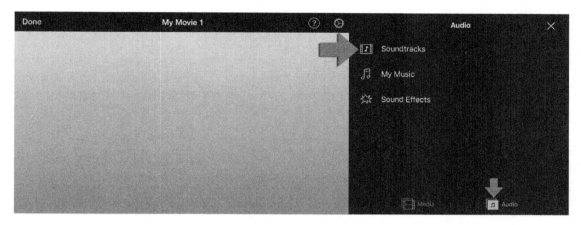

Tap on a track to preview. Tap the '+' icon to add the track to your movie.

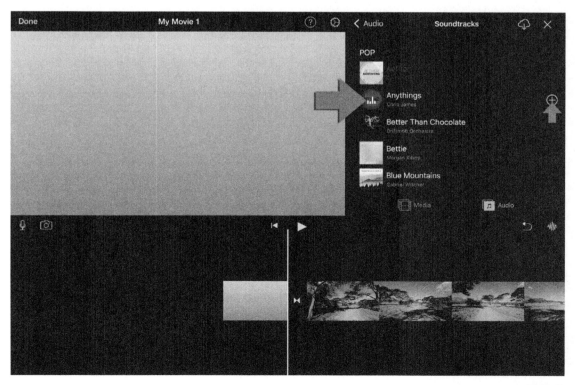

331

Chapter 6: Using Multimedia

You'll see a green bar appear underneath your video track on the time line. This is the audio you just added.

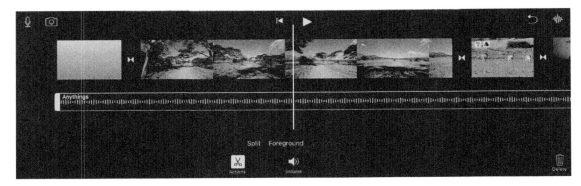

Tap on the audio track to open the audio tools. Here you can trim the audio, or change volume. To delete the audio track, tap the trash can on the right.

If you want to record a voice over, move the play bar to the position in the video you want your voiceover to start.

Tap the mic icon on the left hand side. Then tap 'record' when you're ready to start.

Tap 'stop', then 'accept' when you're done. The narration will appear as another track in your timeline.

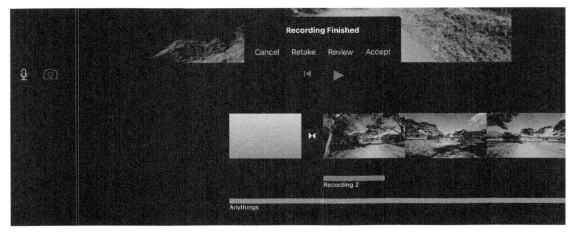

332

Chapter 6: Using Multimedia

If you have music in the background, you might need lower the volume. To do this, tap on the music track, tap the volume icon, adjust the volume slider.

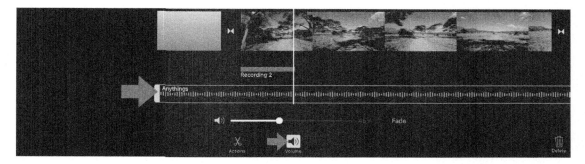

Press the play button in the center of the screen to watch your video. If you're happy with it, tap 'done' on the top left.

Tap the share icon on the bottom. Here, you can save to your files or post directly to social media.

333

Chapter 6: Using Multimedia

Camera App

Tap the camera icon on the home screen.

You can use your iPad as a camera to take photos and record video.

Along the right side of your screen you have some icons. At the top you can turn on/off live photos, add a timer, turn on/off flash, and switch between forward/rear cameras.

The white circle takes the photo, the thumbnail icon underneath shows you the last photo taken. Underneath this you can select the type of video or photo you want to take: time lapse, slow motion, video, photo, portrait, square photo and panoramic photo. Swipe your finger up and down over these to select.

Chapter 6: Using Multimedia

You can adjust the zoom using the slider on the left hand side of the image. Drag the circle on the bar upwards to zoom in, and downwards to zoom out.

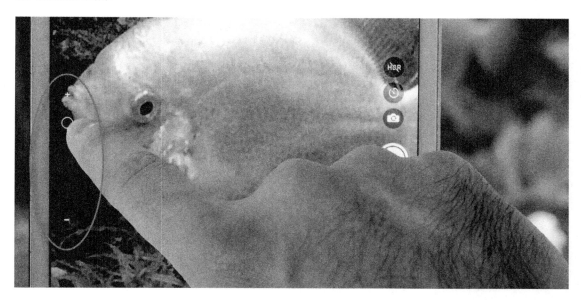

If you're having trouble focusing, tap and hold your finger on the object you want to focus on. This will lock the exposure and focus on that object, so it doesn't change, making it easier to take the photo.

Tap the white circle on the right hand side as normal to take the photo.

Chapter 6: Using Multimedia

You can also adjust the brightness before you take a photo. To do this tap on the screen and you'll see a yellow square show up with a vertical line with a slider on it.

Drag the slider upward to brighten up the image, slide it downward to darken the image.

Tap the white circle to take the photo as normal.

Take a look at the 'taking photos' video demo in the 'multimedia' section of the accompanying resources. Scan code or go to following website.

elluminetpress.com/ipad-mm

Chapter 6: Using Multimedia

Adjusting your Photo

Once you have taken your photo, you can adjust, enhance, crop, or rotate the image.

To do this, tap the photo icon on the right hand side of the screen under the white shutter button.

This will open the photo up on the edit screen.

From here you can adjust, enhance, crop, rotate and share the image. See "Adjusting Images" on page 317.

337

Chapter 6: Using Multimedia

Panoramic Photos

Panoramic shots are great for scenery and landscapes. Photos app allows you to automatically take a series of photos and it stitches them together into a long panoramic image.

To take panoramic photos, open your camera app, select pano from the right hand side of the screen. You might need to scroll down the selections if it isn't visible.

Now, move your iPad to the start of the scene and tap the white circle. You'll notice in the centre of the screen a rectangular box, this will start to fill as you move your iPad across the scene. In this demonstration, I'm taking a panoramic photo of a mountain range.

Position your iPad camera at the beginning of the mountain range on the left, tap the white 'take photo' icon on the right of your screen. Now move your camera along the mountain range until you get to the end. You'll see the rectangular box in the centre of the screen fill up as you do so. Tap the white circle again to finish. Make sure you stand in one spot, the panoramic photos don't work if you walk along with it.

Chapter 6: Using Multimedia

Recording Video

You can record video using the camera app. Select 'video' from the list on the bottom right of your screen.

To take the best looking video, use your iPad in a horizontal orientation as shown below.

Tap the red circle icon on the right hand side of the screen to start recording. Tap on any part of the screen to focus on that point during the video. Use the slider on the left hand side to zoom in and out. Tap the red circle icon on the right hand side to stop recording.

Take a look at the 'recording video' demo in the 'multimedia' section of the accompanying resources.

elluminetpress.com/ipad-mm

Chapter 6: Using Multimedia

Enhancing Video

You can use many of the same adjustments, filters as well as crop, and rotate on your videos. Video editing supports all video formats captured on iPad.

To edit a video, select 'photos' from the side panel. Then tap on the video clip you want to adjust.

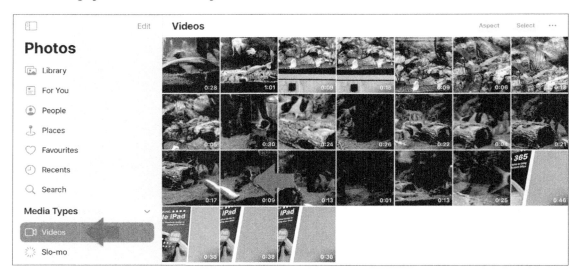

When your video opens up, tap 'edit' on the top right of the screen.

On the left, tap the adjustment icon.

When the adjustment screen appears, you'll see three icons on the left hand side. On the right, you'll see some adjustment dials. These are the same as for photos, see "Adjusting Images" on page 317.

Chapter 6: Using Multimedia

Music App

To start the music app, tap the icon on your dock.

Once music app has loaded you can see all the albums that are currently on your iPad. With the new side panel, the music app works best in horizontal orientation as shown below.

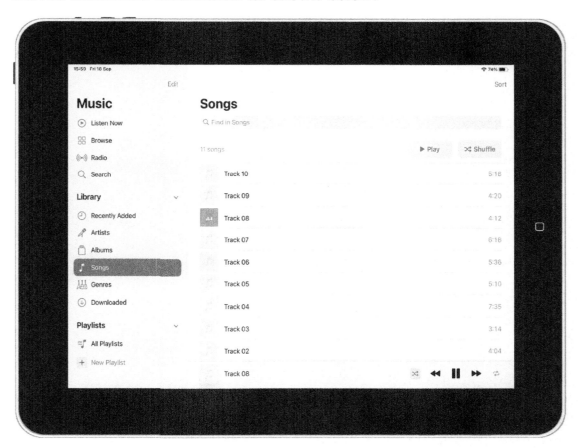

The side panel appears along the left hand side of your screen. If it isn't there, swipe inwards from the left edge of the screen.

Tap on 'songs' in the side panel to list all the songs you've downloaded onto your iPad. Tap 'albums' to view your albums, etc.

There are two ways you can buy your music. You can subscribe to Apple Music and stream any track you like from the music library for a monthly subscription fee. Or you can purchase and download the albums or tracks individually from the iTunes Store (see page 233).

341

Chapter 6: Using Multimedia

Apple Music

Let's take a look at Apple Music. With Apple Music you need a constant internet connection. At the time of writing, there are three subscription options for Apple Music.

- £4.99 a month gives you full access to the music library and is only available for University/College students.

- £9.99 a month gets you full access to the music library and many radio stations available. This is an individual account and allows only one account access to the iTunes Store.

- £14.99 a month gets you full access to the music library and radio stations and allows up to 6 people to sign in and listen to their music. This is ideal for families.

To sign up, open the Music App, then from the side panel select 'listen now'.

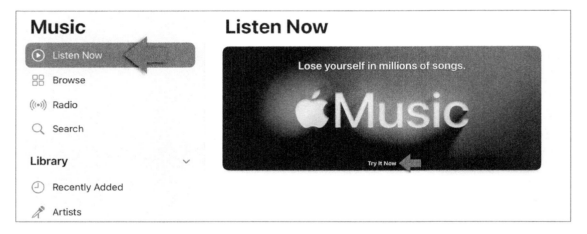

To get started with the individual plant, tap 'start listening'. To change to another plan tap 'see all plans'

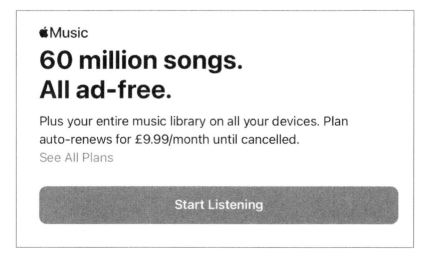

342

Chapter 6: Using Multimedia

Choose a membership programme, then tap 'join apple music'.

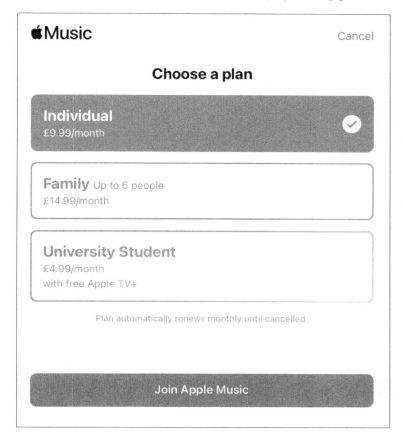

Enter your Apple ID username and password, or confirm with touch ID, if you have this enabled, by placing your finger on the home button.

Tap the genres you like. Tap 'next' when you're done.

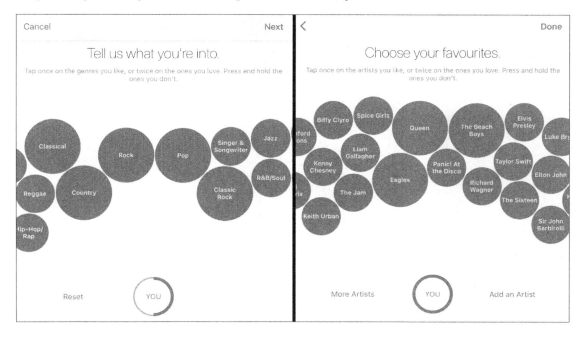

343

Chapter 6: Using Multimedia

The Main Screen

You can use the icons along the bottom of Apple Music to navigate around.

Tap the currently playing track to reveal the album or track details.

Here you'll see lyrics if they're available. Swipe down to close the screen.

Chapter 6: Using Multimedia

Searching for Music

You can search for any artist, band or song you can think of. To do this, on the Music App's home screen, select 'search' from the sidebar on the left hand side.

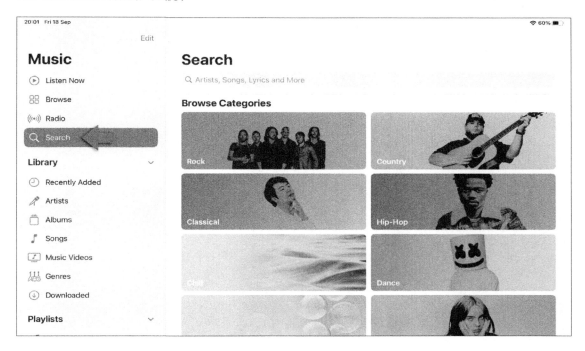

Type an artist's/album name into the search field at the top. Tap 'apple music' to search apple music, tap 'your library' to search songs you've purchased or transferred from CD or MP3 imports etc.

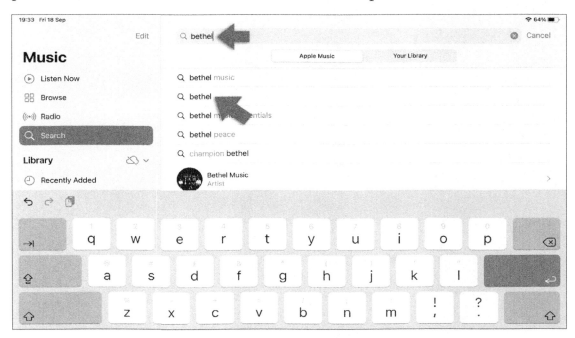

Select the closest match from the search results.

345

Chapter 6: Using Multimedia

Filter your search using the list along the top of the search results: 'artists', 'albums', 'songs'....

Tap on an album, or song name to play it. Tap the + icon next to the song to add it to your library.

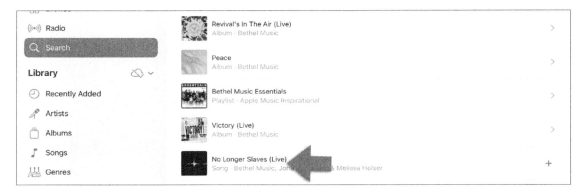

The song will play.

Tap the song at the bottom of the screen to open it up in full.

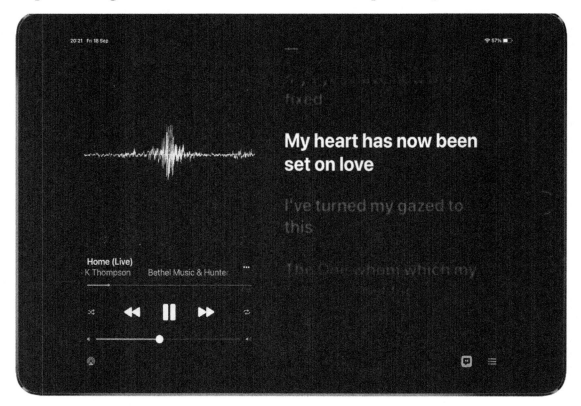

Chapter 6: Using Multimedia

Add to Library

You can start to create a library of your favourite music, so it's easy to find. To do this, tap the + sign next to the song you want to add to your library. If you want to add the whole album tap '+add'.

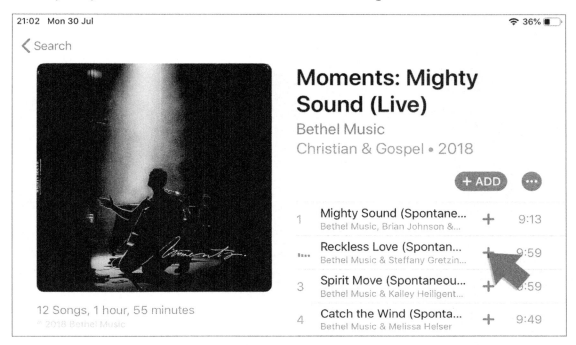

You can access your music library using the sidebar on the left hand side of the screen..

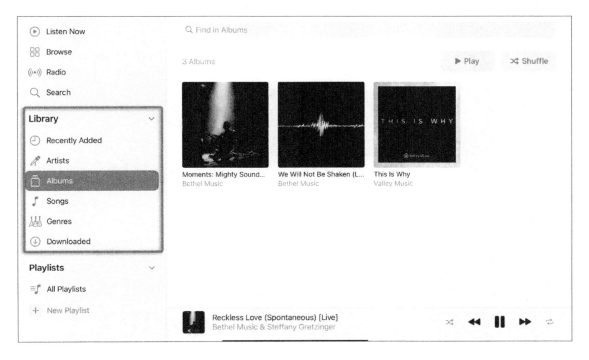

Tap an album to open it, tap on a track to play it.

347

Chapter 6: Using Multimedia

Creating Playlists

You can create playlists to play all your favourite tracks from any album or artist.

To add a track to a playlist, tap and hold your finger on the track in your list of songs, then from the popup menu, select 'add to a playlist.

Select the playlist you want to add the track to, if it exists. Or tap 'new playlist' to add the track to a new playlist.

You'll find your playlists in your library. Tap 'library' on the bottom left. Tap the menu on the top left, select 'playlists'.

Chapter 6: Using Multimedia

Importing CDs

Somewhat outdated technology nowadays, but if you still have audio CDs, you can import them. First you'll need an external CD drive. Plug the drive into a USB port on your Mac and insert a CD.

Open the music app on your Mac, your CD will appear under 'devices' on the left hand panel. Click on the CD to open. Click 'import CD' to begin.

Click 'ok' on the 'import settings' popup.

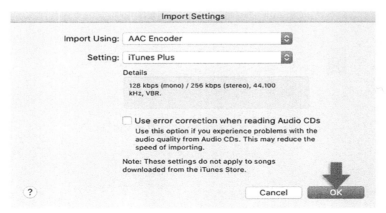

349

Chapter 6: Using Multimedia

Adding Tracks to your iPhone, or iPad Manually

Tracks you download from the iTunes Store or stream from Apple Music will automatically synchronise across your devices. If you want to add music you've imported from a CD or other source you can add the tracks to your device. To do this, plug your iPad or iPhone into your Mac using the USB cable.

On your Mac, open finder.

Select your iPad/iPhone from the left hand pane. Click 'trust' if prompted on your Mac and iPad.

Chapter 6: Using Multimedia

Now, open the music app.

Select the tracks you want, then drag them to your iPad/iPhone under the devices section on the left hand side.

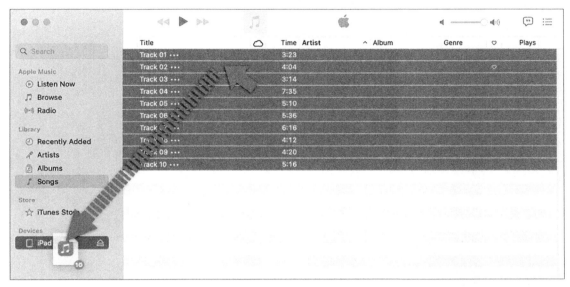

You'll be able to find the tracks on your iPad/iPhone.

Chapter 6: Using Multimedia

Podcasts App

You can listen to all sorts of podcasts. To begin, tap the podcasts icon on your home screen.

Once the app starts, you can browse through the latest podcasts. Along the bottom of the screen you'll see a panel.

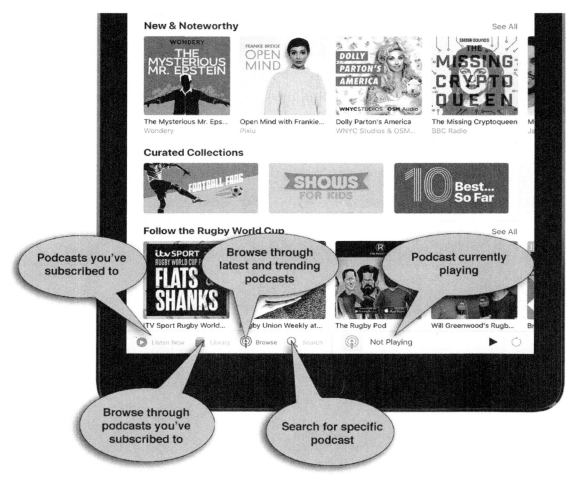

The best way to find your podcasts is to search for them. You can search for artist name, program name, or any area of interest. To search, tap the search icon on the panel along the bottom of the screen.

352

Chapter 6: Using Multimedia

Type the podcast you're looking for in the search field at the top of the screen, the select the podcast you want from the results.

Tap 'subscribe' to get updates when new episodes are posted.

You'll find all your subscribed podcasts in your library or on the 'listen now' tab.

Tap 'recently added' on the left hand side. Tap the podcast icon to open the episodes.

Tap the play icon to continue listening, or tap 'all episodes' to see all available episodes for that particular podcast.

353

Chapter 6: Using Multimedia

iTunes Store

To access the iTunes Store, tap the 'iTunes Store' icon on your home screen.

Once the app has loaded you can browse through music, movies and tv shows - tap the category icons across the top of the screen. You can also type what you are looking for in the search field on the top right of the screen.

Chapter 6: Using Multimedia

Music

Within the music section of the iTunes Store, you can browse through the latest releases, charts and different genres.

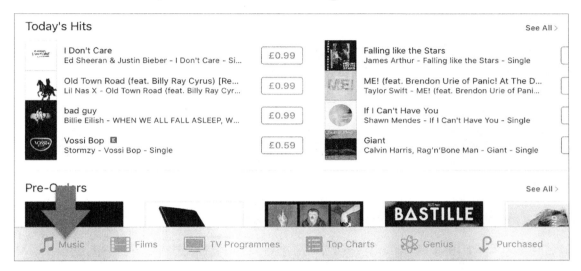

To search for your favourite tracks, artists and albums, type your search into the field at the top. Then select the closest match from the suggestions.

Along the top of the search results, you can view by song or album. Scroll up and down the list to see the songs and albums.

Tap on the price tag to download the song. Once the songs are downloaded you will find then in your recently added playlist.

355

Chapter 6: Using Multimedia

Films & TV

You can stream films and TV programmes directly to your iPad from the iTunes Store. You can buy or rent what you want to watch. To to this, select 'films' or 'tv programmes' from the panel along the bottom of the screen.

You can also search for a specific title using the search field at the top right of the screen, or to browse your favourite genre, tap 'genres' on the top left.

Search for a film or TV programme you want to watch either by typing the title into the search or browse through the genres. Tap on the thumbnail cover to view the details.

Chapter 6: Using Multimedia

On the film details screen you'll be able to read details about the film, reviews and ratings. Tap 'rent' or 'buy'. Verify your purchase using the Touch ID, or your Apple ID username and password.

You'll find your downloaded films and TV programmes in the library section of the TV App.

Chapter 6: Using Multimedia

Apple TV App

Gearing up for Apple's new streaming service Apple TV+, the Apple TV App becomes your entertainment hub where you'll find all your purchased or rented films, music, and TV programmes. You'll find the app on your home screen.

Here, you'll be able to subscribe to Apple's streaming service and stream the latest TV Programmes and movies direct to your iPad.

Watch Now

When you first start the app, you'll land on the 'watch now' page.

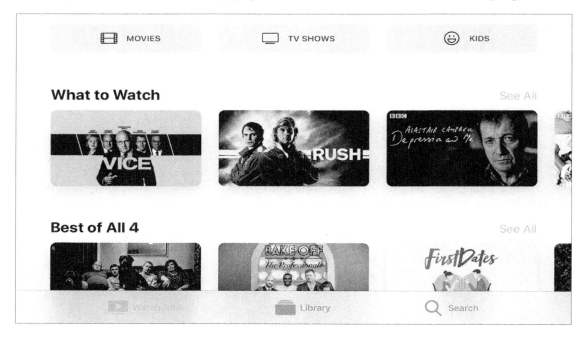

Along the top of the screen you can select movies, tv shows or kids shows.

Along the bottom of the screen you can browse with 'watch now', see your library of media you've purchased or rented, or search for a particular artists, actor, or title.

In the middle of the screen, you'll be able to scroll through current TV Shows and movie releases. Tap on the thumbnail icons to view details, or tap 'see more' on the top right to see more content.

Chapter 6: Using Multimedia

Library

Select 'library' from the panel along the bottom of the screen.

Select 'movies' to see movies you've rented or purchased, similarly select 'tv shows' if you've downloaded a tv show.

Tap on the film or tv programme to begin playback.

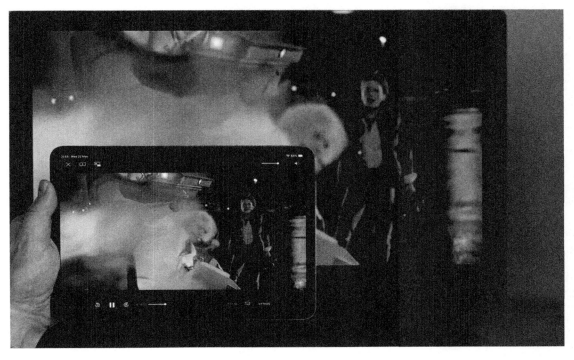

359

Chapter 6: Using Multimedia

Airplay

Airplay allows wireless streaming of audio and video data to an Apple TV or compatible receiver on your TV.

For this to work, both your iPad and Apple TV will need to be on the same WiFi network. This is usually the case in most homes.

To mirror your iPad, swipe downwards from the top right edge of your screen to open your control centre.

Chapter 6: Using Multimedia

Airplay to Apple TV

Tap on 'screen mirroring' or 'airplay mirroring' and select your Apple TV from the list. Enter your passcode if prompted.

If you don't know the Apple TV passcode, go on your Apple TV, then go to settings > Airplay, select 'Onscreen code'.

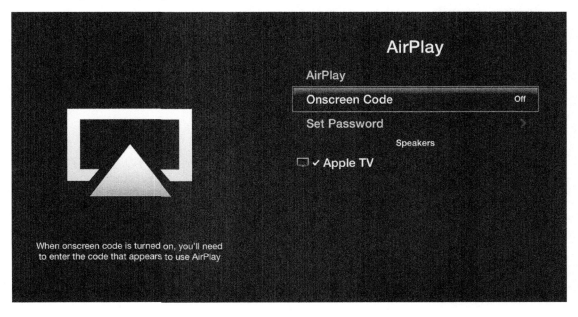

You can turn off the code or set a new one.

361

Chapter 6: Using Multimedia

Airplay to your Mac

This feature turns your Mac into an AirPlay receiver. This means you can stream music and video from an iPhone or iPad to your Mac.

To activate 'AirPlay to Mac', on your Mac, open the system preferences

Select 'sharing' from the system preferences window.

Click the lock icon on the bottom left, then enter your mac username and password.

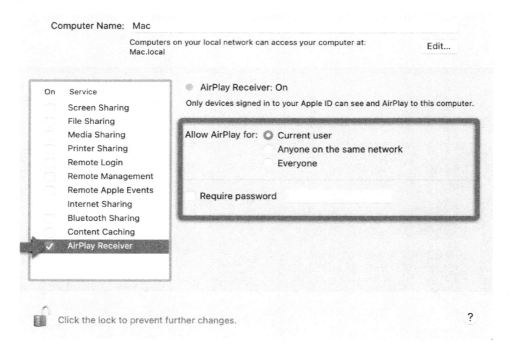

Select 'airplay receiver'. Then select who you want to allow access. Current user is your own Apple ID. Selecting 'anyone on the same network' will allow anyone connected to the same WiFi network to stream media. Selecting 'everyone' will allow anyone to stream media.

You can also set a password.

Chapter 6: Using Multimedia

To stream media, on your iPad select the music track or video, open it up in full.

Tap the 'airplay' icon at the bottom left of the screen, select your Mac from the popup menu.

You'll hear the media play on your Mac.

AirPlay will stream from any iPhone or iPad running iOS / iPadOS 15 or later. This feature works on all Macs released in 2018 or later.

363

Chapter 6: Using Multimedia

Apple Pencil

Apple Pencil is sold separately from the iPad, so you'll need to buy one from the Apple store.

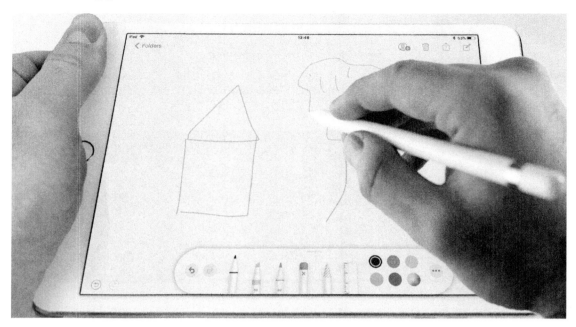

Apple Pencil is a stylus you can use to draw directly onto the iPad's main screen within a variety of different apps.

You can use your pencil in Notes, Pages, Keynote, Microsoft Word, Excel and PowerPoint to add drawings, annotations and handwritten notes.

There are also some artistic apps where you can apply pressure to create darker lines or tilt your pencil to shade in areas.

Just type 'apple pencil' into the search field in the app store and you'll find plenty of apps.

Take a look at the apple pencil video demos in the multimedia section of the resources. Scan code or go to following website.

elluminetpress.com/ipad-mm

Chapter 6: Using Multimedia

Charge your Pencil (1st Gen)

First you should charge up your pencil. To do this, pull the small white cap off the back of your pencil.

You can charge your pencil using the iPad charger. First plug the lightning adapter onto the end of the pencil making sure the small circle on the adapter is facing the pencil. Then plug the cable from your iPad charger into the other end of the lightning adapter.

You can also plug the pencil into the lightning port on the bottom on your iPad. Leave it plugged in for a short while to give it some charge.

Chapter 6: Using Multimedia

Pairing your Pencil with your iPad (1st Gen)

Make sure your pencil is charged up and your iPad is powered on. Plug your pencil into the lightning port on the bottom of your iPad.

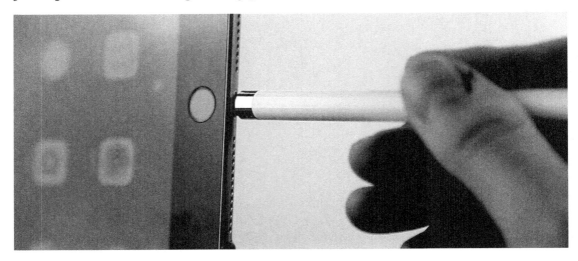

On your iPad, you'll see a prompt. Tap 'turn on' if your bluetooth is off.

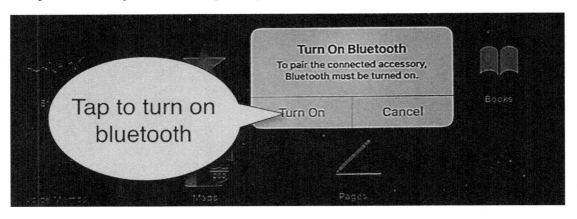

On the next prompt tap 'pair'.

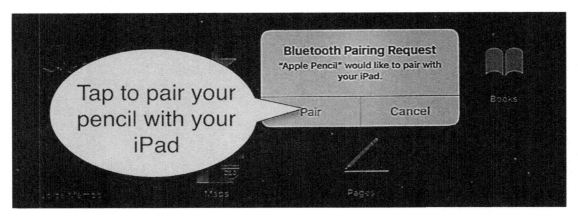

This will connect your pencil to your iPad. Once this is done, you can use your pencil on your iPad

Chapter 6: Using Multimedia

Pair & Charge your Pencil (2nd Gen)

If you are using the iPad Pro series or the new iPad Air (4 gen), you'll need to use Apple Pencil 2nd Gen.

There is a magnetic strip on the side of the iPad next to the two volume buttons.

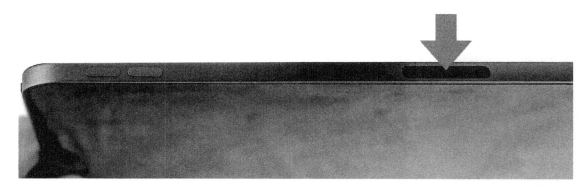

To pair your pencil, attach it to the side of your iPad. The pencil will clip to the magnetic connector.

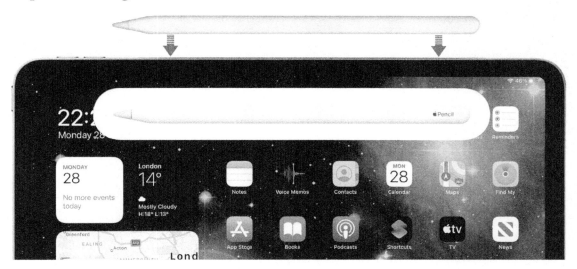

If your pencil won't pair, make sure your bluetooth is enabled.

> Go to Settings > Bluetooth.

You may also need to allow your pencil to charge, it won't pair if the battery power is low.

Chapter 6: Using Multimedia

Using Apple Pencil

You can use apple pencil to take hand written notes. Open up the notes app.

Along the bottom right of the screen you'll see three icons. Tap the markup icon on the far right. Also swipe up from bottom edge.

You can write directly onto the surface of your iPad.

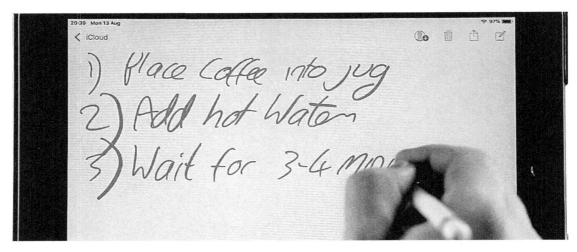

Use the icons on the markup toolbar to select a pen type: marker, highlighter, pencil, eraser and selection/lasso tool, as well as a colour and thickness and opacity (how dark or light the pen is). Tap on a pen type to select, from the popup options, select pen thickness and opacity.

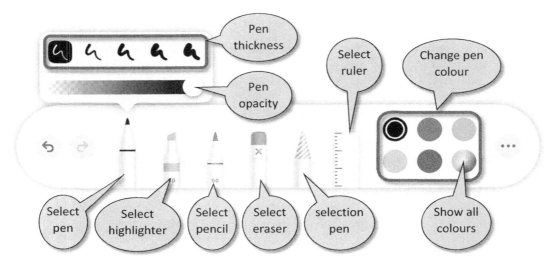

368

Chapter 6: Using Multimedia

You can highlight and annotate using your favourite productivity apps. In Microsoft Word, select the 'draw' ribbon, select a pen and draw directly onto the document. In Pages, you can draw directly onto the iPad screen on an open document with your pencil - the markup toolbar will appear along the bottom of the screen.

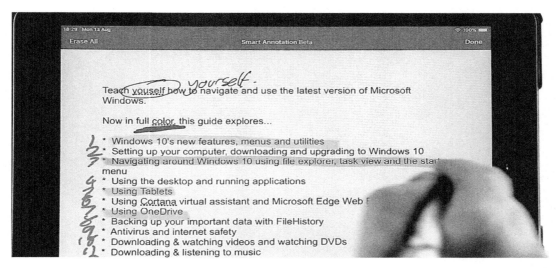

If you are an artist or designer, try out the **Concepts Drawing App** available from the app store.

Have a look at the pencil demos in the multimedia section of the video resources. Scan code or go to following website.

elluminetpress.com/ipad-mm

Chapter 6: Using Multimedia

With the apple pencil 2nd gen, you can double tap the side of the pen to change between the eraser and the last tool you had selected.

You can change this setting in the settings app. Select 'apple pencil' from the list on the left hand side.

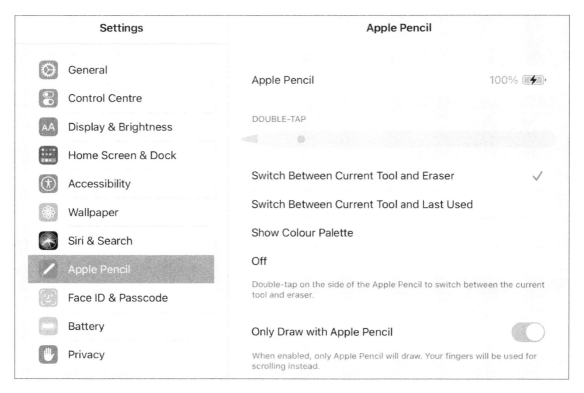

370

Chapter 6: Using Multimedia

Scribble

Apple Scribble is a feature that converts handwritten text into type. This allows you to handwrite in any text field, compose a handwritten email, or a handwritten note and have your writing converted into typed text.

Scribble will also detect handwritten phone numbers or dates, and convert drawn shapes into perfect shapes.

Handwrite in Text Fields

In any text field on your iPad, just write in it with your pencil. You can do this with online forms, and search fields

Delete Text

To delete any text just scribble over the word you want to delete.

Chapter 6: Using Multimedia

Select Text

To select text, draw a line through the words or sentence you want to select. You can also select a word by drawing a circle around it.

Insert Text

To insert a word or text, tap and hold your pencil in the position were you want to insert. A grey box will appear. Write your words to be inserted here.

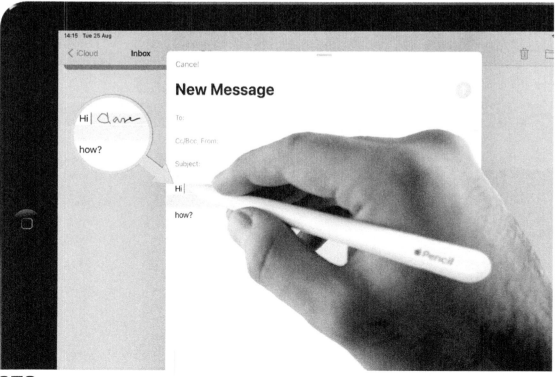

Chapter 6: Using Multimedia

Document Scanner

Within the Notes App, you can scan documents and convert them. From the Notes App, tap the camera icon on the bottom right of your screen, or on the top right of the on-screen keyboard.

Tap 'manual' on the right hand side, this is so you can take a photo of each of your pages and gives you more control than auto mode.

Line up the document in the window as shown below, make sure the yellow box covers the whole document.

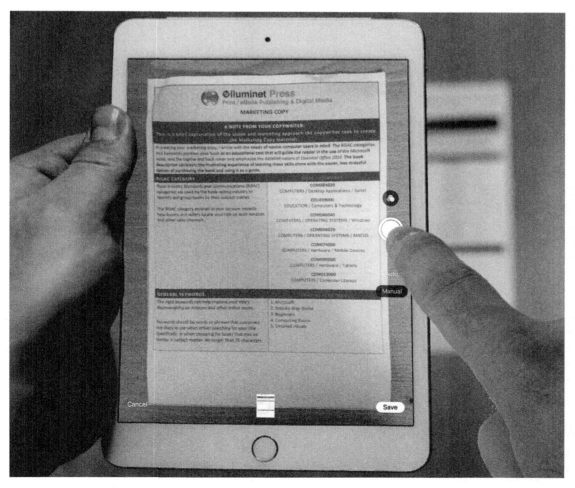

Chapter 6: Using Multimedia

Tap the white button on the right hand side to 'scan the document'. If you have more pages, repeat the process and 'scan' them as well using the white button on the right hand side. Once you have 'scanned' all your pages, tap 'save' on the bottom right corner.

The pages will be added to your note. Tap on the thumbnail to open it up full screen.

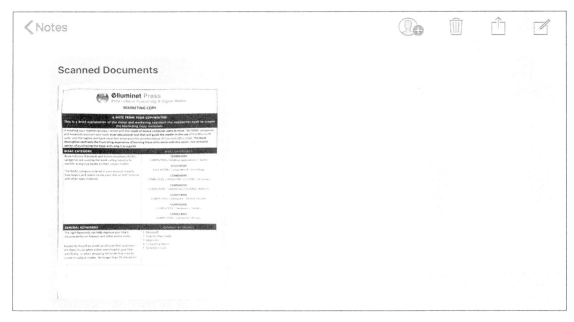

Now you can send the document via email, save it as a PDF, print it or write directly onto the scan with markup.

Tap the 'share' icon on the top right of your screen.

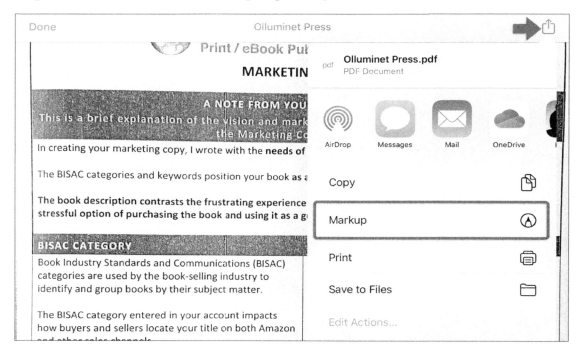

Chapter 6: Using Multimedia

In this demonstration, I'm going to add some annotations with the markup tool. So tap 'markup'.

Select a pen or highlighter from the selection at the bottom left, and select a colour from the bottom right.

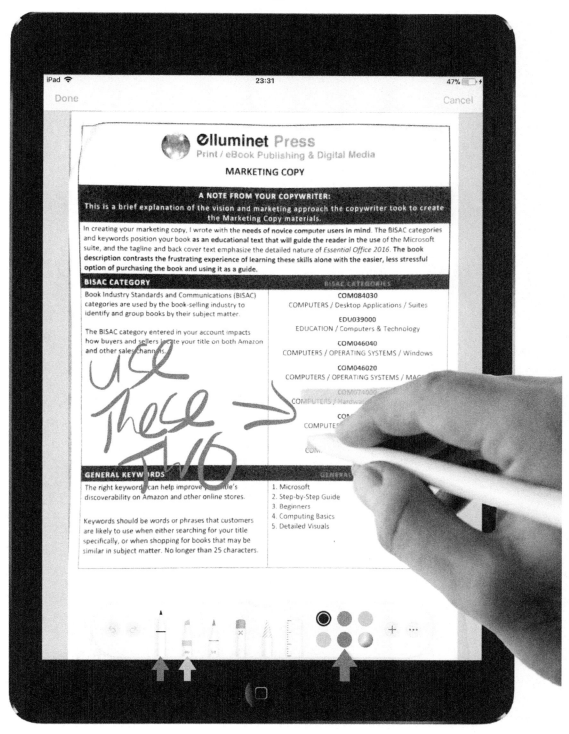

Use your finger or pen to draw directly onto the scanned document. When you're done, tap 'done' on the top left.

Chapter 6: Using Multimedia

Now to send it or save it, tap the 'share' icon on the top right of the screen.

From the drop down, tap 'mail' to email it to someone or 'message' to send via iMessage. From here you can also save it to a PDF or print it if you have air print installed. In this example I'm emailing it.

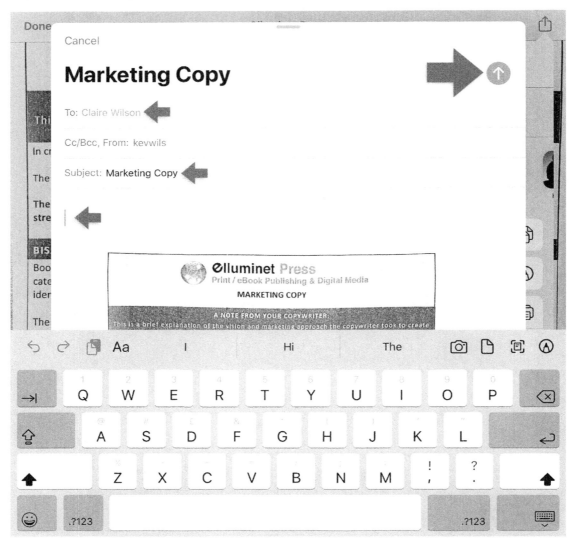

Enter the email address of the person, add a subject and a message. Tap the send icon to send your message.

Chapter 6: Using Multimedia

QR Code Scanner

A QR code (or quick response code) is a 2D bar code used to provide easy access to information through your iPad. This could be a link to a website. These codes are usually printed on signs, flyers, and other printed material.

To scan a QR code, open your camera app, point it at a QR code, tap the code on the screen to focus.

When the camera reads the code, you'll see a prompt at the top of the screen telling you what the code is and where it links to.

Tap and drag the small handle, circled above, down to expand the window to see a preview of the website.

Tap 'open in safari' to open it up in full screen.

7

iPad Accessories

There are thousands of different accessories available for the iPad and you can buy them from a number of different manufacturers, not only Apple.

You can buy keyboards, mice, trackpads, airpods, apple pencil from Apple, as well as various different universal bluetooth accessories such as cases, headphones, and keyboards.

You just need to keep in mind the size and model of your iPad when shopping for accessories. Make sure it will fit the model you have - iPad mini, air, pro, etc.

In this chapter we'll take a look at

- Magic Keyboard
- Smart Keyboard
- Apple Smart Keyboard Folio
- Bluetooth Keyboards
- Mouse Support
- Cases
- AirPods
- Bluetooth Headphones
- Wired Headphones

Take a look at the video resources

elluminetpress.com/using-ipad

Chapter 7: iPad Accessories

Magic Keyboard

If you have new iPad Air (4th generation), iPad Pro 12.9-inch (3rd and 4th generation) or iPad Pro 11-inch (1st and 2nd generation), you can attach Apple's new Magic Keyboard.

Smart Keyboard

The Smart Keyboard is a full-size keyboard made for iPad. You can use this keyboard with iPad (7th and 8th generation), iPad Air (3rd generation) and iPad Pro 10.5-inch.

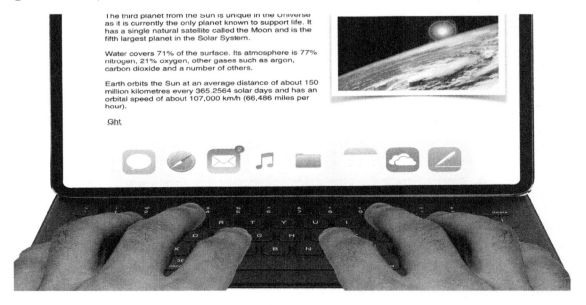

379

Chapter 7: iPad Accessories

Apple Smart Keyboard Folio

The smart keyboard is a keyboard built inside a folio case that your iPad slots into. You can use this keyboard with the new Pad Air (4th generation), iPad Pro 12.9-inch (3rd and 4th generation) and iPad Pro 11-inch (1st and 2nd generation).

The iPad slots onto the keyboard. Align the smart connector on the edge of the iPad to the dock connector on the keyboard.

iPad Air (4th gen)
iPad Pro 12.9-inch (3rd and 4th gen)
iPad Pro 11-inch (1st and 2nd gen)

Apple Smart Keyboard with dock connector

Chapter 7: iPad Accessories

Bluetooth Keyboards

You can also use any bluetooth keyboard. You can pick them up online or at any computer store.

To pair a bluetooth keyboard with your iPad, you'll need to put the keyboard into 'pairing mode' - see the instructions that came with your keyboard to find out how to do this.

Once your keyboard is in 'pairing mode', open the settings app on your iPad and tap 'bluetooth'. Turn bluetooth on if it isn't already.

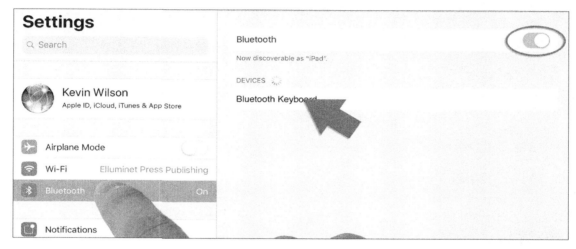

Tap the "Wireless Keyboard" device in the list of discovered bluetooth devices. You may need to wait a minute if it doesn't show right away.

On the keyboard, enter the 4-digit code that pops up on your iPad screen.

381

Chapter 7: iPad Accessories

Mouse Support

You can use any bluetooth mouse. To enable mouse support, open your settings app, scroll down the left hand panel and select 'accessibility', then tap 'touch'.

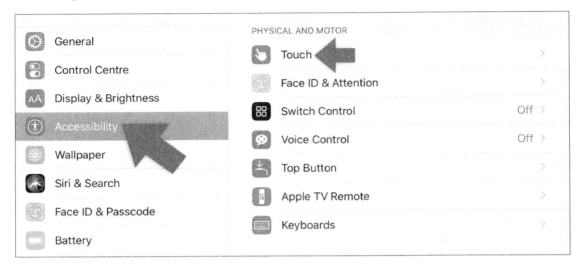

Turn on 'AssistiveTouch'.

Scroll down and select 'pointer devices' then tap 'devices'.

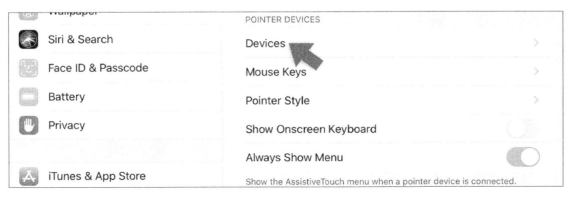

Chapter 7: iPad Accessories

Put your mouse into pairing mode.

Select 'bluetooth devices' to start the pairing process.

Your mouse will appear under the 'devices' section.

Tap on your mouse to pair it. You'll see a big black dot appear on your screen... this is your mouse pointer.

Tap 'AssistiveTouch' at the top of the screen to go back a page.

Under 'pointer devices', you can change the mouse pointer size.

Under tracking speed, you can change the speed of your mouse pointer.

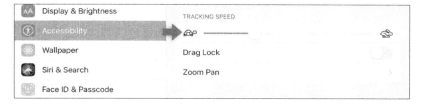

Chapter 7: iPad Accessories

Cases

A case is a must. You can get hundreds of different types. The ones I find most useful are ones that allow you to stand your iPad up making it great for watching movies. The case folds over covering the screen of the iPad when not in use.

Power Chargers

You can get a whole range of chargers from all different manufacturers. The most useful ones I have found are the ones that have a powered USB port on the side, that allows you to plug in your iPad and any other tablet for that matter, using the cable that came with it.

Your iPad will come with a charger so you won't need to buy one unless you need a replacement.

Chapter 7: iPad Accessories

AirPods

AirPods are essentially bluetooth headphones. There are two types of AirPods. The AirPods (shown below left) and AirPod Pro (shown below right).

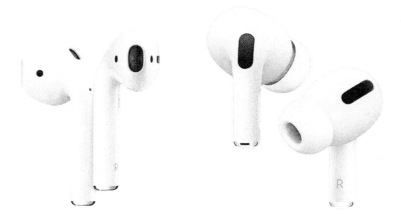

AirPods do have some additional features over other bluetooth headphones. For example, if you're listening to music on your iPhone, you can pick up your iPad to watch a TV show and the AirPods will connect automatically. AirPods Pro also have noise cancelling features, have custom eartips and are water resistant.

Setup

Open the case with your AirPods inside, then place them next to your iPad. You'll see a prompt on your iPad asking you to connect. Tap 'connect'.

Run through the tips and settings on screen. Tap 'done' when you're finished.

Chapter 7: iPad Accessories

Charge

To charge your AirPods, put them in the case and close the lid. Plug your cable from your charger into the power port on the bottom of the case.

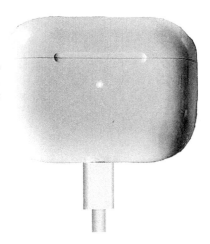

AirPod Controls

You can control various functions using the stem of your AirPod.

Here are the controls for the standard AirPods.

- Double-tap to play, skip forward, or answer a phone call.

The AirPod Pro has some additional controls:

- Tap once to play, pause, or answer a phone call
- Tap twice to skip forward
- Tap three times to skip back
- Tap and hold to switch between Active Noise Cancellation and Transparency mode

Chapter 7: iPad Accessories

Bluetooth Headphones

You can use any bluetooth headphones on your iPad. First, you need to put your headphones in to pairing mode. You'll need to refer to the device's instructions to find specific details on how to do this. On most devices, press and hold the pairing button until the status light starts flashing. See "Bluetooth" on page 74.

Wired Headphones

Your iPad no longer comes with a 3.5mm (1/8") headphone jack. If you want to connect wired headphones or speakers, you'll need an adapter. For the new iPad Air and iPad pro series you'll need a USB-C to 3.5mm headphone jack adapter (below left). For other iPads you'll need a Lightning to 3.5 mm Headphone Jack Adapter (below right).

Plug one end into the port on the bottom of your iPad, then plug the headphones into the adapter.

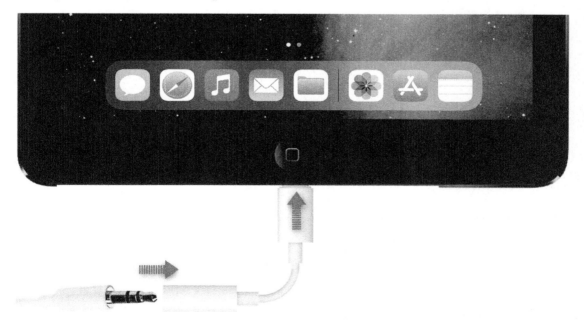

8
Maintaining your iPad

New iPads will ship with iPadOS, but if you can upgrade a previous model. iPadOS will install on the following devices.

- iPad Pro 12.9-inch (5th generation)
- iPad Pro 11-inch (1st - 3rd generation)
- iPad Pro 12.9-inch (1st - 4th generation)
- iPad Pro 10.5-inch
- iPad Pro 9.7-inch
- iPad (5th - 9th generation)
- iPad Mini (5th & 6th generation)
- iPad Mini 4
- iPad Air (3rd & 4th generation)
- iPad Air 2

Before upgrading, make sure you have some time where you don't need to use your iPad as it will be temporarily inoperative while the installation takes place.

For this chapter, take a look at the maintenance section. Open your web browser and navigate to the following site

elluminetpress.com/ipad-sys

Chapter 8: Maintaining your iPad

iPad Backups

You can backup your settings, apps and files to your iCloud account. Go to Settings, Tap on your account name, select 'iCloud', then sign in if you haven't already done so.

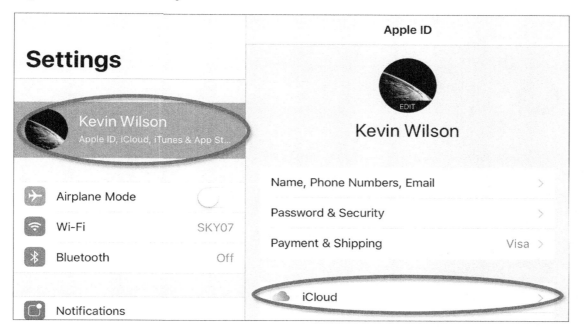

Select 'iCloud Backup'.

Turn on iCloud Backup if it isn't already. Tap 'Back Up Now'.

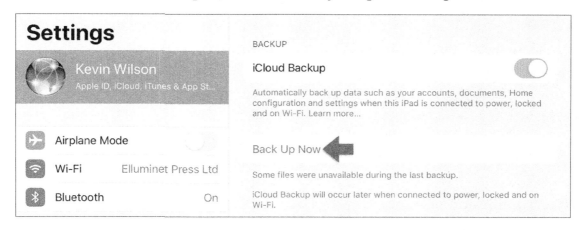

389

Chapter 8: Maintaining your iPad

System Updates

To run the update, on your iPad open your settings app. Tap 'general' then select 'Software Update'.

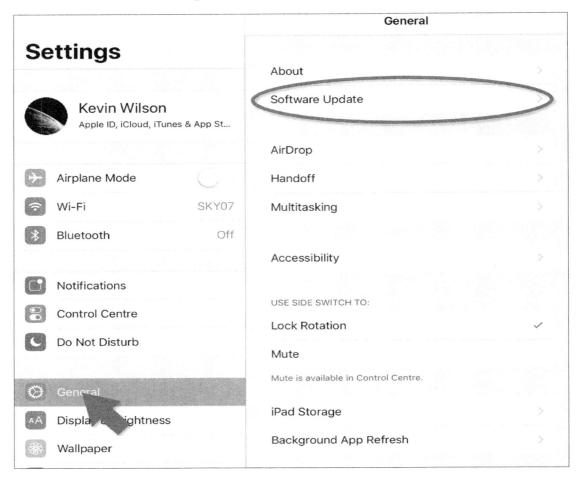

Make sure your device is connected to both Wi-Fi and a power supply, then tap 'download and install' to begin.

The installation will take a while.

Chapter 8: Maintaining your iPad

If you prefer to update using iTunes. Connect your iPad to a USB port on your computer using the cable. Tap the iPad icon on the top left of the toolbar.

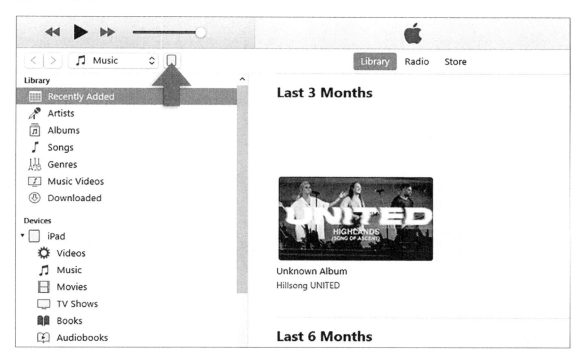

In the summary section, click 'Check for Update', then choose 'Download and Install'.

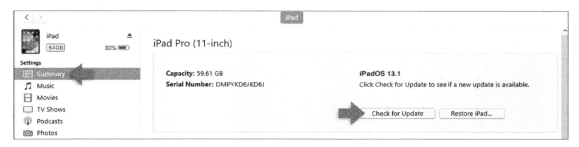

Click 'update' if prompted.

Confirm your iCloud details. Your iPad will restart automatically.

You may have to run through the initial setup again on page 26. After this, your iPad is ready to use.

391

Chapter 8: Maintaining your iPad

App Updates

To check for app updates, open the app store

Tap your Apple ID icon on the top right of the screen.

Scroll down to 'upcoming automatic updates'. You'll see a list of updates that are pending.

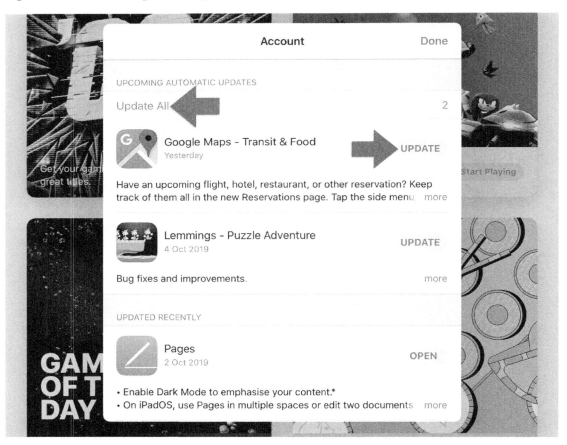

Tap 'update' next to the app to update, or tap 'update all' to apply all the updates that are available.

Chapter 8: Maintaining your iPad

Deleting Apps

To delete apps, tap and hold your finger on an app, until the X appears on the top left of the icon.

Tap on the X to delete the app. Tap 'done' on the top right when you're finished.

You can also delete any of the pre-installed apps you don't use, in the same way as above.

Chapter 8: Maintaining your iPad

iPad Storage Maintenance

You can see what apps an data are stored on your iPad's physical storage. First open your settings app, select 'general', then 'ipad storage'

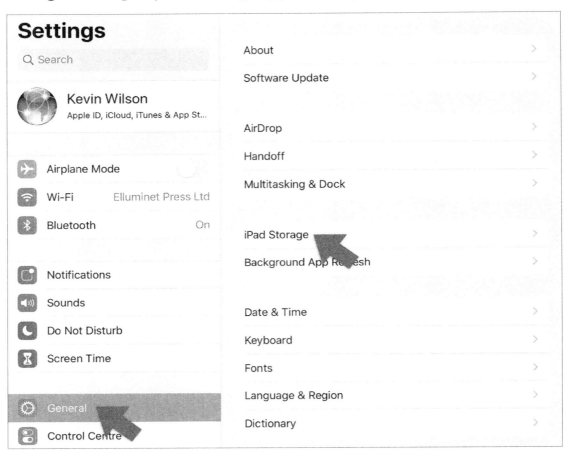

From here, you can see all the apps installed on your iPad. You can also delete or offload apps that you don't use.

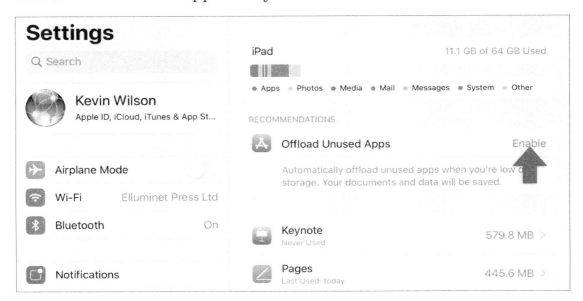

Chapter 8: Maintaining your iPad

Tap 'enable' next to 'offload unused apps'. This will automatically offload apps you don't use but only when you run out of storage. When apps are offloaded, the app itself is deleted from your iPad freeing up space, but any associated documents and data remain. The app icon remains on the home screen, so you can still access it.

When you tap on an offloaded app it will automatically re-install and any documents and data will still be there.

Listed below that on the 'ipad storage' screen are all the apps installed on your iPad. Tap on an app name to see details.

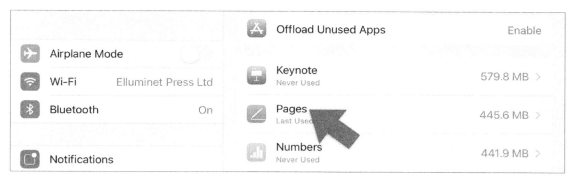

At the top you'll see the amount of space the app takes up (the app size), and the space used for documents and data. From here you can manually offload the app, or delete it. To do this, tap 'offload app' to offload, and 'delete app' to delete.

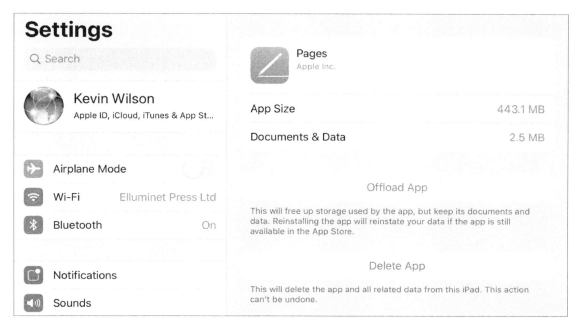

395

Chapter 8: Maintaining your iPad

iPad Recovery

First power off your iPad, then plug your USB cable into the charging port.

Plug the other end of the cable into your Mac or PC.

Open the Music App on your Mac, or iTunes on your PC

Chapter 8: Maintaining your iPad

Now, press and hold the top button and the home button at the same time. This will force your iPad to shutdown. Ignore on-screen the sliders. Hold the buttons down until you see the recovery screen.

Chapter 8: Maintaining your iPad

If you are using an iPad Pro or the new iPad Air, press and release the volume up button, then press and release the volume down button. Press and hold the power button until you see the recovery screen.

Ignore the shutdown slider that pops up on the screen, keep holding the power button until you see the restore screen.

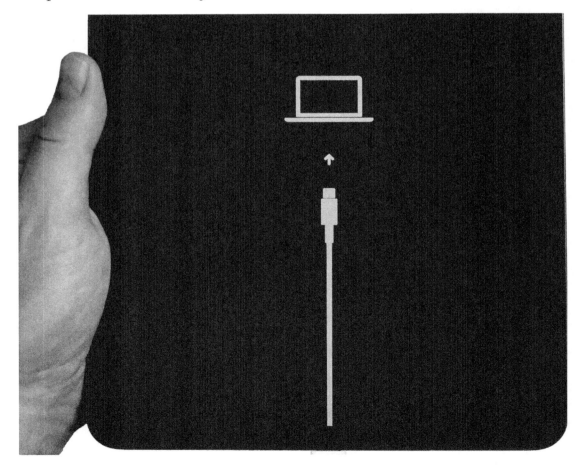

Chapter 8: Maintaining your iPad

On your mac, you'll see a prompt appear in the finder app.

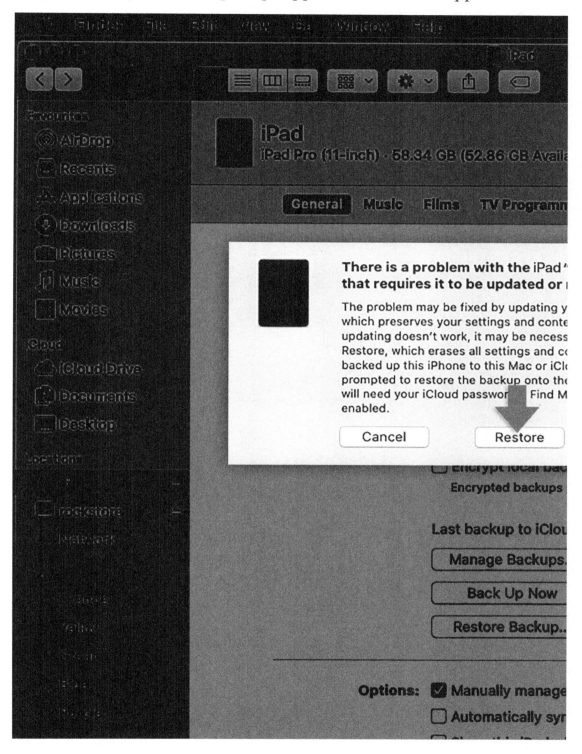

Tap 'update' to update to the latest iPadOS then restore your iPad to factory defaults.

Tap 'restore' to restore your iPad to factory defaults without updating iPadOS.

399

Chapter 8: Maintaining your iPad

Connecting to a Computer

To access iPad from your PC you will need to have iTunes installed. If you are using a Mac, iTunes is now called the Music App and will already be installed.

Tap the Music App icon on your dock or on Launch Pad

If you are on a PC then you will need to download iTunes from the Microsoft Store. You'll find the Microsoft Store on your start menu.

Type 'itunes' into the search field on the top right, then select 'iTunes' from the drop down menu.

Click 'install'.

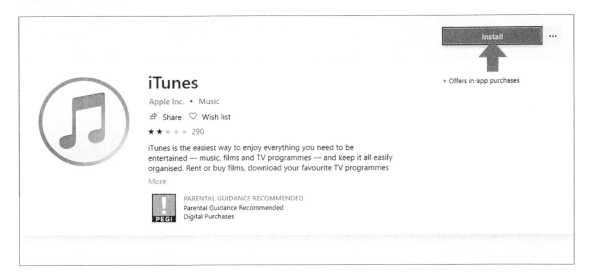

You'll find the iTunes app on your start menu.

Chapter 8: Maintaining your iPad

Select the 'account' menu, click 'sign in...', then enter your Apple ID and password. Click 'sign in'.

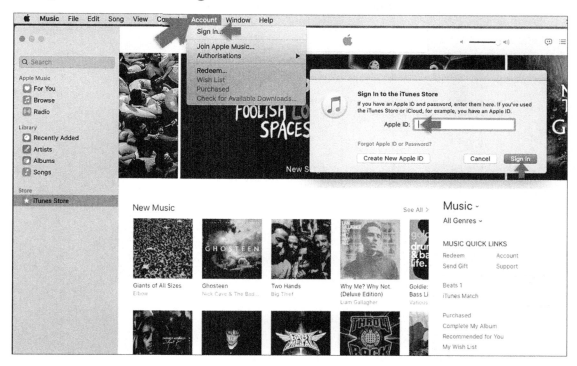

Sync your iPad/iPhone with your Mac

Plug your iPad into your Mac. Tap 'trust' on your iPad/iPhone if prompted. Open the finder app. Your iPad/iPhone will appear under 'devices' on the left hand panel. Click on your device.

If this is the first time you have connected your device to your mac, click 'get started'.

Chapter 8: Maintaining your iPad

Here you can manage your iPad. Select 'general' for general settings, click 'music', 'films', 'tv programs', 'podcasts', 'audio books', and 'books' tabs to set auto sync between your mac to device,

From the 'general' tab, you can check for updates, or restore iPad if you're having problems. You can also back up your iPad to your computer or restore your iPad from a backup.

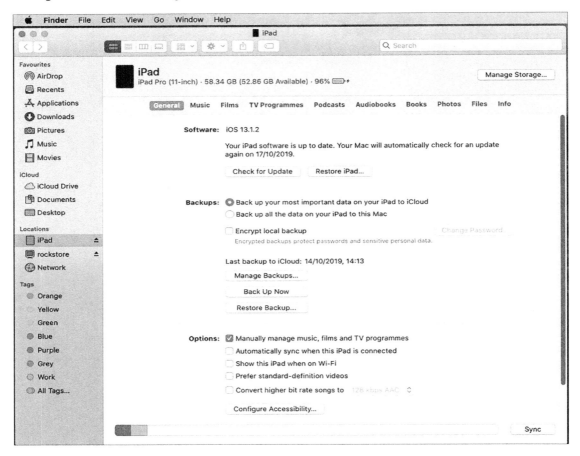

In the 'options' section further down the page, you can 'manually manage your music'. This allows you to drag and drop the music you want on your iPad from your mac. This is better if you prefer to choose what you to sync rather than syncing your whole music library on your mac.

Along the bottom, you'll see a data bar. This shows you how much space has been used on your device.

402

Chapter 8: Maintaining your iPad

Restore iPad

You can restore your device to its factory settings if you have problems with it.

Turn on your device and connect it to your mac. Open your finder app and select the device under the 'locations' section on the left hand panel.

On 'general' settings, click 'Restore iPad'. *If you have downloaded a restore image (IPSW), hold the option key and click 'restore' then select the image file.*

Click 'back up'.

Click 'restore and update'

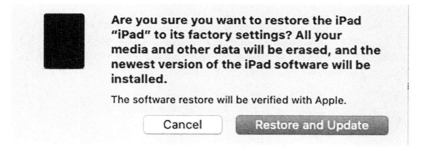

This will wipe your data, apps, music and settings, so you'll need to restore from a previous backup if you do this.

Chapter 8: Maintaining your iPad

Erase iPad

If you want to erase your iPad, this will delete all your data and personal information. This is useful if you are selling your iPad or giving it to someone else. To erase your iPad, open the settings app, select 'general' then tap 'reset'.

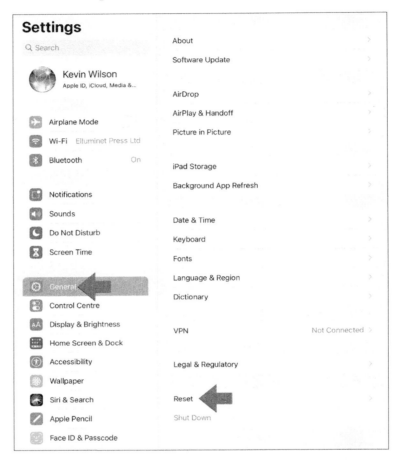

Tap 'Erase All Content and Settings'.

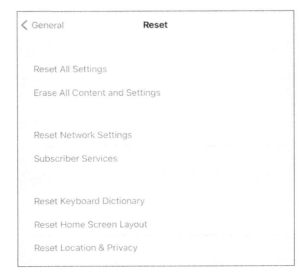

Chapter 8: Maintaining your iPad

Tap 'erase now', then enter your iPad's passcode.

Enter your Apple ID password to turn off the Activation Lock and remove the device from the 'Find My' app and your Apple ID Account.

Your iPad will reset. You'll land on the 'hello' screen when the reset is complete. From here you will need to run through the initial setup to set the iPad up again.

See page 26 for information on how to setup your iPad.

Video Resources

To help you understand the procedures and concepts explored in this book, we have developed some video resources and app demos for you to use, as you work through the book.

As well as the video resources, you'll also find some downloadable files and samples for exercises that appear in the book.

To find the resources, open your web browser and navigate to the following website

elluminetpress.com/ipad/

Do not use a search engine, type the website into the address field at the top of the browser window.

At the beginning of each chapter, you'll find a website that contains the resources for that chapter.

Video Resources

Using the Videos

When you open the link to the video resources, you'll see a thumbnail list at the bottom.

Click on the thumbnail for the particular video you want to watch. Most videos are between 30 and 60 seconds outlining the procedure, others are a bit longer. When the video is playing, hover your mouse over the video and you'll see some controls...

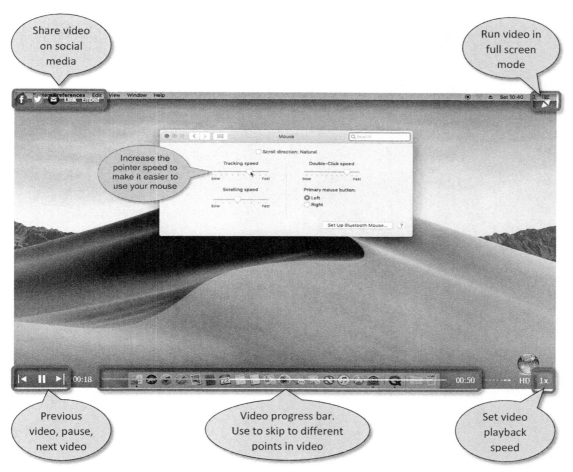

407

Video Resources

Scanning the Codes

At the beginning of each chapter, you'll a QR code you can scan with your phone to access additional resources, files and videos.

iPhone

To scan the code with your iPhone/iPad, open the camera app.

Frame the code in the middle of the screen. Tap on the website popup at the top.

Video Resources

Android

To scan the code with your phone or tablet, open the camera app.

Frame the code in the middle of the screen. Tap on the website popup at the top.

If it doesn't scan, turn on 'Scan QR codes'. To do this, tap the settings icon on the top left. Turn on 'scan QR codes'.

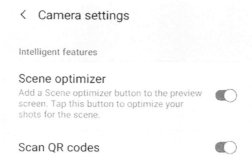

If the setting isn't there, you'll need to download a QR Code scanner. Open the Google Play Store, then search for "QR Code Scanner".

Index

A

Address Book 272
AirDrop 307
   Receive a File from Someone using AirDrop 310
   Send a file to Someone using AirDrop 308
Airplay 360
   to Apple TV 361
   to your Mac 362
AirPods 385
   Charge 386
   Controls 386
   Setup 385
Air Print 236
Apple Books App 186
   Browse the Bookstore 187
   Downloading Books 189
   Opening a Book 186
   Search the Bookstore 188
Apple ID 48
   Creating 48
Apple Music 342
   Cast to Apple TV 344
   Library 347
   Lyrics 344
   Main Screen 344
   Playlists 348
   Repeat 344
   Search for Music 345
   Shuffle 344
   Subscriptions 342
Apple Pay 81
   Setup 81

Index

    Using 83
Apple Pencil 364
    Charge your Pencil 365
    Draw 369
    Highlight Text 369
    Pair & Charge your Pencil (2nd Gen) 367
    Pairing your Pencil with your iPad 366
    Using Apple Pencil 368
    Writing text 368
Apple TV App 358
    Library 359
    See movies you've rented or purchased 359
    Watch Now 358
App Library 116
App Shelf 134
App Store 149
    Arcade 153
    Browsing the Store 150
    Download App 156
    Download Apps 155
    Search 155
App Switcher 124
A Series Chip 21

B

Background 45
Backups 389

C

Calendar 277
    Adding an Appointment 278
Camera App 334
    Adjusting Photos 337
    Adjust the brightness 336
    Enhancing Video 340
    Focus 335
    Panoramic Photos 338
    Recording Video 339
    Switch between forward/rear cameras 334
    Zoom 335
Cases 384
Cellular Data 61
Chargers 384
Charging your iPad's Battery 23

Index

Child Accounts 88
Clock App 201
    Alarm 203
    Bed Time 204
    Stop Watch 206
    Timer 206
    World Clock 201
Close a Running App 129
Close Slide Over 133
Close Split View 133
Connecting to a Computer 77, 400
Connecting to the Internet 59
Contacts 272
    Add a Recurring Appointment 279
    Adding an Appointment from a Message 280
    Add New Contact 272, 274
    Delete a Contact 276
    New Contact from a Message 275
    View Contact Details 273
Control Center 118
Cut, Copy & Paste 125

D

Dark Mode 43
Date & Time 41
Deleting Apps 393, 395
Devices 74
    Bluetooth 74
    USB 76
    Video 76
Dictation 143
Display 41
Dock 109
Drag 121
Drag & Drop 132

E

Email 264
    Attachments 269
    Block Sender 271
    Flagging Messages 270
    Formatting Messages 268
    Forward a Message 264
    New Message 267

Index

    Replying 264
    Signature 266
    Threads 265
Email Accounts 70
Erase iPad 404
External CD drive 349

F

FaceID 49
    FaceID Unlock Settings 50
    Setup 49
FaceTime 281
    Effects 286
    Group 289
    New Call 282
    SharePlay 292
    Share Screen 291
Factory Reset 404
Family Sharing 84
    Add a Family Member 87
    Child Accounts 88
    Setup 84
Files App 191
    Create New Folders 192
    Delete Files or Folders 193
    Drag Files into Folders 192, 193
    External Drive Support 194
    File Servers 196
    Rename Files or Folders 195
    Share a File 193, 194
flashlight 102
Fonts 233
    Downloading 234
    Installing from File 235
Forgot iCloud Password 69

G

Gestures 120

H

Headphones (bluetooth) 387
Headphones (wired) 387
home button 103

Index

Home Screen 105
    Anatomy 105
    Arranging Icons 106
    Removing Icons 108
    Reveal Home Screen 123
    Switching Between App Pages 107

I

iBooks 186
iCal 277
iCloud 64
    Forgot Password 69
    iCloud Sync 67
    Settings 65
    Sign In 64
    Sign Out 64
    Storage 68
iCloud Password 66
iCloud Personal Details 65
iMessage
    Adding Effects 298
    Animated Gifs 304
    Annotate a Video or Photograph 302
    Digital Touch 300
    Emojis 306
    Payments with iMessage 305
    Replying to Messages 294
    Sending Photos from Camera 297
    Sending Photos from Photos App 296
    Sending Voice Messages 295
iMovie 325
    Add Additional Media 330
    Adding Media 325
    Audio 331
    Editing your Movie 327
    New Project 325
    Reorder & Trim 328
    Transitions 330
Initial Setup 26
    Auto Setup 26
    Manual Setup 29
iPad 20
iPad Air 20
iPad Backups 389

Index

iPad Mini 20
iPadOS 15
iPad Pro 19
IPSW 403
iTunes 341
iTunes Store 354
    Buying Music 355
    Films & TV 356
    Main Screen 354

K

Keyboard 39
    Change or Add 39
    Settings 40
    Text Shortcuts 39
Keyboards
    On-screen Keyboard 136
Keyboards (external) 379
    Bluetooth Keyboards 381
    Magic Keyboard 379
    Smart Keyboard 379
    Smart Keyboard Folio 380
Keynote 219
    Templates 219
Keynote App
    Adding Media 222
    Animations 223
    Editing a Slide 220
    New Slide 221
    Text Boxes 225

L

Language & Region 38
Light Mode 43
lightning port 101
Liquid Retina 21

M

M1 21
Mail App 264
    Attachments 269
        Drawing 269
        Insert from Photos App 269

Index

    Scan a Document 269
    Take Photo 269
  Block Sender 271
  Create a Mailbox Folder 270
  Flagging Messages 270
  Formatting Messages 268
  Forward a Message 264
  Mark as Unread 270
  Move Message 271
  New Message 267
  Reply 264
  Signature 266
  Threads 265
Maps App 173
  3D Maps 181
  Create Guide 177
  Driving Directions 177
  Drop a Pin 180
  Explore maps 174
  Favourite Locations 173
  Flyover 181
  Guides 175
  Home Location 173
  Look Around 176
  Satellite Map 174
  Share Location 177
  Street Map 174
  Transport Map 174
  Work Location 173
Mobile Data 61
Mouse Support 382
M Series Chip 21
Multitasking 128
Music App 341
  Adding Tracks to your iPhone, or iPad Manually 350
  Importing CDs 349
  Playlists 348

N

News App 183
  Personalise your News 185
  Reading the News 183
  Searching for News Sources 184
  Selecting News Sources 184

Night Shift 42
Nit 21
Notes App 157
    Creating Folders 165
    Dictating Notes 163
    Handwritten Notes 160
    Inserting Photos 159
    Inviting other Users 166
    Organising your Notes 165
    Paste Handwriting as Text 161
    Quick Note 164
    Shape Recognition 162
    Typing Notes 158
Notification Center 119
Notifications 57
Numbers App 228
    Copy, Cut, Paste 229
    Data Types 229
    Entering Data 229
    Formulas 232
    Functions 232
    Inserting Rows & Columns 231
    Resizing Rows and Columns 231
    Text Formatting 230

O

Offload App 395

P

Pages App
    Adding a Picture 217
    Collaboration 218
    Formatting Text 215
Passcode 53
Payment & Shipping 66
Pencil 364
Personal Details 65
Photos App 313
    Albums 320
    Browsing Through your Photos 315
    Editing Photos 316
        Brightness 317
        Contrast 317
        Crop 318

Index

    Exposure 317
    Highlights 317
    Rotate 319
    Shadows 317
  Importing Photos from Card 313
  Import Photos 313
  Sharing 322
Podcasts 352
Power Button 101
Power Up 23
Printing Documents 236
  Air Print 236
  Older Printers 237
Privacy 54
ProMotion 21

Q

QR Code Scanner 377
Quick Note 164

R

Recording Screen 147
Recovery 396
Reminders 168
  Adding a Task 168
  Create a Reminder 168
  Create New List 169
  Reminder at a Location 172
  Reminder When Messaging Someone 171
  Schedule a Reminder 170
Reset 404
  All Settings 404
  Erase all content and settings 404
  Reset home screen layout 404
  Reset keyboard dictionary 404
  Reset location and privacy 404
  Reset network settings 404
  Reset subscriber services 404
Restore from Image File 403
Restore iPad 403
Reveal Dock 123
Reveal Home Screen 123

Index

S

Safari 239
  Autofill
    Using Autofill to Fill in a Form in Safari 259
    Using Autofill to Fill in Payment Details in Safari 260
  Autofill Passwords 253
  Bookmarking a Site 245
  Browsing History 248
  Download Manager 251
  Edit a bookmark 247
  Forms Autofill 256
    Add Contact Info 256
    Adding Credit Cards 258
  Generate Automatic Strong Passwords 252
  Page Zoom 250
  Password 254
  Password Monitoring 261
  Reader View 249
  Revisiting a Bookmarked Site 246
  Share Menu 241
  Sidebar 240
  Start Page 239
  Tabs 241
    New Tab 242
    New Tab Group 243
    Reopen Tab Group 244
    Show All 242
    Tab Bar 241
    Tab Groups 242
  To Delete Bookmark 247
  Toolbar 240
  Website Privacy Report 262
Scanning Documents 373
School Accounts 63
Screen Recording 147
Screenshots 146
Screen Time 92
  Allowed Apps 97
  Allowing and Blocking Content 98
  App Limits 95
  Content & Privacy Restrictions 97
  Downtime 94
Scribble 371
  Delete Text 371

Index

    Handwrite in Text Fields 371
    Insert Text 372
    Select Text 372
Search 139
Search Settings 55
Settings
    Home Screen & Dock 47
    Opening 37
    Search 37
Shortcuts 207
SIM card tray 102
Siri 141
    Settings 55
    Translate 142
Slide Over 131
SoC 21
Social Media Accounts 73
Split View 130
Spotlight 139
Status Bar 109
Storage Maintenance 394
Storage Management 68
Switch Between Open Apps 122
Switch to Another Running App 128
Sync your iPad with your Mac 401

T

Text Selection 127
Touch Gestures 120
    Drag 121
    Swipe 122
    Switch Between Open Apps 122
    Tap 120
    Zoom 121
TouchID 52
Translate 142
True Tone 21

U

Universal Control 78
    Moving Between Devices 135
    Setup 78
Unlock iPad 24
Updates 390

Index

Updating Apps 392
Updating your iPad 390
Upgrading 36
USB-C port 101

V

Voice Control 144
Voice Dictation 143
Voice Memos App 197
    Recording Memos 198
    Renaming Memos 199
    Trim a Memo 200
volume buttons 102
VPNs 63

W

Wake iPad 24
Wallpaper 45
Widgets 110
    Add to Home Screen 110
    Add to Today View 112
    Edit Widget 114
    Remove Widgets 115
WiFi 59
Work Accounts 63

X

XDR 21

Z

Zoom 121

Printed in Great Britain
by Amazon